ASYLUM BOOKS

Painting the Rainbow

Wayne Clay was born in 1961 in Sheffield where he still lives. After leaving the City Council Works Department where he was a notoriously unproductive painter and decorator he became a prolific painter of pictures. Painting the Rainbow is his first book and narrates his life up to 1993. He is working on a sequel to this biography as well as a definitive text on football.

Peter Bullimore who shares this experience of Sheffield working class life is co founder with Terence McLaughlin and Alec Jenner of Asylum Associates, an international training and development cooperative. Asylum Associates are the producers of Asylum: an international magazine for democratic psychiatry, psychology, education and community development.

WARNING TO THE READER

This story is told in the vernacular! Some will argue that such grammatical variation is not permissible and others that it preserves the authenticity of voice. Rules have been broken. The reader will be the judge.

Wayne D Clay
Painting the Rainbow

With a forward by Peter Bullimore

Published by Asylum

29 Heathbank Road, Cheadle Heath, Stockport SK3 0UP

Series editor Terence McLaughlin

Designed by mano@elmano.co.uk

Printed by RAP Spiderweb

Clock Street, Hollinwood, Oldham, OL9 7LY

Distributed by Asylum Associates

Limbrick Centre, Limbrick Road, Sheffield S6 2PE

ISBN: 0-9544030-1-0

978-0-9544030-1-0

CONTENTS

Forward

This is a story of one man's struggle with manic depression. The story will take you on a journey of manic depression - not just the author's journey but your own. You will experience the lows as you read the sad events of his life but you will experience the highs with the great humour he also shares with you.

I first met Wayne at Myers Grove School in Sheffield in 1972. I must mention this was a place we both hated attending, the over zealous nature of the school being met with an early form of indifference. Both of us underachieved on the academic side of things. It was bad enough that we had to attend, let alone do the work we were given. We both did physical science, a lesson that was given in a room that that was situated right at the top of the science block and well out of the way of the other pupils. This sort of summed up our school years in the fact we were better off out of sight and mind of the rest of the class. Had we been provided with a compass and a map it could not have been made more clear that we were not thought of very highly.

School life rapidly came to a close in the summer of 1977 with us finally leaving Myers Grove, the `Stalag 13' of schools. If we thought school was bad it was going to get a lot worse with the world we were living in now wanting us to find a job. Work for Wayne was painting and decorating for Sheffield Council this would prove to be the biggest ordeal of his life.

Wayne and myself started drinking regularly with the commencement of work. There was one incident that sticks in my mind, when he put his fist through a window after a night out. He did many things that people described as stupid, but the reality was the sheer frustration of his life He had begun to feel trapped and totally weighed down, a deep sense of responsibility hanging over his whole frame and with no way of shaking it off.

There is a major difference between my own breakdown and Wayne's in that Wayne orchestrated his mental state to go into psychosis in order to relieve himself of the burdens he had carried around for nearly 26 years. He felt it was part of his destiny. He thought that of all the people who have been in the

Sheffield psychiatric system, he was the greatest case for treatment ever known. His delusion was that it would all go away very quickly, something that could not have been further from the truth. His deep depression got the chance to get out of its bottle and the resulting years have been extremely hard to get over. His journey started out with him being wracked with doubt, continuing for many years with him finally releasing the energy that he thought he was carrying. Today he thinks the journey was worth it, but it caused much pain to his family.

This story is all true and I hope as you read his life story that you enjoy his journey as much as I did, and as much as he enjoyed writing it enabling him to get so much anger and misunderstanding off his chest. We sometimes think we know people but we don't really understand what's going off in someone's mind. Having known Wayne for so many years I only now feel I really know him and I have the utmost respect for the way he has reclaimed his life from his demons.

His true friend Peter Bullimore.

Introduction

A t the beginning of 1987 I started to experience insomnia but I did not pay much attention to this fact as I felt well in myself, which had not always been the case in my life. I was doing plenty of studying for the exams that lay ahead, so I hoped that I would get good results on the back of my efforts. I was also in the habit of playing a dictionary game, where I would start with a word and see what it led up to into definitions. My body was in need of some exercise and I was going on runs around the houses where I was living with my mother and brother. My weight was going down, but I would find out this was not such a healthy thing to do when it is in any way connected with my nerves.

The time was nearing and I was making pots of tea many times in a day and going to the toilet to have a crap at all times of the day and night. This was my way of shedding the years or that's what I thought it was. I was coming up to the time I had waited so long for. My trips to the toilet in the night were upsetting my mother because she knew it had begun. My head was now getting warm and staying so throughout the days and the nights. The things that I wrote down during this period, I now look back on as muddled thoughts that were a right load of drivel.

When I was not working on revision and didn't feel like doing much I would play my records. The albums that I played the most in this period were Kate Bush and U2. On the U2 album, `The Unforgettable Fire', I started to play one track over and over again as I could identify with what was happening to me in the words of the song. The track was called `Bad'. It would turn out to be a favourite song of someone I had been waiting to meet for a very long time. The song was touched with great meaning for me and I wrote out the words to the songs when the time was reaching its climax.

My relationship with my mother and father was not good, with me disappointing both of them in different ways. My mother told me she was fed up making excuses for me, and my father was unhappy that I didn't have a job since I was sacked from the Council. With me living with my mother when my parents divorced, I called my mother silly names and hated doing the decorating, of which there was plenty in the house she had taken on after the separation. I had not seen my father for three years before the Christmas of 1986, but I did agree to go to a dinner dance that my father paid for, where I met him, and my brother and sister were present. The dance was held in a place at the Northern General Hospital, which I hadn't been near for quite a few years. The reason the dance was held at the hospital was because one of our relatives drives an ambulance.

This was a very important meeting with my father because the time would arrive soon enough and I would need the help of both my parents. The real thing about all this is that I had gone into myself at an early age to protect myself and to hide feelings affecting my judgment and because of this I was cut off from the world around me. I had appeared to hate, and even despise my parents, but this was just a front to make life a lot easier to get through, till the time would come to show who I really was.

I sat in the dark in the front room of my mother's house, listening to Kate Bush on the record player I started to cry which was something I had given up many years before. The reason for my crying was that I loved my parents even though I had shown both of them very little up to now. It was a relief to have real feelings again after so long of having to play the living dead because it was the best way of being anonymous. I wondered if I was mad, even at this stage, yet reality, fantasy and insanity had been such close companions in my life, which made it hard to tell. This left me with just my own instincts to follow and they would hopefully get me through the biggest and meanest test of my life. The story you are about to read is true but you may not believe it to be so and to you who do not believe I hope you enjoy what I have written anyway.

1 Painting the Rainbow

I got out of bed and opened the curtains to see a light frost had turned the grass into a snowy white blanket that crunched when you walked on it. I put on my clothes and made my way to the kitchen to make myself a pot of tea and a couple of slices of toast for breakfast. I was soon on my way walking to my old school, Myers Grove, for an English lesson. The air had a cool chill to it and even with a light wind it would blow through you. A thought crossed my mind as I walked that here I was walking willingly to a school I had hated so much as a pupil, it took some believing that I could be going back to a scene of much personal unhappiness. I was one of the first students to turn up but my friend Michael was present so I sat down next to him. We talked about the weekend football results and discussed the projects we had chosen to do. On this day we were to have a private discussion with our course tutor, John Edwards, about the way our work was going. Being the brave type, I was the last student to be seen by John Edwards just before the tea break. He was holding these chats in a little room, which had previously been a cupboard. I sat in a chair opposite him and he was doing most of the talking. While he was talking he kept putting his hand on his forehead as if he was in pain. The conversation, if you could call it that, had reached a point where we were discussing how languages come together and how thoughts can be realized. He seemed to have a lot of trouble following this line of thought and was pulling his head back with both hands. Eventually, I asked him if he would like to be relieved of his pains and traumas, he said, "Yes please!" while he held his head in desperation. I still don't know how the conversation got round to redemption but that is what the outcome of our little chat had brought us to. This was the signal I had been waiting for and I made my way out of the small room to make myself a cup of tea as all the other students had already got theirs. I needed a drink to settle my nerves as I was now on edge after my chat with John Edwards, which had decided my action that was to come. I had not slept the night before and I had a slight burning sensation in my head, my breathing was starting to cause me problems because I was snatching at each breath. When break time was over, I told the rest of the class that I had things to do and got my gear together and left the school. I had decided to see my symbolic mother who, if she were still a lecturer, would be at Stannington College, where she would be teaching English. She had been my tutor when I did an 'O' level in English at the college a few years before. It was just a matter of walking up the hill from Myers Grove to the college and I was soon there. I made my way to the lecturers' rooms and knocked on the door and when someone said "Enter", that's what I did. I was not sure how Ms Emsworth was going to take what I had to say so I was slightly apprehensive.

At first I went to the wrong woman because I wasn't wearing my glasses and now I was very short sighted. Eventually not having to use Braille I found the lady I was looking for. I asked her if we could discuss something that was playing on my mind in private. We left the office and ended up going for a fair walk in order to find a place where we could talk. While we were walking I told her I thought of her as my symbolic mother and she said someone also had said this before to her. We entered a small room, which was at the side of the foyer in the college and had a big window looking out into the corridor. Having sat down I started to tell her about parts of my life and how they had affected me in my life up to now. I mentioned Catherine who I hoped I hadn't alienated myself to. It was just going through certain aspects of my mission, which didn't seem clear to me at the time - in other words I was looking for reassurances. My breathing was very noticeable because of the noise I was making whilst gulping air. I don't know what Ms Emsworth thought of it all but I was glad that such a bright and nice person had given me some of her time, to listen to my ravings. The thought entered my head that I probably would never see her again yet here I was talking about some of my deepest thoughts to a near stranger. I also thought that the help she had given me during my time as her 'O' level student was something that I could never repay her for. She helped my English come on greatly at a time when I was very willing to hear and expand my knowledge. After about twenty minutes we had discussed all I wanted to and we left the little room and said our goodbyes, with me thanking her for giving her time. It also crossed my mind that I had better be sane with all the things going through my mind or I was on the edge of sanity and staring madness in the face.

I made my way home, where I began to out my thoughts and the words of a particular pop song that seemed to me to have great reference to what was going on. I was full of energy and felt really good in myself now that I had got certain things off my chest. The whole thing appeared to me to be one big meant happening. I was so wide-awake and willing to think about anything. Before I went to bed I cried about my parents because I loved them and didn't hate them. I think this was because of the way I had treated them in the past and it had all been part of the way things had to be in order to carry the operation to a successful conclusion. The great thing about crying is that afterwards you feel so much better and I was already moving towards the big high that was to come.

During the night I was unable to sleep being so full of myself and thinking over parts of my past, which had brought me to this time and to a day that would alter everything after it.... The way in the past I had always had time for people and been there for plenty of people who were feeling down..... The way I had swapped from a team that was winning to a team that was losing when we were playing footie in the schoolyard with a tennis ball came back to mind.... All the people I had met in my life from the good to the bad and who were indifferent. Where were all these people now and would they remember me if I was to bump into them, probably not? ... The way my life had taken a path that had encompassed so many different types of people who had different thoughts about life in contrast to my own. I recalled so many of the good and bad times I had been through in nearly twenty six years of living and now wondered if certain events had a far greater significance than they had at the time. The way in my time at Myers Grove School I had been so anti-discipline and gone around in a daze most of the time with just art and history to console me. By not doing well at school and not getting good grades it meant getting the job of a painter and decorator - a lot more easier than if I had swotted for my exams. In the scheme of things it would have not made too much difference if I had played truant but that's just an after thought. The way things were I could pretend to myself that I was more clever than a lot of the people around me by just being part of the crowd and not standing out too much.... Of my time on the Council of all the strokes I pulled and so many of the jokes and the jibes aimed at me plus the hatred that was directed at me by so many small minded cretins.... The times I spent at college during my apprenticeship, of all the unhappy times I had there, of the times when I was daft and all the times I had too much to drink.... The thoughts since of going back to education which was something that would have been out of the question when I was at school, after all my bad memories. But between the years I had changed and now enjoyed reading and writing and doing my studies. It had been virtually a new experience actually enjoying education and it opened up a world I had in my earlier life shunned. I could now walk into a library without wanting to hit some of the people present. Of the way the song `Bad' by U2 had so mirrored my experience that I was now going through and couldn't have been written any better with me in mind. The way that just at the right moment I had got my signal from John Edwards to move to the countdown of the operation could not have been any better arranged. I felt confident in myself and didn't fear anything that was in front of me. The next phase if I had told anyone about it they would not have believed me. My going to see my symbolic mother I hoped, would not be taken in a wrong way but was something that I felt was important at the time. That night I was so full of myself which for me was unnatural because I was in the main down in the dumps most of the time. My thoughts in my mind I hoped were not an illness that had come over me because of living a semi-hermit existence in my life. Or was it all true that I was capable of doing something that would blow most people's minds away. That I had a promise to keep and finally get a very weighty burden off my shoulders and then be able to live my life in the same way as everyone else. All these thoughts were going through my mind, making my head feel warm, with the pain still to come. The night could not go fast enough before becoming morning. I lay on my bed waiting with anticipation for the right moment to go downstairs. With the dark slowly turning brighter I looked at the clock and decided to wait at least till six o'clock, as I didn't want to upset my mum anymore than the minimum. At six I made my way downstairs and put on the kettle to make a pot of tea. When I had drunk my second cup I went back upstairs to my bedroom and put on my tracksuit. The thought in my head was to go for a run as I had been working on my body for the last few months. I had started to eat bran when I felt hungry, and also had cut down on the fry-ups that I was used to having. My mother had got up by now and as I opened the back door I said to her "It's over!"

It was a cold and fresh morning, and my breathing even before I started to run was very exaggerated and my head was very warm. I made my way from Hawksley Avenue to the top gates of the park on Middlewood Road and when I started to run it began. My heart was beating faster and faster even at the beginning and my lungs felt tight like someone had got them in a vice grip. The park appeared to be empty and because of the morning dew everything looked fresh and clean. I made my way past the library and went down the slight slope. I went past the duck pond that was on the right as I ran along the path, the main grass area of the park was to my left and I had decided that this part of the park was the area I was going to run around. I ran passing the trees and going to the bottom of the park which had Penistone Road running along part of it and I reached the area just in front of the building that was used for children to do things in the summer months. This would be the first of my circuits and I was nearly in position for starter's orders. The imaginary starter's pistol was fired and the race had begun. I ran as fast as I could with my heart pumping and my lungs fighting for air as it felt like there was a clamp across my chest. The pain inside my head was increasing with every stride until the pain grew to an implosion inside my brain. The power from this happening was fantastic and it felt like my head could come off with the force because it was so strong and pounding on the inside of my head. The whole experience made me run even faster around the circuit that I was running and I completed my first circuit by running on the inside of the trees to my right. The grass was hard and crunchy with the frost that had been during the night and I've always run better on a hard surface. Snow started to fall on this area in the park and I felt that it had something to do with me. The park was mine or so I thought at the time and now no one could stop me even if they wanted to. I began the second circuit and the snow came down even harder and was settling on the grass and the path areas of the park. My head felt like it was at breaking point and seemed that it might explode at any moment. Even though I felt a great sense of wonderment over what I had done I also had a fleeting thought about the damage that this could bring me in the future. The snow kept falling as I ran and I now realised the power of what I had done. My head had somehow triggered off the snow downfall that was happening at this moment. My lungs felt tight and the muscles in my legs were starting to give out great pain and I was learning I had muscles in places where I had never had them before. I began the final circuit and felt if I ran any faster I would have to fly. This was the greatest high of my life and I knew there was no turning back, this was really happening and all the uncertainties were cast aside for a time at least. This was the sort of high people who take drugs or drink heavily are always in search of but never find, and here I was on tea and fresh air going into wonderland and leaving everyone else in my wake. Let go of this lifeless line was going through my mind as I ran, throw this lifeless line into the wind and the wind of change would be released at last. I'm dreaming I can do it... I know I can do it... this is happening. To set my spirit free and hear my heartbeat, as it has never done before, with my lungs trying to gasp air, the cobwebs falling off me as I ran. At last I was coming out of my hibernation to be alive at last. The days of protecting the power were now over and it was time to use it to help change some people's lives and give them a second chance. After the bloom there is the fade away and the cocoon that had been wrapped around me inside my head was now free at last. It was now time to be the person I had always been underneath. Never in my life had I felt so wide awake and in charge of my senses, which were in hyper-drive. To feel alive and being myself was just sinking in. Here I was on one of the days of fulfillment. It had finally arrived and I felt euphoric about it. At long last I am free and soon I will be as free as other people with the great weights of responsibility no more. Can I live up to the challenge that is now before me and I'll get through it with out too many scars, well I hope I can. Or will it all become too big and make me mad for the rest of my life? At this moment in time I would gladly run through a brick wall if it were required to complete my mission. I keep saying to myself that nothing can stop me now, no one can stop me. Its too late, the power had been unleashed and it will go on its course. People will find they have a destiny to face very shortly whether they like it or not, they have decided it for themselves and now it is on its way. The energy I can feel in my body is so invigorating I have never felt such a feeling in my life. I'm so full of it I want to scream to let others know what I am going through but it will be known soon enough by people I know and by many

17

people who I don't know. Will I be able to complete all I have to do before I go out of my head? When the force becomes too much, as it will, I must be in care by then or it could all go wrong. Time from this moment on is now speeding along and racing like my head. I am now fighting the clock with plenty to do now I have entered a new dimension. Even if I don't survive this morning has been one of the highlights of my life and suddenly it all seems like its been worthwhile, all the waiting, all the pain and all the doubt that I've been through to here. The pounding of my heart feels like it could burst out through my chest at any moment. They're going to find a man in the park with no heart and no brain if they keep pounding so. My head is burning with my mind saying I've got to survive, I will survive and surviving is something I'm good at I survive by doing whatever it takes. To be so wide awake after all this time, it's like I've just opened my crypt and come out alive again after being dead for twenty five years. But now I am wide awake and at last full of myself with a self confidence filling out my body but how long will it last? My lungs feel like someone is squeezing them inside my chest as I gasp for air. It's just great to be alive and kicking even if I am gasping for air. I wonder if anyone else has ever been in the same position as I find myself in now. Did they manage coming down from the high to land on earth again or did they stay trapped in a world of madness? Then again what the heck and who cares anyway, here I am and that's all that matters at this point in time. The cold wind in the park seems to be getting stronger by the second and is taking what little breath I have as I run. Then suddenly the wind leaves the park to go around the world or so I thought at the time. I'm so out of breath but the feeling is one of excitement and of expectation of what is to come. This really is happening and it is definitely not a hallucination. The snow comes down like a blanket making the world seem like a spilled bottle of milk. I wonder what all the people I've known will think about this when they find out it is me, will they just deny it or will they even realise what I have done and anyhow, do I really care what anyone else thinks? My head is burning and the snow and the cold weather don't seem able to cool it down. What a moment is ones life, though a line from an old movie struck me as apt "I'm on the top of the world ma!" as James Cagney said in the film I'm thinking of. I really was on top of the world but then a nagging doubt came over me and I could feel the power leaving my body and ebbing away slowly. My muscles felt like they needed a rest and a good soak in the bath. I'm out of breath with my lungs feeling like they're going to burst open at any second. Maybe I should have trained harder to get myself into better shape. My head is starting to go into a confused state of mind and suddenly I am not too sure about what I am doing running around Hillsborough Park early in the morning with snow falling all around me. I headed back home in a little trot being the best I could manage. Thinking back to when I said, "It's over!" to my Mother I now felt that this was a premature statement to make because it really was just beginning. The consequences of my actions on this morning were going to change my life forever.

When I got back home I took my training gear off and had a wash down in the bathroom. The tracksuit was wet through inside and out and I was glad to get it off. I put my clothes on, which were a pair of blue cord trousers, an orange shirt and a red jumper. It was toast for breakfast and I went into the living room to play some records because there was plenty of time before I had to leave for college. I was thinking about Catherine and being with her after all this time. My Mother left to go to work and my brother hadn't got up yet, with me paying little notice. Eventually, the time came for me to leave the house, with my getting in a queue for a bus just before the Barracks. When I arrived in town I looked all around me in the hope of meeting Catherine before we got to college. The history lesson was held at Granville College with me making my way by foot looking for a glimpse of Catherine but she was nowhere to be seen. The history lesson was held in some out buildings on the right side of the road because the college is split into two parts on either side of Granville Road. Today's lesson was to be on British history and the tutor would be Mark Davis. I was the first to arrive with only two other students turning up on this day. The lecturer asked us if he had got bad breath or something because of such a poor turn out. I put it down to what I had done that morning with me somehow attacking people's nervous systems. This was the reason behind the low turn out or so I thought at the time. I asked Mark Davis if I could have a piece of chalk and he gave me some. I started to write on the blackboard all the thoughts and ideas that were going through my head. The things I wrote were the answers to all the unanswered questions that had been bothering people for years. It was the first and last time I tried to explain the madness that had come over me. One of the students who were present only came to class every other week and he commented that what I was doing was boring. It struck me the whole thing had been boring me for years so he had nothing to come with his cheap observation.

After writing on the blackboard Mark Davis, who was in a very confused state himself, seemed very distant. He sat down beside me to hear what I had to say as I tried to explain what I had written in a clearer way. I told him I got a tick for everything I had written. The main theme of what I had written was my mother and the Mother of all Creation. It was she who was behind what I was attempting. The message of `Mother Weeps No More' was something that was going through my head with me thinking it was a message from some distant ancestor. I tried very hard to convey what was about to happen with thinking I had somehow affected all the members of the class in some physiological way. I had brought about chaos in order to attempt change on a massive scale. The tables had been turned as I was now the tutor trying to explain what I thought was going on. While we had our chat the other two students did some work Mark Davis had given out. I don't think that he took much in of what I was trying to explain to him. He was concerned a great deal with a member of his family who was ill at the time and this made his thoughts wander. Later I found out from my dad that Mark Davis told the class I had gone to commit suicide. I told him that I had managed to go back to the first Mother in the history of the human race in order to set myself free from my promise. `Mother Weeps No More' was going through my head over and over again. This of course is a very heavy thought and I could be also viewed as a total load of crap, coming from someone who had gone out of their mind with a ready made excuse. I gave up trying to get through to Mark Davis but at least I had tried to point out what was going on inside my head. We took our morning break just a little early, with us making our way to the canteen. When we got in the queue for a drink Mark Davis bought me a cup of tea. The four of us sat down at a table. There was the lad who only came very rarely, a total knob head, and I didn't like him because of his reactionary politics. The other student was Jake and I got on fairly well with him. Talking to Jake I asked him where Catherine lived, with him giving me her address. My thoughts would always return to Catherine no matter how I had tried to block her out of my mind. It struck me while I was in the canteen that I had to see her and nothing was going to stand in my way of doing so. After the break we made our way back to the classroom and I tidied up my desk, put my coat on and said goodbye to Mark Davis and Jake as I left the room. I was going to Catherine's house because I wanted to explain to her what was going on and also tell her it was me who would be making things happen that were not normal. I knew Catherine lived in Stannington but now I knew her address. The house was on a fairly new estate of stone built houses, just a couple of minutes away from my friend Rory's house.

Nearing her home I walked down the slight hill with me soon standing in front of the door to her house. It never dawned on me she might not be in on the way to her house but now I wondered. I knocked on the door and waited, no answer so I knocked again. This time Catherine opened the door with a big dog playfully coming out to greet me. The dog was very excited so asking me in she put the dog in a room and shut the door. She then asked me if I wanted a cup of tea that received a resounding yes. I gave her a Mars bar, as I knew she liked them and she said, "no one has ever given me anything before!" Next I gave her some things I'd written. There was a song we both knew and I had written out the words of the song from `The Unforgettable Fire' album by U2. The song was called `Bad' and while she was reading what I had written, I asked her to put the record on. Before she put it on she said "it's my favourite track on the album!". I tried with little success to try and get through to her that things would be happening that no one would want to admit to. Catherine looked great with her eyes always looking like they were going to cry; this made her look so vulnerable and young. I know some of you out there are thinking that she was near tears because she had me to look at, but that was not the case. Looking back maybe I should have tried harder to get her to understand and get over how much she meant to me. The time I spend with Catherine seemed to fly with her soon having to leave to go to a lesson. I walked with her to the bus stop and got on with her but I got off at Hillsborough corner to go to my mother's. Having said goodbye to Catherine I wondered would the next time we meet, would she be mine?

The clock was racing against me and now that I had opened my head by implosion, I would soon be in no fit state to do anything. When I got home I made myself a pot of tea and took it into the front room with me. I was playing records time and time again to while away the hours. My breathing was now very strained and I was taking great gulps through my mouth, plus my head felt like it was on fire and about to burst open at any moment. It was my turn to cook the meal and we were having roast lamb and vegetables. When my Mother came home with my Brother I put the meal on the plates and we got stuck in. When we had finished the meal I washed the dishes. My mother was concerned about the way I was eating strangely even by my standards. When I had finished my chores I went back into the front room to play my records. My head was now burning and I knew that I only had so much time left. The thought in my head was that I would get Catherine after doing my bit and would be free after all this time. Not exactly a new thought but very much a recurring one. If I was compared to a normal person I would be thought out of my head but the experience I was going through was not beyond belief. I watched a little television before going to bed and I knew I would get no sleep because I was so awake. I lay on my bed thinking about my meeting with Catherine and how fantastic she looked. There was no doubt in my mind about one thing, if I ended up with Catherine by my side the whole ordeal I had been put through in order to get to this moment would seem like a fair deal. There are not many women who you could say are gorgeous but Catherine was definitely one whom you could say that of. The fact is I was hooked and she was like no other person I had ever met. To think she was going to be in my arms in a short while was something to really dream about. My mind also thought back to the moment when John Edwards said "Yes please" in such a sad way, which was more like a plea than anything else. The pain on his face at that moment in time will always be with me and I could only feel sorry for him even though he had a lot of bad things written in his face. Just because John Edwards had asked me to help I would not be going through everything just for him but all those like him and others who were not would get something out of what I was attempting to do. The task had been up to this week one of waiting but now it was full steam ahead and get out of my way I've got something important to do. The hours were slowly moving along and some things from the past came to mind such as my time on the council while I was a painter and one of my charge hands called Grunty would not have to wait much longer to get his reward for the way he treated me, which he'd brought on himself with me just helping along.... Of all the days I'd hated so much in my time on the works, of the cold days when I was so miserable and so near to jacking it in.... Of the years at Myers Grove I spent and the very little I learned while being there. Most of the people in my year will be married by now and here I am and I haven't even been engaged yet. I would have a lot to catch up on but that was how it had to be in order to carry this great task out. The responsibility I had carried around with me was one of the reasons I'd always shunned any attempt to make me responsible for anything else. The strain that I had been put under from an early age would at last be lifted off my world-weary shoulders. The sexual repression was something that I had thought a lot about and its effects over me could lead me to being a person I didn't want to be but I had become over the years. The night was full of stars when I looked out of my bedroom window with me full of excitement. There was a state of expectancy about me and I could hardly wait for the sun to rise again so I could go for a walk outside.

It was the early hours of what was a Friday and would certainly be a memorable day in my life the way it unfolded. I was downstairs at six o'clock making myself a pot of tea just for a change. There was no reason for me to get up early, as I had no classes on a Friday to attend. My mother didn't sleep too well either during the night but unlike me she looked like she was missing it. I was so full of myself and I couldn't recall feeling any better than I did this morning. When my mother had left for work I went in the front room to play my records. My brother went out to do a course he was doing at the time. I felt like I could fly and a lot of the songs seemed to have significance with what was going on in my mind. The morning had soon passed by and the afternoon was upon me. It suddenly came over me to go to Hillsborough library, which was in the park. When I entered I had in mind that I would take out ten books, which would cover human achievements, in particular if they were from the twentieth century. It took me a while to get the ten books I wanted and I can only recall two of the books I took out because they had a picture on the front. One was about Hitler and the other was about soccer skill with a picture of Pele on the front of it. I had gone out without a bag so I held the books in front of me and made my way through the snow. My destination was my old school Myers Grove or as I called it when a pupil Myers Grotto! It meant a walk up

Stannington Road hill and then turning right on to Wood Lane hill. The English language course I was on was meeting in what had been the teachers' mess room when I attended the school in the seventies. But now it was just a room for the English course. The main doors of the school were open so I walked in and went to the room I was going to decorate. Putting the books on top of a large desk I arranged them so they could all be seen. When I took my hat off my hair was wet with sweat and I put it in my coat pocket, I then removed my coat. Then I started to unravel badminton nets that were all in knots. When I had a net unraveled I laid it across chairs and started to decorate the room in a fashion. What with the snow falling outside it could be said to be Christmas in March. There was a stepladder and I put a net over it with the rest on the chairs. My head was burning by now and I felt thirsty so I had a look in the fridge, which was in the room. There were two bottles of milk, which I drank in gulps and feeling a lot better after doing so. It felt like I was experiencing my own personal melt down inside my head with it at any moment bursting open. I wrote a joke on a scrabble board game - "Why did Jesus go to Germany?" "Because he got tired of being hammered with tacks!"

I arranged the letters from the scrabble board and was going to throw them in the air but didn't get around to it. The room began to take shape with my moving chairs and waste paper bins into the positions I wanted them in. I left the room to go to the toilet and passed one of my old teachers who said to me "It's not that bad is it?" If only he knew. When I made my way back I went into the art room that was just across the corridor from the room I had been decorating. When inside the art room I arranged desks and put some of the pupil's models around the room. The best part was when I started to throw all the paint pots all around the room. It was such a great release. How the colours seemed so bright I couldn't remember seeing them as bright as they looked now in front of my eyes. The power of the colours could blow the mind away; they looked radiant. Was there some sort of code here that I had forgotten and was now coming back to me? The sheer beauty of the colours could overpower me and it all seemed to make sense out of the nonsense that I was thinking. My senses felt like they were at a peak and my body already had been. Is this the way true colour looks like all the time and before I was never capable of seeing it but now had the enlightenment to see it in all its glory. The way it makes me feel happy and glad to be alive is certainly a different experience for me. How many before me I wonder have seen such wonders with their eyes and emotion come over them? My head was somewhere in the stars and I felt great to have gotten to this point in my life. It was suddenly worth the struggle that it had taken to get here. I thought they'd be scraping me off the ceiling before I'd done. The brightness of the colours must enlighten the world or so I thought at the time. Will the brightness consume me and make me disappear? How long will this last? Is it temporary or a long-term happening? Will the brightness lead to insanity or will it change me forever in a good way? A thought crosses my mind, have I already gone beyond the barriers of sanity with no return and that the reason for this experience is that I am mad? That my very ideas that I can change people's lives is just an excuse for my mind to make me think that everything is fine when in fact, I am fighting for my existence. Only time will give up the answer. It could well be I've damaged my brain with the pain I'm feeling and the warmth of my head is very worrying. If it was possible for everyone to see the colours in this way would we be living in a better world crosses my mind. It was certainly another memory that would stay with me for the rest of my life and make me thankful that I could have such an experience in my life. The room certainly looked colourful when I had finished. One of the cleaning ladies came in and smiled at me and then left the room. It was as if she was in a trance. The teacher who I had known when I was a pupil at the school looked in from the doorway in the corridor and asked me what I was doing. I told him I was in the English Language class and that I had permission to be in the room. This seemed to get rid of him and clutching some emulsion tins I made my way across the corridor to the English room that I had been decorating. Going through my head was that song "I can paint a rainbow", you know the one, "red and yellow, green and blue, orange and purple too, I can see a rainbow, see a rainbow, can't you?" Well it goes something like that and I can remember seeing a hallucination of Tribal dancing rites by people with paint on their faces dancing around a massive fire. What a strange feeling of emotions were going through me. I was in a place that I had previously hated but here I was now gaining one of the greatest highs of my life. This was definitely a great experience and it would soon be over with me then having to pay the price for this amazing high.

The teacher who had words with me while I was in the art room had gone for another member of staff who was his superior. She poked her head through the door and asked me what I was doing. I replied, "I'm decorating!" She left and no doubt went to telephone the police to sort out what was going on. I had been at play for the best part of four hours and had enjoyed my time no end. Running around the park had been great; this was the metaphysical part of me after the physical part had run around the park. I was on edge but it was all positive waves that were going through me, which for me was a nice change from my usual morbid thoughts on my life. Art had always been something of a refuge for me when I attended this school and now I was using art to make my stand against the world. This was a beacon to tell everyone who wanted to listen that I had finally arrived and intended to take over everything I could. It was all giant symbolism to announce my presence and I had done it in a very peaceful way. Some people when they blow a fuse inside their heads get a machine gun and mow down passers by, I painted a rainbow which isn't as news worthy even though it is a lot less common than an idiot with a machine gun. By using a rainbow I was making my mark and also letting everyone know who I was in the process. Even if they didn't realise at first who I was it would dawn on them eventually when they thought it all through. I daubed the paint from the emulsion tins with my hands and I got paint all over my clothes with me just finishing my imaginary rainbow when the police came in. One of the policemen asked me to leave the room while another picked up my coat. Because I had paint all over my hands I was given a towel to get most of it off. Before I was handcuffed behind my back, I was led to a police car and had difficulty getting into the back of the car with my hands behind my back. That was the end of painting the rainbow but only the beginning of my adventure that was before me. I had pulled in my audience with the 'Here I am, come and get me' routine. When I got into the police car one of the policemen said "It's Wayne - I went to school with him!" Things seemed to be going to plan. The other policeman asked me why I had done it and I said "For my mother!" That was the first thing that entered my head and it seemed about right anyway. We waited in the car for about ten minutes before making our way to the Hammerton Road Police Station. Getting out of the car was awkward with my arms being behind my back but I managed it somehow. I was led to a desk in a room with a chair either side. The policeman who knew me from our school days asked me to empty my pockets of both my trousers and my coat onto the table in front of me. There was another policeman in the doorway and I thought it strange that they let the youngest member of the crew who went to the school to pick me up to go through police procedures. Not that I would have complained, I liked the idea of someone knowing me being around. The policeman who knew me mentioned, "He's got his passport" in a way that made it seem significant. He told me after looking through what I had emptied out of my pockets that they could not bring any charges against me because I had done nothing wrong. It seems that painting rainbows are a lot less punishable that gunning down most of the population. I told him that I would pay for any damage I had caused in my inspired time at my old school. But with him saying they could not charge me that seemed to be the end of the matter as far as the police were concerned.

When the interrogation was over I was allowed to use the toilet. I returned to the room and the policeman who was watching over me stood in the doorway. I asked him "How's your mother?" and he replied "None of your business!" which of course was the case. I must have been very much mother orientated at the time. Now began a long wait. I don't know how long I waited but nothing seemed to matter anymore. My mother had been sent for and that's why it took a while, as she hadn't come home from work yet. She finally turned up with my brother. We were taken outside with two policemen, and all sat down in the back of a white Maria. The destination was the Northern General Hospital. While we were on the way there, my mother asked me "Will

I get through it?" and I replied, "Of course you will!" I had put my wet woolen hat on again, which always makes me look stupid but then again I didn't need much help in that direction as I was stupid most of the time anyway! When we got to the emergency department of the hospital complex, our party entered the hospital. One of the policemen took my handcuffs off and we sat down after informing the duty nurse of our arrival. We would now have to wait to see the Specialist or more like I would have to wait to see the Specialist. My father turned up at the hospital and shortly after so did my sister and brother-in-law. I had the whole family around me in what seemed to me to be the start of a fantastic adventure. I was high as a kite and it all appeared to be one big game. The Specialist was ready and for some reason he wanted to see my mother and father first. I was still waiting to see the Specialist. When my parents came out of the little office, my father told me that they didn't tell him about the incident with the whiskey. This meant that as far as the Specialist knew I had no previous escapades that could point out my present state. It was now my turn to go into the little room and face the Specialist, which didn't seem like much of a task. The Doctor looked a little like Bjorn Borg, the tennis player, and he started to ask me questions about myself. I kept answering that I was fine and had never felt better because I was experiencing the greatest high of my life. The interview was a success, I had passed my entry test and I was going to be detained for observation.

The two policemen, on hearing this, said goodbye and left the hospital. One of the policemen visited my mother to ask how I was going on with my illness the following week. We now had to wait for an ambulance to take me to the psychiatric hospital unit where I would be put under observation. The ambulance arrived and my mother and brother got in the back with me and my father and sister following us in their cars. We were shown to ward 54 and I had to have a little test of my reflexes. I went into a room with a Doctor and she tried to check my body's reactions when she touched me in certain areas, but she came to the conclusion that I was messing about and wasting her time. I was full of myself and nothing else mattered to me at that time. To keep me for observation I had to be put under Section 28 of the Mental Health Act. In order for this Act to be made legal, my doctor had to be called for even though I had never seen her. I was given a little room all to myself and my parents and relatives left me for the night. The ward was a mixed ward with both sexes in separate sections and there were big curtains you could pull round your bed if you didn't want to be disturbed by the other patients.

The first night is a bit murky in my memory. I felt there was nothing wrong with me so I decided to leave the ward and then leave the hospital. I put on my coat, my hat and also my gloves and then told the staff that I was going home. That was what I thought because they would not let me leave the ward and I can remember kicking a door in frustration at my situation. The room I had been given was stripped of everything except for a mattress. Then they asked me to take my clothes off and all I had on was my underpants. They then informed me that I was going to have an injection to sedate me and the very thought of a needle going into me made me shiver. During my life it was I who had pricked at people's nervous systems and I knew the power of what I had released in Hillsborough Park was no longer inside me. This meant I was powerless and very vulnerable to attack; it was the sheer weight of these thoughts that filled my mind with terror. I knew that once that needle was placed inside me I would loose my feelings of just being alive and happy in myself and that it would lose my feeling of euphoria with it being the start of the low. I was told to lay face down on the mattress and that I would be held down by the staff if I resisted against having the injection. I told them to get on with it and I said, "You're a load of bastards!" The needle could not have hurt more if the nurse had used a knife - the pain was really severe. The nurse must have hit a nerve or something and I think it might have been so painful that I blacked out through the pain and had my first hours of shuteye for sometime. The pain was just the beginning and before I was done in the hospital I knew I was going to have to get through a lot more pain to get what I wanted, which was mainly Catherine. How I would be glad to think of something that was so worthwhile when I was facing despair in the face. The needle marked the end of the high and the start of the low but it ended much more than that, it ended my nervous system as in regards to one's health. The Wayne Clay who entered the Northern General Hospital, with that one injection was gone forever. It would take a long time to sink in that when, or if, I got through this ordeal, I would be a new Wayne Clay and would have to face the world as I was now and not as I was before the incidents that changed my life. My new world had begun with a nightmare and before it was going to get any better it was going to get a lot worse.

2 Childhood to Teenager

Thinking back to my childhood it's hard to think of what was my earliest memory. I can remember being afraid of the dark and having the landing light on to help me sleep. During my sleep I would wet the bed, which I did from the age of two. I was nearly eleven years old, which looking back on it was not exactly a confidence booster. I can recall being put in a nursery school very early on so I was out of the way for my mother. They used to get us to queue up in a line and give us a spoonful of cod liver oil. In the afternoon we would get out the camping beds and have a rest, whether you wanted one or not as the case might be. My mother would collect me or sometimes it would be a neighbour. I went to the nursery until I was able to go to proper school. The day I first went to Malin Bridge Junior School I felt very nervous as I walked up the hill with my mother and when she left me my heart sank. I so much wanted to leave with my mother instead of going into the classroom and meeting my teacher. Because of my bowel disorder, on one of my first days at school, I had an accident and had to go and clean myself up and put on some shorts. I was allowed to leave the classroom without asking permission to go to the toilet. I think because of these distractions my schoolwork was very poor and I didn't do too well in my learning. On the plus side I made a good friend in Mark. Its funny I'm not sure of the name of my first teacher but I'd make a guess that she was called Fox. We would have an assembly in the morning in the hall that was between the classrooms that were either side of it. I can recall singing Onward Christian Soldiers and Dance Now for I am the Lord of the Dance said He. During one assembly all the books were thrown in the air, which ended the assembly earlier than usual. One time there was a visit from someone from the Health Department about how important it is to clean your teeth. They gave us a badge plus an apple each with the old motto: an apple a day keeps the doctor away. In the morning break we would all be given a bottle of milk to drink and sometimes there were leftovers and I would have a second bottle. Thinking back to people visiting us there was the Tufty Club that I think was something to do with road safety and we did get a visit from the Police to tell us about road safety as well. As my time passed by in my first year at the school, I got involved in a gang and I can recall one day we went into the outside toilets and started to kick the doors in. Because of the noise this alerted one of the teachers on break duty who caught us and took all of us, of which there were about seven, to see the Headmaster. We were allowed in the room and stood in a line in front of his big desk while the teacher told him what we had been up to. He caned all of the lads except me, who he said was easily led and told me not to hang around with these lads again if I didn't want to be in trouble all the time. At dinnertime I had the school meal until we were allowed to bring sandwiches. One day at dinner time, when I was still having the school meal, there was leftovers of mincemeat and I went back twice to have some more, for seconds it was rice pudding and there was plenty of leftovers of that too and I made a right pig of myself going for more three times. Things had certainly changed from Oliver asking for more gruel that's for sure!

When I went out into the playground after my dinner I could hardly move because I was so full. In the breaks we had there were plenty of corner shops to go to and we would have 1-penny and 2-penny drinks of pop. When we had finished our drinks we would all go to the shed and play Bulldog. Someone would stand in the middle of the shed and we would all run whilst the one in the middle tried to grab somebody who would then also stand in the middle and try to grab someone else and so on until there was only one person left, who when we started the game again, would be the one in the middle at the start. This game was very rough but no one seemed to mind the confrontations that could arise from the game. I was very slow in my studies and can recall having to read to one of the teachers in a room with just us two in it and I felt embarrassed about the situation, making me blush and redden in the face. When I was at home one day at Holme Lane, the doctor came and had to show me how to blow my nose with the aid of a piece of cotton wool. During my early years I had plenty of nosebleeds and dizzy spells. I really liked it when we lived at Holme Lane even if the toilet was in the yard, which certainly made life interesting when you had to go when it was pitch black outside.

Next to our yard there was a much bigger one that had the back doors of four houses. I think that family was called Blackburn. They had two sons who were both older than me yet my sister and I would play with them. When they wanted to get rid of me they would pull their jumpers over their heads and I would run into the house crying and saying the bogeymen are after me! When I watched Doctor Who I would be hiding behind the settee and one of the stories was about yetis that had a ball in the middle of their stomachs; that really scared me at the time. My favourite television series at the time was The Man from Uncle, which had one American and one Russian working together to stop the evil doings of another organisation that didn't care how they got power just as long as they got power. In the other yard there were a couple of old ladies who were called Nellie and I thought that all old ladies were called Nellie because of this. My sister and I would go in their houses and play twenty questions to do with vegetable, solid or mineral as the game went I think, or they would tell us stories. When it was summer time the Blackburn's and I would go up to Rivelin and catch newts but they never seemed to live longer than a couple of days and I don't think there is any of them left in that area today. One of the Blackburn's put frog spawn into their fish tank and I can remember their house being overrun with about one hundred frogs which were less than an inch long. When it was bonfire night, as the other yard was a lot larger, we would have our bonfire there and everyone would give out toffee that seemed to take forever to chew. My sister and I would play with some sparklers. In our yard there was the back door to the chemists and also a tailors and not forgetting my mother's Donway Dress Making and Alterations shop. The Chemist, whose son I think was called Elton, whose shirt always seemed to be hanging out, would make us chips. There is something that still sticks in my mind when we lived at Holme Lane and it is the dead chicks that had fallen out of a nest in the gutter above. It was so sad that they would never be able to fly and had such a short life after all the effort their parents would have had to put in.

My early years were far from idyllic with my parents having rows most of the time that would happen throughout their marriage. Plus I had co-ordination difficulties and bed-wetting problems that were not helping me in my development. I can remember my dad saying he would give me a ten bob note if I could learn the alphabet when I was nine or ten years old. I did it and nearly got sick from all the chocolate and bottles of pop I bought. When it came to Saturdays I would dread having to go with my mother to the other shop on Langsett Road, so I would hide in next door's toilets with one of the Blackburn's and my mum would leave ten pence for my dinner and that was when there were two hundred and forty pennies to one pound. I usually had tomato soup, which was my favourite soup. Of course I didn't get away all of the time and spent many hours on the back of the shops when I was a child and sometimes I would help with unpicking on certain jobs. If I went with my mother it would be chips for dinner and they were the greasiest chips in town or so I thought at the time. We had a sewing class at Malin Bridge School and we would be dropping our needle and thread on the floor so we could look up the skirt of the teacher who was supervising our work. In my last year I think my teacher was called Potter and he showed us the rules to chess and that's about all I can remember about him. There was an incident at school that showed the way things would go in my life. I tried to trip up my friend, Mark as we went back into class and instead tripped myself, catching my left ear on a desk as I did so. I had cut open a piece of my ear and blood was flowing down onto my shirt. One of the members of staff helped find a towel that I could use to catch the blood that was coming out of my ear. I was given a sweet while they tried to get in touch with my parents. In the end one of the teachers who had a car gave me a lift to my mother's shop and from there he gave us a lift to the Infirmary Hospital that was just down the road. Both my mother and I made our way to the emergency department and I can recall having an injection in the muscly part of my thigh, which made me cry at the time. The doctor put some stitches in my ear and I kept asking him "Have you done yet?" as I wanted to leave as soon as possible. The doctor didn't have much patience and said when he had finished that we should have gone to the Children's Hospital in town.

A week later I was told to go and see the Headmaster who asked me if anyone had tripped me up and I couldn't really tell him I was trying to trip my friend up so I just said no and that was the end of that. With not having to go and have a meal at dinnertime now we could bring sandwiches. A group of lads and I would play around the church that was opposite the school. Sometimes we would all pile into a shop and some of the lads would pinch bags of crisps. After a while it got relayed back to the headmaster and he mentioned it in assembly, telling us we could not play around the church at dinnertimes anymore. One day a couple of older lads were going to have a fight on the ground behind the church out of the way of the teachers. There must have been about one hundred of us after school going to watch. It was all over very quickly with our lad pulling the other one to the floor and kicking him in the face, which gave him a nosebleed. So we all dispersed and went our separate ways to go home.

When I was nine years old I joined the Sutton Cub Scouts. My next-door neighbour and I had tried to join the Pollicarp Scout group which must have had a good fifty members on the night we went to join, but thankfully as it turned out, there was no room for us at that time. So the following week, with two lads off the same drive that we now lived on, we joined the Sutton Cub Scouts who were based on Beechwood Road just off Taplin Road. It was a small hall compared to the Pollicarps and there were only about one dozen members, which I felt was about right. We swore I think, an oath of allegiance to the Queen, but I am not sure if that was later. With the two lads from my Drive it was a lot better to go rather than be by yourself. By now we had moved house to Woodend Drive - a newly built house with three bedrooms and an indoor toilet. It was a lot bigger than the house we left behind on Holme Lane. I was still going to Malin Bridge School - it was a little further away that's all. It was just a matter of down one hill and up another and the same to get home. Not forgetting the lollipop ladies at work on the busy road who made sure we got across the road safely. When my time at Malin Bridge ended it was with regret after getting over some of my nervous disorders I had a fairly good time playing around. In the last week before the six-week summer holidays I had a severe pain on my right side on the Thursday. It was the doctor who said it was nothing to worry about. The following day I was a lot worse and I was taken to hospital where I had my appendix taken out. The day after the operation I was taken to a rest home for children. There were a lot who were there who had more serious problems than my own. I was put in a bed next to a girl who was in her early teens. She had the hands and feet of a baby but everywhere else she was the right size for her age. I can recall she was very brave about it, which is something I don't think I would have been, in the same circumstances. As I was still wetting the bed, my mother would bring me a fresh pair of pyjamas to wear every night and take home the pair I had worn the previous night. During the week of my stay at the home there was one of the worst storms that had ever hit Sheffield and I wonder looking back, did I have something to do with it by having my insides opened? Maybe it's just a silly thought after the event. I was having a little fight one day with a lad and I kicked him hard on the leg, he then pulled up his trouser leg and it was covered with varicose veins. I felt sorry for what I had done, he must have been through some right pain and it certainly was not a pleasant sight. One night we were given the alternative of watching a western or having one of the nurses read us a story. There was no contest - I was going to watch the western whereas all the other patients who could move wanted to hear the story. My dad asked me if I'd watched the western and I told him of course I had.

I was only at the convalescent home for one week when Cousin Jennie's husband Tom picked me up. There was a little song around at the time that went "Tom and Jennie working for a penny". My sister and I would usually sing it to them or after seeing them. In fact I don't think they were married at the time or I'm not sure at any rate. Jennie's mother was my dad's sister and of course, my auntie is called Irene like the song "Goodnight Irene". I was told that when my dad's mother was still alive I had thrown Auntie Irene's wage packet onto the fire and my Grandmother stopped them from hitting me. I don't remember doing so but funnily enough I have always gotten on with Auntie Irene, who when she had been shopping would bring back some clay to play with or potato faces that you put on a potato, I suppose that's self explanatory!

With my time at Malin Bridge coming to an end, I would be starting after the six weeks holidays at Myers Grove School that was just across the road from our house. The two lads who went with me to the cubs, Michael and Grant also joined the Sutton Scouts. They were a lot more active than the cubs. There was a changing over ceremony with us leaving the cubs and joining the Scouts. By being a Scout there would be plenty of opportunity to go camping.

Even though I missed the first camping holiday I could go on because of me still wetting the bed, which finally ended around this time I'm glad to say. The stopping of my bed wetting came about because my mum was fed up with it, so was I. She asked how to deal with the problem and was told to wake me up in the night and I was then to go to the toilet. After about a week of this my bed-wetting was a thing of the past after the best part of nine years. With this problem being over, come to think it must have helped my development at the time to advance to new levels. When the next big holiday came along I would be able to go on it, which made me happy inside. It turned out to be some journey. We met at Beechwood Road and I think we had changed our name from Sutton Scouts to Beechwood Scouts. When we were all present with our gear in rucksacks and kit bags, we made our way to the train station where we would be catching our train to Scotland. It turned out to be the baggage car because it was no doubt cheaper. I think it took us around eleven hours to reach Scotland and we got there in the early hours of the morning. We had to leave the station and make our way to another one to catch the train that would take us to our desired destination. It was, I think, a couple of hours to our stop. When we got there we had to walk to the campsite that had been arranged for us to use. The site had a river down the side of it and a Loch was just the other side of the road. When we finally arrived it was time to put up the tents, which we had plenty of. There were two tents for the Scouts, one for cooking in, and one tent each for the two scout leaders, one of whom had brought his wife and their baby. When the tents were up we had to dig a latrine and put a windbreaker round. The place was so peaceful and you could see the big house whose owner also owned the land we were camping on.

The first night we were all tired, not surprisingly after our journey so went to bed early but then had a job sleeping because we were all excited. In the morning after breakfast and a wash we put up a volleyball net that we would play a lot in our two week stay. We also made a raft that we used to go on the Loch with. The Loch had a spell bound silence that was only broken with fish jumping out of the water. There were two older scouts who were close to sixteen and at night they would make their way to a pub that was a fair way down the road. We went on many day trips, one of which was to see how they made tartan and the history of its development. In fact, when we left the place we ended up being chased down a side road by some fifth formers who wanted to beat us up. I can recall one trip we made to the Isle of Mull, we had to use a boat to get there and during the trip we saw hundreds of seals even if it wasn't a clear day by any means. There was a mist over the water on this day. When we got to the Isle of Mull we were given a tour around the castle. There were plenty of Claymores on the walls, with lances and old guns adorning them too. There were banners and lots of old wooden furniture. We were shown around the dungeons where they had dummies being tortured made out of wax and not out of flesh as the previous ancestors had once practiced. I took some photographs on this trip but sadly only two photos came out when they were developed and I've hardly taken a picture since.

At this time I was still trying out smoking but then I just gave it up and gave away my cigarettes to the other scouts. When we didn't go on a day trip there was plenty to do like playing volleyball or going for a swim in the river or go on the Loch with the raft, plus the scout leaders could always think of something to do. We could always go for a long walk and look at the beautiful countryside. One day we visited a dam that produced electricity and it was massive because we went down below into the mountain by bus, which must have taken a good ten minutes to get to what we were going to look at. It was certainly a memorable experience; the sheer vastness of it took a long time to sink in. On the next trip we visited Edinburgh to buy presents to take back home. While we were there we bumped into some other scouts from a different part of the country and swapped badges with them, for which when our scout leaders saw us again, told us off and not to do it again.

Because we were a few miles away from the shops we had a tuck shop. One of the scout leaders, who had come by car, bought a whole box of Mars bars wholesale and also tins of pop in a bulk buy. This meant we could have at least some sweets without having to become tired in the process. The two weeks passed quickly and to celebrate the end of the camping holiday we would have a binge, this meant everyone putting in fifty pence and spending the money on food of which there would be plenty of. We just made pigs of ourselves and it really had been a good holiday. The tents had to be packed up and all our things put into our rucksacks and kit bags for the trip home. Because I didn't want to go back the journey to Sheffield didn't seem to take as long as the trip to our campsite. This was usually the case after a trip away I would wish that we could stay for a lot longer and feel disappointed when I reached home. It was always strange after camping going back to school on the Monday and landing with a thump. We didn't just go for two week holidays of course. We would go for a weekend from Friday to Sunday evening. One of the destinations was Hesley Wood, a campsite that catered for Scouts. It had plenty of things to have a go at, like canoeing or climbing, long jumping and high jumping, plus nature trails. Even though one of my memories of Hesley Wood was not particularly glowing. It was raining on the Friday that we went there and it rained and rained throughout the whole weekend. We left early on the Sunday and we were still drying the tents on the following Friday in our hall at Beechwood. There was also a cabin out in the countryside that we could use. It was a scout cabin with a snooker table and bunk beds and tables for us all to sit round at meal times. Which reminds me of one of the times I was cooking meatballs, the flame from the gas stove caught hold of a curtain and it was going up in flames and I was motionless but one of the scouts filled a pan with water and threw it at the curtain but he missed the curtain and hit the meatballs. This had me in hysterics and I was nearly sick because I was laughing so much. The good thing about it was that the meatballs didn't taste too different to normal, with the water and ash that had fallen over them not damaging their rifting abilities. We certainly had plenty of laughs! There were also times when we would go to a farm of one of the scout's relatives. It was a chicken farm in the main and you could certainly smell the shit when you arrived but after a while you became adjusted to it and then you really couldn't smell it unless someone trod in it. We got told off for running around the chickens because it made them nervous and the eggs they produced were deformed.

By this time a lot of the scouts who were members of the Beechwood Scouts I had brought to the troop, so they were my friends in a select club. This would become important in a couple of years; to raise money for the halls upkeep we collected newspapers and got one hundred pounds per tonne. It took a lot of effort to get that much together but we managed it a few times. Moving to the next summer holiday, I had with the Scouts was a trip for two weeks at Filey. The train journey this time was a lot shorter than going to Scotland. We even had a train carriage reserved for us so there was no problem of getting a seat. The campsite was very near the sea and we spent many hours playing in the sun. There was a problem with jellyfish though because they could sting, we would throw stones at them to try and break them up. When we were doing this, one of the scout leaders said that we were Clays Commandoes. The holiday was fine and there was a teenage girl on the campsite who was one of the scout leader's relations. There was one lad in our group who would always be talking a load of rubbish so much so that he had a badge sewn onto his shirt that was of a big mouth. We did go to the Butlin's Camp for a day and waited our turn to have a go on the amusement rides. I was certainly glad that we hadn't gone there for two weeks, as one day was more than enough. I can't remember as much about this holiday as the one in Scotland. We had a binge at the end and the lad with the big mouth finished off the food for a bet, it was enough to make you sick just watching him.

To raise money to keep the hall open on Beechwood Road, we started to run a disco at the hall. It was very popular and soon there were more people than there was room to let them in. In many ways because it was a Child to Teenager Group it was filling a gap that exists for that age group. Inside you could have a drink of pop or have a Horlicks, plus there were plenty of sweets to choose from. This was the height of my time as a scout even though our troop was small and more like a boys club we had out lived it or so we thought that night. We all agreed to walk away and never come back, it was strange that we disbanded looking back on it but that's what happened. I did hear that a few went the following week but after a short while they merged with another scout troop, so that was the end of the Beechwood Scouts and now even the hall has gone as it had been turned into flats. I still have fond memories of my time as a scout and it was a very good thing for a time.

Going back to my school days after the six weeks holidays with me finishing at Malin Bridge in 1972 it was time to go to the comprehensive school, Myers Grove. It was a day I had started to dread during the holiday period with everyday taking me just a little closer to the first day of term. I had butterflies in my stomach as I made my way to the school wearing my school uniform. All the other new students were told to form a queue and were shown to the assembly hall. We sat on the floor with our satchels and one of the teachers asked for silence. He told us some things about the school and how we were supposed to behave in our time there. One of the teachers, Mr Burgin, was going to be our year tutor throughout our time there for the next five years. They told us who was going to be our form tutors who we would report to in the morning and take the register to make sure who had turned up or who was absent. Our names were read out so we didn't get it wrong. The next stage was to go to the classrooms we would start in everyday from now on. The first classroom I had was one of the science classrooms so there were gas switches and plugs all around the room. My first form teacher, Mr Bloomfield, was a Geordie and turned out to be one of the more likeable teachers at school. The rest of the morning was spent writing down which lessons we would be doing on such a day and the times of the lessons. The lessons could be held in any of the classrooms so we had to know our way around the school, which on the first day was overpowering. I was very apprehensive on the first day and wondered to myself how was I going to cope. When it became time for dinner I made my way back home as it was less than ten minutes away. My sister and her friend were already at the house as they would be for the next two years as my sister was three years older than me. I was feeling a lot better in myself after I had eaten my dinner but the first day at school was a real strain. I made my way back to school and we went over some more things to do with our stay at the comprehensive in the afternoon. We had a badge on our blazers we wore to school, which was a motif of an acorn. The motto was "From little acorns big oak trees grow". We also had to wear a tie. Thankfully my first day nerves had been overcome and it certainly took a lot of time to get into the routine after the way things had been at Malin Bridge. It could be said that it was a culture shock. I made a friend who was called Peter; he was in the same lessons as me throughout school. In the last two years you had to make choices of the subjects you were going to do, so the class could be full with many people who were not in your form. The thing that hit me about the lessons we were to do was that they wanted us to do more of the work ourselves unlike at Malin Bridge. In my French class I ended up with the same name I had at my previous school, which was Geor, which in Yorkshire is the way people pronounce give over. Doing French was a joke as I had enough problems with English, never mind learning another language that I could be as illiterate in! The lesson that the rest of the pupils and I looked forward to was history which was taken by Mr Farmer. He would tell us stories about the people and events of the Anglo-Saxon era. We would have his lesson on a Friday afternoon, which was just right for putting you in a good mood for the weekend. Because I lived so near, my friends at the time and I would play football on the grass pitches or play tennis when the nets were up. After a couple of months at school I felt a lot better about it than at the start. We did metal work in the fist year and then woodwork in the second to give us a chance to choose which course to take in the latter years or you could take domestic science, which mainly was cooking with plenty of writing involved in all three subjects. The metalwork teacher who I had in the first year was Mr Tompkinson, who was known as Tommo. He was a short stocky man who was just below five feet tall and because of his height he had the piss taken all the time. It was said some fifth form pupils had locked him in a storeroom so they had no lesson to do. One of the stories about him was he had asked a lad what he was going to do when he grew up and the lad replied with the same question to great laughter from the rest of the class. He was the most parodied teacher at school and so many people were cruel about his height. In contrast to Mr Tompkinson being the butt of countless jokes there was a teacher called Mr Wardle who seemed to strike fear into all the pupils. He was a religious education teacher and thinking back he was probably a practicing pagan. When he walked into a room your could hear a pin drop because of his presence. I remember one day though one of my friends at the time who was very big for his age not seeing Mr Wardle enter the room, so he was still talking when Mr Wardle had put his book down on his desk. He noted who the lad was and asked him to come to the front of the classroom, when he asked it was like a command. The lad made his way to the front very slowly with trepidation. Mr Wardle asked him what he had been talking about that was so important, he got no reply and hit the lad across the head, the force of which made him hit the wall. I think Mr Wardle was trying to make a hole in the wall. Thankfully that was the end of my problems such as asking a question, for the class was silent for the rest of the lesson and what a relief it brought when we left the classroom and were in the corridor. This was the way things were done at Myers Grove and fully backed by the Headmaster, many pupils got the same treatment but you could say they were fair - they treated us all like dogs! Even sadder than that is that some people actually need rigid discipline to know where they are in the scheme of things all the time to stop them from doing stupid things.

My first English teacher draws a blank as far as my memory in concerned. I have no idea who it was. Strangely enough I can recall my French tutor but that's probably because she was a right bitch who had a grudge against the male species. She was called Miss Oldfield and known as Annie Oldfield behind her back. In one of the lessons we had with her she started to put initials up on the blackboard of anyone causing a disturbance in the class. When she put mine up there was laughter all around the classroom because they are WC. I've always like putting the D in between my first name and my surname and I didn't find it very funny at the time going a brighter shade of red. Even though going bright read when a teacher asked or said something to me was the norm during the time I had at the school. I would bottle up what I wanted to say most of the time and then blush like a beetroot, it was something I eventually overcame but it hampered my school years. Talking about embarrassment, as soon as I had started going to Myers Grove I started with acne in a big way. Acne was something that really affected me and how I felt for years and I was very jealous of those who never seemed to get a pimple, never mind the big boils I got on my nose or my chin. In fact, some of those who didn't get acne probably didn't have nappy rash either. I went to the doctors about my acne but none of the tablets or creams ever seemed to work. The best stuff I ever used was Germoline, it didn't get rid of the acne but it took some of the soreness away and helped make the spots loose their bright redness. The teacher who took me for maths in my year was nicknamed Touché Turtle, as he was also a fencing instructor. It was good to know he was good at something. Because he was known as Touché Turtle everyone wanted to poke fun at him and very few pupils took him seriously. It certainly added up that we didn't have much of a clue about the maths he was supposed to have been teaching us.

The physical education we were given included most outdoor sports and all indoor gymnastics. Well they did for those with a better-coordinated body than yours truly. The discipline factor certainly came into what we did when we stayed indoors in the gym. If you hadn't cleaned your slippers, which were supposed to look white all the time, you would get a slipper across the backside. Those who didn't take part for whatever reason would be given something to write out during the time the rest of us were giving our all becoming breathless. Mr Burgin, our year tutor, was also the PE teacher and in the main he was fair without being soft.

It was during an assembly that Mr Burgin started to tell us that old tale of the boy who cried wolf one day and I didn't agree with the outcome. What kind of society would place someone in a job they obviously couldn't do and then blame them for larking about when they became bored. It was simple to me if you had someone who was not happy with their job you could try to find them some alternative employment. In the story, the boy is put in charge of the sheep and becomes totally bored with looking after them. So to make the night shift a little bit more interesting, he runs through the village crying, "Wolf!" for a lark. The shepherds come out and run to the field where the sheep are and realise there is no wolf and they've been having their leg pulled. After this incident do they get rid of the boy for being an idiot? No they don't, they tell the lad not to do it again and you've still got the job whether you like it or not. So the next night arrives and the boy is again on his own looking after the sheep. Surprise, surprise the boy gets just as bored as the night before and being such a holder of an imaginative mind, runs into the village again shouting "Wolf Wolf!" The shepherds come out and rush to the field in order to protect the sheep from attack but they soon catch on that the boy has duped them. This time when they get hold of the boy, after giving him a load of verbal, they still let him be the watcher over the sheep. Are these people stupid or what? Why don't they give the job to someone more reliable to someone who cares what happens to the sheep because it is obvious to a deaf, dumb and blind man on a bolting horse that the village idiot is being put in charge of the valuable sheep. The third night comes along and low and behold a real wolf appears on the scene to eat and kill some of the sheep. The boy runs through the village crying "Wolf Wolf!" but no one listens and they just turn over in their sleep. Meanwhile the boy tries his best to get some men to leave their huts to protect the sheep but can get no one to believe him. With the light of the next day the shepherds see plenty of carcasses littering the field where the flock was situated. They turn on the boy and for some reason they kill him for the loss of the sheep. What a criminal waste over a stupid job in the first place but how can they blame the boy for these collective incompetences? Why did they not try to find someone more suitable to look after the sheep instead of the boy? This always left me puzzled but I suppose the story wasn't based on fact because surely no people could be that dumb over the protection of their livelihood. What always got me about this story is they kill a fool to balance the books when in fact it is their own stupidity by using the boy that ends in his death. It seemed obvious to me after the first time the boy cried "Wolf!" that he wasn't happy with his work and that he would be better looking for a job doing something else. The second time he cried wolf should have been his last night in charge of the sheep because of his disregard for looking after the sheep. But for some reason known to the shepherds he kept the job and the third night when a wolf did appear to attack the sheep no one in the village believed the boy and stayed in their huts. If someone had gone around lynching all the stupid people in this village they would soon have nobody left, for how can you explain that the boy who was put in charge of the sheep was brainless yet they put him in a very trustworthy job, which was beyond him. I am really glad to have gotten this off my chest, as it was always something that came to mind when discussing morality tales. It always hit me as a weak tale being too contrived and all round no starter, even if the boy was the only capable person to watch over the sheep it still can't justify the lad getting killed because of his obvious stupidity while being given a position of trust. This is one dumb village and I feel the shepherds are very much to blame for this situation. I know one thing I wouldn't stay long in their village for anything.

I think I've named all the teachers who taught me in the first year other than the art teacher who I can't recall at this moment in time or my science teacher either. The year passed slowly and I did so-so in my first exams with confidence in myself being in short supply. It was something that was going to affect all my years at the school. The one subject I did well in throughout school was history; I always was close to being top of the class after an exam.

In the second year in the biology class we did human reproduction, which had everybody interested for some unknown reason, only kidding! The second year is much of a blank to me except for a different French teacher. This one was known as Boris the Bold because he looked a little like a cartoon character from that time. He was, if I remember correctly, quite a rubbish teacher who during his lesson, would be contemplating the meaning of life and is there life on other planets? I know I haven't mentioned the Headmaster who was known as Wart Hog. His real name was Mr Hill and I was told by someone that he wanted to protect the girls at school from the students at Stannington College, which was just a couple of football pitches away. So he wanted a chain mail fence erecting between the college and the school but he didn't get what he wanted because I don't think he was taken too seriously. The second year passed by and my grades were up and down as the first had been and I was starting to really hate the school and just didn't want to go and I certainly didn't want to do my homework. It's funny, when I was at school there always seemed lots of programmes on the television that I didn't want to miss, limiting the time I gave to my studies. Maybe it was that I hated doing homework so any alternative, however poor, was an excuse for not spending more time on the set homework. When I started my third year my sister had left, doing well in her exams for a job at the TSB bank. I was now alone at dinner times and would have radio 1 on when it was the Johnnie Walker Show. He had a pop quiz called Pop the Question. The show was open to the public to test their knowledge of popular music and some nominal prize would be given them if they got the questions right. On one occasion, they had Elton John on the programme just for a change and the other caller on the show got one of his albums as a prize. When I said I was alone in the dinner times, that is not the whole case, as some days my dad would be home due to the fact he was a shift worker. He worked for the British Steel Company as a maintenance pipe fitter. The men who worked for the firm called it by another name 'Billy Smart's Circus'. My dad's cooking abilities were few and far between. If he was at home I would be having beans on toast. On one occasion I was walking to the house when I began talking to a girl who lived opposite on Woodend Drive and told her if my father was home I would be having baked beans on toast. Sure enough, my dad was home doing something to his car when I asked him what was for dinner in front of the girl, he replied "Beans on Toast!" We both started laughing when he said it and my dad wondered what we were laughing at until I told him. I can recall one day I was talking about going home for dinner when one of the girls in the class said "Don't you get lonely being on your own?" It had never crossed my mind that I was alone so it never bothered me even though the girl hinted that she would have hated to be alone.

One of the biggest forces on my childhood is something I have so far not mentioned and that was the weekly visit to my granddad's. I say my granddad and not my grandparents because my grandmother died while I was very young and I can barely remember her other than a kiss she gave me once. My granddad lived in a semi detached council house on Wolfe Road just past Wadsley Bridge Club. The house was still heated by a coal fire in the living room. There was a lino covering on the floor with a carpet over it that touched where it fit. My granddad's chair was very big in contrast to him, and was designed in a practical manner stopping the draughts hitting his back. Just above and behind him was a photograph of his dad wearing a cloth cap and having a bushy moustache. There was an old solid table to the right of my granddad as he looked, then there was an old cabinet with a pot-made fish bowl on top of that, and looking out of place with the other furniture was a large black and white television. Going further along in the room and near the door was an old radio on a very old looking small table. The kitchen had very old taps and I can still smell the metal now. There was a toilet opposite the coal stack and my granddad used the hard type of toilet paper, probably because he had always used that type; all I know is that it was very uncomfortable for me. When we went on these visits to my granddad's we would usually watch some television first then turn it off and he would start to tell us stories of his past which there were usually three of. I just liked looking into the fire and all the images you could see in it. On the table there was always Fox's mints and I usually managed to get one. When it was time to leave we would follow my granddad into the kitchen where his coat was hung up and put his hands into the pockets to bring out some money for my sister and I and also eventually my brother. I've missed out what he looked like - I'll make up for that here! He was no taller than five foot two, he always wore a cloth cap, he wore a corduroy waistcoat which he kept in the pocket a watch on a chain, he also wore a kerchief around his neck, his trousers were also made of corduroy and on his feet he had a pair of heavy duty boots which now and again he'd tap them on the floor making a fair bit of noise to make sure of the circulation. In many ways it was like looking at a museum piece from a time long before.

When I was about ten my dad took me to see granddad at work. Granddad's workshop was on West Street and you went up a Dickensian looking wooden staircase to his workshop. My granddad was a knife maker known as Little Masters in their time. The thing about my granddad still working part-time at Richards was that he was around eighty years old when my dad took me to see him. He retired at the age of eighty-two and said of his pension that it was the best people he had ever worked for because he got paid every week! The knives he had made throughout his life were sold in the main by my Uncle Jack (my dad's brother) and would be worth a small fortune today. There was always talk of a blueprint he had made of a knife he wanted to make that he left in his workshop. I visited my granddad sometimes on my own and would cut his privet for him when it was growing all over the place. I can remember also eating the rhubarb that was growing in his garden and the visits to the toilet afterwards! My Auntie Irene, granddad's daughter, in the main looked after him and made sure he was all right and that he was still capable of doing things for himself. In fact, I've only mentioned one brother and one sister that my dad had, which is not all of them by any means. In their time my grandparents had nine children - four boys and five girls. Of the nine, only six reached adulthood - three sons and three daughters. One of my uncles, Bill, died in an accident on leave during the Second World War. My other uncle, Jack, who I've already mentioned, died in a motorcar accident after a visit to see granddad and my dad. One of my aunties, Anne, also died but before then we were regular visitors on a Sunday having our tea there. In many ways it was similar in furniture to my granddads except it was less sparse. So I still have two aunties left, Elsie who lives in Southampton, and Auntie Irene in Darlington. On one occasion I went to my granddads on my own to see him and before I left he told me to wait while he went upstairs and when he came back downstairs, he gave me a small penknife. I was really surprised because I had thought all of the knives had already long gone. My granddad was ninety when he died and he lost it in his last year. My Auntie Irene looked after him at her flat for the last year and when I saw him he kept calling me Darryl (my brother's name). I didn't see him much that last year because I wanted to remember him as he was. In some ways I got on better with him at one stage in my life than I did with my father. Of course there was quite an age gap between my dad and granddad who had been in his forties when my Dad popped out and was the last offspring, the baby of the family. My granddad was born in 1888 in Victorian times and died in 1978, thankfully before that stupid uncaring and worthless bitch, just like her policies, called for a return to Victorian values in the following year. I'm not saying I was glad that my granddad had died, but the way old people get treated these days he was better off out of it.

My third year at Myers Grove had some changes in the way of teachers. The form tutor was different for a start. It was now a woodwork teacher, Mr Lamb who wanted us all to tell a story about ourselves and I recall I was the first to refuse and they're still waiting for my story now! The maths teacher, Mrs Robinson, was very good looking but even she didn't improve my Math! In English there was also a change, I had a Mrs Smith who was married to the Deputy Head. She didn't like me and this was mutual, I came fourth in the exam yet she put me in a lower class the following year on her supervision. The English lessons really dragged especially during the book reading days, I can remember Call of the Wild by Jack London as one of these class reads. It might not have entirely been the fault of the book as I only read a couple of pages an hour and spent most of the time dreaming of an escape attempt to get out from Myers Grotto, the Staleg 13 of schools! I did well in history coming top of the class, but the teacher didn't like me much and was some sort of bible pusher so we didn't have much in common. The geography teacher we had was a total klutz, who after one lesson hit me on the back of the legs with a ruler; he was such a bad teacher no one got more than 15% in the exam results. At the end of the third year it was time to make some choices about what lessons to do and what to stop doing. We got career counseling and when I say we, my mum was present at the discussion stage. I know I wanted to do history and art because they were my favourite subjects. There was no choice with English, maths and religious education as they were all part of the syllabus. Then technical drawing, woodwork and a new course called physical science were chosen by me even though I still had no idea of the job I would choose when I left school. The physical science subject was both chemistry and physics in alternate weeks. The room we had in the science block was right at the top, out of sight and out of mind so I thought at the time from the other classrooms.

The tutors we had now would be, unless they moved to another school, our tutors for the next two years. Mr Hopkins, who was nicknamed Hair Bear because he looked like a cartoon character at the time, took starting with history, my favourite subject and class at the time. He was tall and big, a former rugby player who had played for England in the juniors. He was probably the worst history teacher I've had. His method of dictating the history we were covering was not a style I particularly liked, especially because I'm a slow writer. The course was made up of continuous assessments and an exam at the end of the course. He was another teacher who was feared and he hit a lad I knew one day in his lesson very similar to what Wardle did. There's no doubt about it they were all liberal thinkers at Myers Grove - very liberal with hitting people in particular. My art tutor was Mr Saunders who never got too cross with the fact that I produced very little work and I never did work out a project. It was certainly one of the more relaxing lessons and there were plenty of my friends in the same group. There was Peter, Ledger, Wadey and Grogsy and I, all together so there was never much shortage of laughter in this class. My English tutor was Mr Daniels, nicknamed Danny Boy. He was my favourite teacher because you could talk to him without getting into trouble. He was in his mid-twenties and this was probably one of the main reasons for my liking him, the other teachers were from a different time warp and were not exactly friendly other than to creeps. In the same class was Michael, who had become a friend over the last year or so; he was always a bit giddy and getting himself into trouble. My maths teacher was Mr Thorne who was a nuclear fall out victim, due to his dandruff covering his shoulders all the time. He tried to keep us interested by pulling faces but it didn't work. The whole math class was united in the belief that we were wasting our time to remember some equations so we could answer questions in the final year's exam which I don't think was entirely the fault of the teacher, we were resigned to our fate from an early stage and that was that.

I chose technical drawing as one of my subjects in the final two years as I had come top of the class in the last exams. In fact, in the test I got all fifty questions right. They covered shapes and angles of metal, because I got them all right we had to do a further ten questions. I had enjoyed the technical drawing up to this point when it became too much of an effort. The technical drawing tutor was an ex-army man but which one; he had blond hair, blue eyes and kept clicking his heels definitely a member of the Aryan race. He was called Mr Maslin. I chose to do woodwork because I liked it a lot better than metalwork and I didn't want to do domestic science. The teacher for woodwork was Mr Ward who was no bag of laughs. He was a very strict teacher who threatened those in his class with the cane if they did not do the homework he set. I can recall him standing in for a teacher who had been ill one day and one of the girls in the class was chatting away to her friends when Mr Ward was talking, he came over to her and hit her across the face. What a lovely man he was. The Religious Education tutor was the one and only, Mr Wardle who many a time had me in fits of laughter when he was laying into someone for no real reason. I had to bite my lip to stop me from bursting out when some poor soul came under the spotlight from Mr Wardle's cold wit. I don't remember him hitting anyone in the last two years, which must have been some sort of record for him. The funny thing about the R.E. lesson is that I can't recall a single thing from any of them.

The Physical Science, I chose to do, was the first of its kind, combining Chemistry with Physics. We had two separate teachers on the course; one was Mr Prince, who took the Physics part of the course, and Mr Oakley, who took the Chemistry side of the course. It's a funny thing but I reckon Mr Prince was one of the few teachers without a nickname. What I can tell you is that he was always telling us about his gun collection, one of the class members would start him off and that would be the end of the Physics with Mr Prince rambling on about his pistol collection. That gives me an idea for a nickname, he should be known as Sex Pistol. The chemistry tutor, Mr Oakley, was known as Annie Oakley and the most I can think of saying about him is that he left the school and went to help out in India and so meant another teacher for us in our final year. One more thing about Annie Oakley was that he was very religious and I think it was something to do with a Christian group that he was involved with that he went to India for.

In the games lesson for the last two years, we had Mr Royston who was known as Perm Boy because his hair was rarely out of place. He took great pleasure in hitting pupils in his charge and I can remember him hitting a lad in the face that gave him a nosebleed. What a born leader Perm Boy was with setting such a fine example. There was one games lesson that was something like the football match in the film 'Kes'. Royston and his team in the game were losing the match and it was time to go home. We could see all the other pupils leaving the school but we played on. Royston was a right dirty bastard during the game, kicking anyone who went near him. We were all starting to say "Aren't we calling it a day?" and "Isn't it time to go home?" Thankfully his team scored so the match was now a draw, but this wasn't the end of the match by any means. He wanted to be on the winning side so Grogsy, who was in our goal for the game, when a shot came on target he jumped over the ball, skillfully, so Royston's team had won, yippee. We all rushed back to the changing rooms and had a quick shower and the dressed quickly. A day at school ended at twenty to four usually, but on this day it was twenty past four when we started to make our way home. Like I'd said, Perm Boy set a fine example for us to follow, if you wanted to be a bastard all your life.

Around this time, we would go in groups to the cinema or the lads would have a girlfriend to spend their time with. I can recall going to the pictures when there was about six of us to go and watch 'Rollerball'. A film about a game in the future that would help those watching it to vent their emotions and get their violent urges out of their system. The queue was massive, we tried to get in and we decided we wouldn't get a seat this Friday night at the Gaumont.

45

So we made our way to the ABC cinema and went in to watch 'Earthquake', one of the many disaster movies that were around at the time. The film was made in Sensoround, which made it seem like the earth truly was moving in the cinema while we were watching it. The next Friday, we went to see 'Rollerball' and this time we got in and I really enjoyed the movie, which starred James Caan. Going to the cinema every week was something I did right up to being sixteen and starting work. I was even a member of the ABC minors, which were held on Saturday mornings and cost a whole five pence to gain admission. Altogether now, 'When I was a lad....' I had all the badges what were sold at the time, but when I started Myers Grove School I grew out of it. What they showed were cartoons and the old Flash Gordon series with Buster Crabbe, even my dad said that he had seen those when he was a lad too, so it didn't put the theatre out too much to do with cost. Its odd but until I wrote about going to the cinema I hadn't thought of all those Saturdays when I was young that I had spent with friends going to ABC minors.

Something else I haven't mentioned is my grandparents on my mother's side. My mother's parents had divorced when she as still a child and my nanny, as we called her, had remarried in the intervening years. I still called my step-granddad as he was granddad. When we would go to see them it would take over four hours of traveling to get to where they lived. They lived near Twickenham Stadium in Middlesex; I think it is, in a large terraced house. They had four sausage dogs and one cat that liked to try and hit you with its paw when you walked past it. Because the dogs had grown up with the cat, they left it alone but barked and chased any other cat that comes into the garden. The dogs were spoilt when it came to meal times because granddad and nanny both gave them food off their plates. One of the dogs was called Bunny and he used to walk on his hind legs to try to persuade them to give him some more food which they usually did as he was so cute. Granddad had a massive record collection with many albums by Sinatra, Martin and Tom Jones. You name them; he had an album by them in the genre of his taste. He also had a library of paperback books. Nanny always seemed glad to see us when we had made the trip down, which always was an ordeal. Seeing the same things for miles on end on a motorway is one of the most boring things you can do. Nanny's face was very wrinkled and she sounded southern which is a softer way of talking than the way we talk in Yorkshire. It never took my mum long on our trips down there to start coming out with a more southern accent than she normally had. I can recall nanny going on a holiday we had and there was one day when the sun was very hot and it made nanny's bags under her eyes puff up. It looked like someone had hit her in the face two times and she was fairly ill with it for a couple of days. On one of the trips down there, my mum's brother, Ivan, who still lived with his mum, let me have some of his stamps as I was a keen collector back then. I called him Ivan the Terrible. I hope no one thinks that I made up all of these nicknames, perish the thought.

There was also a half brother. My Uncle Lionel I think married a woman called Jeanne, he was nicknamed Leo the Lion. At the time of this in the early seventies, they were living in a squat, which was very common, in the South of England. In many ways both my uncles were dropouts. My Uncle Ivan had been a draughtsman but he packed it in to work on a building site and Lionel also was working on building sites. The last I heard of Ivan was that he was a teacher at a school in West Bromwich and that Uncle Lionel was living with him. Both nanny and granddad are dead now so I have no living grandparents anymore.

I always liked our visits because it was like going to a different world from that one I had in Sheffield. One thing about when nanny lived at Twickenham was her next-door neighbours. They were thieves who, on one occasion, walked into a shop with a little trailer, put a cooker on it and walked out as bold as you like with it and took it home. That particular story has always made me laugh! I think it's the pure cheek of the thing that hits a chord inside me. How anyone can have the nerve to do something like that I will never know, I know I for one don't have the bottle to do it!

My mother, I should point out, also has a sister who lives in South Africa and on one of our visits to nanny's we went to her sisters who was just preparing to move in the next week, which is over twenty years ago now. The reason I mention this is because I got a Joe Ninety machine gun that could fire a rocket out of the front of the gun. In my early years I was gun mad and of course, cowboy daft! It sure is funny what you remember sometimes.

After the school holidays in 1976 the new term started at Myers Grove which would be my last year at school and would affect my life in the near future depending on how well I did in the final exams in 1977. We had a mock exam, which was the last chance for the teachers to say what they thought about my course work, in the main it was thumbs down, with the overall view that I didn't like school discipline and that I was very apathetic about my schoolwork. At the end of the report, which basically told me nothing new and there wasn't much time to have a change of heart now. The last of my school years was dominated by what was I going to do when I left school. We had career lessons and personal chats to try and find a clear path to what job I would pick and be happy in doing. I couldn't think of anything that I really wanted to do and I got fed up with the question of what are you going to do when you leave school? There was a comic moment that came out of this when one day at the morning register I was told off by the teacher for making a disturbance in the class. The teacher told me to write down what I was going to do when I left school in the way of work. When I was really young I would always tell people that I wanted to be a clown, this had changed however to be nothing. I was fed up with being asked this question so I wrote that I wanted to be the Jolly Green Giant and handed it in to the teacher before leaving the room for my lesson. The following day was on assembly day and it was our year tutor, Mr Burgin who was taking it. He talked about some things that I've forgotten now but then came to the subject of work and I like so many around me were nearly falling sleep when he read out that some pupil who would remain nameless had written that when they left school that wanted to be the Jolly Green Giant! I went as red as a beetroot when he read this out and wished I have never written it because I was so embarrassed by it.

The reason I used humour to stick two fingers up to the school is that if I told them to fuck off I would have got the cane and would not have gotten much satisfaction out of that, but this way the absurdity of the question as I saw it was made fun of and I think on that occasion, I broke even with the system but only just. Maybe I got my wish of old and I was a clown for a day at least in my life.

The art class that I attended was great because a lot of my school friends were also in the class. Grogsy, Wadey, Ledger and Peter usually had a good laugh during the lesson. Mr Saunders the art teacher because he was a bit slacker than the other members of staff, was seen as a soft touch even though we all did the homework he set. I can remember that he set us homework, which was to draw a cabbage. I drew a cabbage whilst watching television and shaded it in and it looked more like a golf club head. He tore into the class and said that only one person had drawn something that had remotely looked like a cabbage. So we were set the same homework and this time I drew something that resembled a cabbage - believe it or not. One day we had a female substitute teacher to take the art class. Because we always had a laugh when we got together the lady teacher also laughed with us and said that someone close to her had just died and this was the first occasion since that she had laughed. My artwork never managed to be about anything in particular which meant I wouldn't be getting a good grade but I really enjoyed the art class anyway.

The school asked all the pupils to pay in seven pence, a contribution to the maintenance of the school vehicles, which took pupils to other schools to compete at sports. There was Grogsy, Wadey and I who hadn't paid in the required seven pence, not because of the money but of the principle that we didn't take part in these sport competitions so we didn't have to pay towards the upkeep of the vans. Our form tutor told us to go and see Mr Burgin who you know was our year tutor. So we made our way to his office, and out of the room he came as we got there. Wadey and Grogsy started arguing with him over the money that was still outstanding as far as us three were concerned. It was so comical having an argument over seven pence and I started laughing. Mr Burgin said, "Wayne's embarrassed!" I might have been but I wasn't going to pay the seven pence whatever he had to say and I never did pay in the seven pence.

In my history class I have done the course work of the continuous assessment and was on course to being given a grade 1 in CSE. The teacher, Mr Hopkins had lent me a book to do some writing about Roosevelt the American President during the pre-war depression times and the Second World War. I had written my piece and had the book to return on the table at home but I forgot it when I left the house to go to school after dinner. I was on edge all during the history lesson thinking Mr Hopkins wanted the book today and I hadn't brought it with me. When the bell went to signal the end of the lesson, I felt a great sense of relief and afterwards thought how silly I was to get worked up over nothing. Before I left the school Mr Hopkins came to my table and said that I had got a CSE grade 1, which didn't make me full of joy but made me feel something of a traitor having joined in with all the arse lickers and attaining a good grade.

One day in my English class, Mr Daniels, my favourite teacher at Myers Grove screwed up something I had written and put it in the bin; I got up and put it back in my folder. Our class of English was only up to grade 2 at CSE standard. That is no matter how well you could write in the exam or course work you could not gain a higher grade in that class. I would write silly stories that made the Jolly Green Giant episode look very normal. I felt that I had been given a raw deal in getting put in this class so if that's how they wanted it that was fine by me, but they weren't going to get much work out of me. Mr Daniels, I recall, married a math teacher from our school which made me feel sorry for their children if they ever had any that is. I think Mr Daniels left Myers Grove at the end of the year and went to another school.

My work in woodwork was always on the slow side and maybe I was getting some practice in for my time working for the Council. The teacher, Mr Ward, as I've already mentioned was a disciplinarian, would now and again have a look at my work, which in the final year was a stool. He would come around and talking to the whole class, would say how slow my output was and comment that I was close to falling asleep. I somehow managed to finish the stool, which is after all probably the only stool I will ever make, and I still have it today. I used cord for the seat, but some of the other pupils had cloth over foam to make for a softer seat. Ledger who had used the foam to build the soft seat hadn't done a good job of sticking the cloth over the foam and his seat was falling off and unmanageable. Wadey, on seeing this and being such a good friend, got hold of a six-inch nail and knocked it through the cloth and foam into the wood. It was such a mad thing to do and Ledger's stool looked to have been a wasted effort as the nail had split some of the wood but it didn't half make me laugh! In the final year's exams I got grade 3 at CSE in woodwork and was glad to be out of the company of Mr Ward who had been a right bastard.

In my technical drawing class, Mr Maslin went about things in his usual military way. A fellow pupil had not done his homework for some reason and Mr Maslin said of him "Leech you're a leach by name and a leach by nature!" In the final year there was too much effort required to keep up with the work being set that I totally lost interest and cannot recall getting my satisfaction out of the whole course and I dare say I wasn't the only one. The funny thing about Mr Maslin was that he had a military feel to him and how he behaved, but underneath he was a real softy who made me laugh a lot at some of the things that he would say to the class.

The math lessons were a waste of time and all we ever seemed to do was matrixes. The teacher, Mr Thorne, was a right load of rubbish who also gave one half an hours' computer course a week, which was him writing on a blackboard and us pupils trying to write it down as fast as possible. Because I am a slow writer I kept losing my place, as he kept moving up the board for more apace to write this intelligible, useless information. It was very much like his math classes - no one learned anything from the computer course either. When it was close to leaving school Mr Thorne wouldn't talk to us because our grades were so low and I somehow managed a grade 5 at CSE in the final exam.

With Annie Oakley making his way to India before the final year began, we ended up with a replacement teacher who was a bigger religious nut than old Annie had been. The other pupils got around to asking him why he wanted to marry a virgin because of his religious beliefs. That question took up a good half an hour with us still in the smallest classroom in the school, it's a wonder they didn't give our class some roadmaps to get lost with, they loved us really of course. When the virgin issue was over for this particular week we now got into why he believed in Jesus and I said I wouldn't believe in Jesus if he appeared in front of me right now, he'd certainly have a hard job because he would have to know his way around the science block for a start! I don't remember this teacher's name and I very much doubt if the other pupils who were in his class remember it either. By the way, the lesson he was supposed to take was Chemistry even though we talked more about religion than science, and in fact we probably talked more about religion with him that we did in the religious education classes.

Mr Prince was still our physics teacher, who had plenty more things to say about his gun collection. He did give us a good piece of advice to do with drinking alcohol though, which was when you get back to your home after a night out drinking; try to drink a pint of water which will help you stop having too big a hangover the morning after! I'm not sure if I even got a grade for this subject known as physical science even though I did chuck a lot of screws out of the window of the small room which I had taken out of some desks that I sat at and wished I had started earlier than I did in doing so.

I think I've already mentioned that I had Mr Wardle for religious education classes. It was not a subject that I ever felt much about, if it gets some people through the day that's fine by me. It's just that I personally don't want to hear it, even though I can hardly recall anything that we did in the lessons. So much of it was out of date anyway and it was just another lesson to dream in while the time passed by. In sport I entered the shot-put event to represent the country I was in at school, which was India. The others were Canada, Australia and I think Ghana. Why they chose these four countries I honestly don't know but we were all put into one of these groups. The reason I'm going through all this is that I won the competition for India and in the next assembly Mr Burgin was giving out certificates for the winners. When he read my name out I went as ever, a brighter shade of red and stood up, then I thought this is embarrassing with the only reason I won being because a lot of the bigger lads couldn't be bothered enough to enter. I sat down again but Mr Burgin had seen me, worst luck, and told me again to collect the certificate which I did but with little relish and acute embarrassment. It was a record of bright redness even for me!

The last week at school had arrived and only on the Thursday had I been told that we really didn't have to go to school anymore as we had completed our exams. It was the week when Liverpool became Champions of Europe in a great final. In the English class we had a bet on the right score of the game with both Peter and I guessing at 3-1 to Liverpool. I can still remember Peter and I playing a little game of football on the playing field on our last day and I cut myself on my arm and we both went back to our house to have a glass of orange squash. What a relief that it was all over. The school reports we got through the years, in the main say one thing and that is "Could do better" but on this occasion I would like to say back to the school system that they could do better themselves. My thoughts on school are that the reason we go to school as children is because our mums and dads go out to work and the state system provides parents with a place to put their children for the day where they can find them. This goes on for five days a week from the age of five to the age of sixteen in which time I learnt how to read and write and be able to count. Other than these achievements I got very little else from my time in the school system. I learned more from watching television than I ever got from school. The other things I learned in my lifetime were from the hard school of knocks and being able to pull myself off the floor to keep on trying and continuing my trek through life to meet my destiny which was only around the corner but would seem like a lifetime to get there. The last day of school I told my mother how much I had wanted to finish with school because I had hated it so much. When I told her she was surprised that I had hated school and that she never knew I felt that way about it, which in many ways sums up the communication problem I had with my parents. The finishing of school was just another beginning in my life with me looking for a job but first things first, I signed on and was entitled to nine pounds a week of which my mother took five pounds from me for board and lodgings.

3 Work

Ileft School near the end of May 1977 not having decided what job I would like to do and because of this I kept going to see my careers officer. At the final push it was between moving boxes in a warehouse or becoming a painter and decorator. I didn't like the sound of moving boxes in a warehouse so I filled out a form to apply for a job on the council for becoming an apprentice painter and decorator. The Council got in touch with me and I had to go and do a test, plus there was a short interview afterwards. A letter appeared through the door and it was a confirmation that I had been accepted to start an apprenticeship in September. I watched a lot of television between finishing School and starting work. The time drew nearer and soon it was September the 5th the first day.

All the apprentices had to report on the first day to some council buildings at the bottom of Snig Hill. I was nervous and in the same boat as the other apprentices in knowing no one in the group. I think we went through who would be responsible if we were involved in any accidents at work and through some other standards of practice that we would have to adhere to. In the main though it was highly forgettable and I for one was glad to see the back of the first day. Interesting to note there was no paint brush or paint about on the first day; if only the other days could have been the same as the first day. That was Monday out of the way and on the Tuesday we had to report to the paint depot which was down Attercliffe. To help us fit in and have a smoother beginning the paint gaffer tried to place us close to home. I lived at Stannington and one of the paint gangs were due to go and do some houses in Stannington Village so I joined their particular gang. This didn't quite workout at first because the gang were still finishing off an estate at Birley, which for me was the other side of Sheffield. The men who I was first posted with seemed to be a happy go lucky sort or so I thought in the beginning. In time I would think some more realistic thoughts about those who surrounded me in my experiences on the Council. The gang were moved from Birley to Stannington on the Friday and I tried to help as best I could, well I sort of moved around a bit, the things you do to keep warm. In saying I lived in

Stannington I exaggerated slightly because we lived at the bottom end of Stannington and a good twenty five minutes walk from Stannington Village to Woodend Drive where I lived with my family. In fact there was an apprentice who lived in Stannington but he was late arriving on the Tuesday when we were given our destinations, his name was Rory and in time we would become firm friends and with names like Rory and Wayne it's a surprise people thought we were a couple of cowboys.

So I got posted to Stannington and he didn't, even though he did join us for a day because the job he was on was closed for a day for a strike. Some of the men were slightly odd, one of whom spoke very high pitched and was known quite cruelly as squeaky Pete. If you were a block away and could hear him he sounded like a woman. There was a song in the charts by Eddie and the Hot Rods and I remember this because there was an Eddie and a Rodney on the paint gang. There was one who was in his early twenties and was a right nutcase but he was moved to another job which I'm sure was a relief to the tenants If not the rest of the gang. When you're the apprentice you usually get the job of going to the shops or going for chips but on the Stannington job we all went to the Peacock pub because they did a lovely liver sandwich and they didn't seem to mind us all going in with our overalls on. The weather at the time was not too bad and I can't remember it raining in what turned out for me a couple of weeks of being on the gang before starting the College part of the apprenticeship.

The first twelve names in the register which I was one of were to under go a 26 weeks fulltime attendance of Shirecliffe College. We could only go back to site work when the College was shut for its holidays. At the time we were the first group ever to be given a fulltime apprenticeship at the College, the other group consisting of twelve apprentices were going to be two weeks at College and then two weeks at work in their first year and complete their 26 weeks at College in this way. I don't think anyone realised what this was going to do to the behaviour of our group but there was going to be many a heated argument in the future. I for one didn't know what was in front of me and if I had I might have changed my course in life except for my conscience which throughout my life kept going along, carrying me along with it for better or for worse. The reality slowly sank in here I was expected to learn yet I had just finished off School life where I had hated virtually everyone and was in no mood to start to learn anything. I had finished one hateful environment for another which the only thing I would learn would be to hate my work environment even more. There's no doubt about it I was not the stuff for making much out of and I couldn't change the way I was set in order to get through my challenge.

The first day at Shirecliffe College was the usual outlining the course we would be starting and who would be taking us for the various lessons. The head man the Top Honcho, the big cheese, our leader, our saviour was John Joseph a man made of putty if ever there was one. The second in command was Kenneth Ball a man of the people except he didn't seem able to find them. The next of this motley crew was Bob Moody a Morris Minor owner enough said. The fourth Musketeer was Ted Fillet who would give many a lesson over the next three years which I would doze through and try and stay awake in. Another member of staff was only a now and then type, was Mr Claterus. The main gist of the first day was to show us around the workshop where we would be spending most of our time and to see who could be the stupidest apprentice... believe me there was plenty of competition. Luckily for me Rory and I were already becoming firm friends so I wasn't totally isolated and alienated, with him being in the same group as me. When we got stuck into the work we were to do the following day we were all given a board that had to be rubbed down for re use by us to do some of the course work. I can still remember when I actually started to paint the large board that was on castors that I didn't have a clue how to paint properly so Mr Joseph showed me how to lay off and that was that , from that moment on - no Niagara falls from my paint work. The same could not be said of Rory's work as it was three years before they let him paint the floor. Only kidding but I don't think he was called Ruffinsky for nothing.

In mentioning Rory I might as well go through most of the rest of the group who I can recall the names of. There was Tom Bowler well that was his nickname which I think its best that I stick to as many of the guilty would perhaps want there shady past forgotten. The reason he was called Tom Bowler was because his name sounded something similar. There was Boris who it was said of had never washed his face but you certainly couldn't have called him a racist as he looked like one big blackhead. Who knows with the technological world in which we live in Boris might have come into contact with a piece of soap by now. One of the lads came to the college with a full length overall made out of very thin plastic which in one day was in tatters so he got the nickname of teabag for the rest of his stay at the college. I for awhile was known as Houdi Elbow, the man of mystery, which must have been because I'm too cryptic for my own good and it reminds me that no one understands me, which could well be my epitaph. The others in the group were the usual sixteen year old psychopaths from the mean streets or were raw babies, which is the way it goes in life. For our dinner we would usually go to the canteen and have a chip buttie which didn't cost much and have a cup of tea. The rest of the time we would go and sit down in the foyer to pass the time. I even in the first week was fed up and wanted to be somewhere else away from all the idiots and all the rubbish they wanted us to learn. Also at the college there were other students doing bricklaying, woodwork, plumbing and learning to be electricians and also the more academic minded. The college was all over people with wide backgrounds and very varying futures.

In the main at the start of our course in painting we had Mr Joseph and Mr Ball for our practical lessons and concentrated on this side of the work. At the start I might not have felt too good about the situation I was in but I was prepared to give of my best. The boards that were on castors were at first our main outlet in regards to work we were then given smaller boards to do some sign writing on. In our time at the college we would cover sign writing, stencilling, wood graining, rag rolling effect, spray painting and many other forms of work that would never be used in our normal onsite work. They even entrusted us with some gold leafing work. In the group there was a fair bit of friction between some of the members and one day a sponge was thrown at me and I had had enough at the time so I went and threw it back at the lad who I thought threw it at me. We had a little set to that didn't last long which was probably a good thing because he didn't throw the sponge; it had been Tom Bowler who was laughing at the whole incident. I made it up with my wrestling partner and that was that finished. One night a week we had to stay for an evening lesson which didn't finish till quarter past seven. I really hated these Thursday nights and resented the fact that we were the only group who were staying behind after our lessons. We would do a form of stencilling in these night time classes. Sometimes we would get let out a little earlier and go and watch Wednesday play at Hillsborough.

It was in December when I did something which when I think back was one of the most stupid things I have ever done in my life. It was a Thursday night and I was on a whopper of a downer. I ate a big meal in the canteen and then with my rucksack on my back I walked to the Tesco on Herries road. I went inside and bought a pint bottle of whisky which on my way back to the college I opened the bottle and gulped down a couple of inches. When it was time for the night group to begin I made my way into the workshop and told of what I had done. I took the whisky bottle out of my rucksack and made my way to the toilets where I just supped three quarters of a pint of whisky like it was a pint of milk. After about ten minutes I started to hit the walls of the workshop with my fists and staggered about before I was helped out side and collapsed in a heap on the floor. I had really blown it and an Ambulance was called for to take me to Hospital. I kept regaining a sort of consciousness but not much. I was given the stomach pump and there was sick all over my jumper and shirt. They put me in a bed in the Northern General Hospital for the night. My father came and he brought my brother to see me and it was the one night of the year that my mum went out with her friends for a meal. I can remember a lot of old men looking at me and laughing at my state and the next thing I remember is going for a drink of water at four in the morning. When I said I had gone for a drink in the night the Doctor said that he didn't believe me. I went for a wash and some of the acne on my face was really bright red, which on this occasion I couldn't careless about. I felt like death warmed up and could still taste the whisky from the night before.

My things were given me in a plastic bag which was a good job as my clothes were covered in sick. My Dad brought me a coat and they said I could leave the Hospital without seeing a shrink. When we had gotten home I had a bath to get rid of some of the smell, I then ate a meal which made me feel a lot better and steadier on my legs. My hair was very long and I needed a haircut which is something I have always hated having done. I don't know if it was being taken to Tony's by my Dad and having the same awful haircut or watching what happened to Victor Mature when he was playing Samson but I hate having my haircut. Because of the booze I was a brain dead Zombie, what do I mean that's nothing fresh for me. It was a simple task of just sitting in the chair and losing all my curls as I had always done but on this occasion I didn't feel a thing. The weekend was here and I was glad of the time I had to get over my hangover.

On the Monday after reporting for the register I was told to go and see the Principal of the college. We had a little chat and with it being the last week of term and nearly Christmas he was prepared to put the incident down as high spirits. There was one condition that I should write a letter of apology to my tutor of the Thursday night class and to say I would not be doing a repeat performance. The incident didn't get back to the Works Department because the college were keen to keep a low profile. The week ended and so did college for 1977 so I went back to the same gang I had been with before college began. The charge hand on the job was called Barry and he was a friendly enough bloke and I got on with him fairly well. Because I was the only apprentice on the job it was my duty to go for the breakfast sandwiches the men were having while we were working on the Burngreave estate. They could have sausage, egg, bacon and tomato anyway they liked them in their sandwiches, which were very filling. With it being December it was bitterly cold working outside and I was dressed up like someone working on the Siberian Express and I even had the string to wrap up the heavy coat that I wore at the time. Fortunately for me my dad got me some gloves from his workplace and I was able to work in them. It was in such weather that I realised the importance of getting a cup of tea out of the tenants, which I would later have down to an art form. This was the survival of the fittest and if you wanted a cup of tea it was no good squashing your nose on a tenants window or behaving like you were a mute, it was come out with it time and I came out of my introvert shell in this way. When it was nearing dinnertime I would go round and take orders for chips or anything else some of the gang would want such as biscuits. At this time some of the gang would go to the pub for their dinner and I would join them when I had brought back the orders from the shops.

One day Barry asked me if the pub had any slot machines in the toilets and I didn't know what he was on about till he said he wanted some johnnies. There were always some women on the jobs who were happy to have sex, whether they were married or divorced. Christmas was on us and when it was our last day we were all ready to go to the pub for the afternoon session. I was pissed again and totally out of my head and when I could drink no more I started throwing my beer over people as they went past, plus I was going into the women's toilets when I went for a slash. Making my way out of the pub I slipped on some muddy grass and wet my arse. When I got my bus to take me home I dropped my money and it took a lot of effort to pick it up again, well it does if you're seeing treble at the time. When I got home I went straight to bed, when a friend rang to see if I was going out I told him I was not well, which was the case. I wonder if I said on this occasion never again, I probably did. Well looking back over my first few months of work and going to college I was in a deep depressive state and didn't know what to do about it, there seemed to be no alternative but to bite the bullet and get on with it. One good thought about college was that the course had already past the half way mark, which was something to be cheerful about at any rate.

When the New Year came in and all the dust and booze were laid to rest I was back on the Burngreave Estate for a week before the college doors would open to accept me again. Barry got me to paint a kitchen ceiling for an elderly tenant who was no longer very mobile; I didn't mind doing the job even though it was unofficial. But by the end of the week the tenant had died and some of the men cruelly said it was because I had painted his ceiling. I have a habit of getting blamed for everything. The week passed quickly except for one day when I took an order for chips and was told there was a chip shop with a white front in another area of the Burngreave Estate. So with directions I set off at about twenty five minutes to twelve to find this fabled white front chip shop. I found no such chip shop and kept on walking; when I finally knew where I was I had made a big circle. I came out onto the Wicker, where there was a chip shop open but not alas a white front variety. Buying myself some chips I slowly made my way back to the cabin, my dash for freedom had not proved a success. When I got back I had been gone for over two hours and the men had been looking for me, they are still waiting for their chips to this day. If any one had asked me for a skirting ladder they would not have seen me till going home time because I would have taken such a request as serious so therefore it must be done in a proper way and take as long as it takes.

Well after the short interlude it was back to the lovely Shirecliffe College. Back to our loveable boards and some new techniques that I would forget before I finished them. I've forgotten to tell you about General Studies a lesson we had which was not taken by the painting tutors. I haven't told you because I have nearly forgotten the whole sorry episode. There was one trip we went on that I can recall though and that was a guided tour of the Sheffield Wednesday Football ground. Wednesday were in the third division back then and Jack Charlton was the manager. We were shown around the ground by the grounds man. One of the most vivid of memories I can recall was of the Wednesday trophy cabinet, I've seen better trophies in people's houses. It certainly wasn't Anfield that's for sure. Other than this day I have no more memories of what we did in general studies, perhaps the whole thing was too much like school so I naturally shut myself off from it.

When we had finished what we were doing to our boards in the workshop we were taken to what had been a school. It was called Salmon Pastures and was situated down Attercliffe. The river that had given the place its name had long since killed off the salmon with industrial waste. The school was in a fair state of repair and we would be just part of all the work crafts doing their bits to restore the school to its former self. It was ideal for us really, giving us practise and also to do parts of the course that couldn't be completed in the workshop. When it was our days for Salmon Pastures we would make our way there for the register. To me at the time it was one more place where I was expected to do some work, which the thought of didn't please me in the slightest. There was a canteen that had already been cleaned up before we arrived and there was an older woman working there. One of the lads in my group chatted her up and started going out with her, which earned him the nickname of Casanova or Cas for short. I myself would wag some of the days because I was so unhappy with the situation I was in. What had I done to deserve this went through my head and surely I was born for something better than this. To get paid for the missing days, which I didn't do at first, I would go to the Doctors, pay a pound to get his signature on a sick note which covered me for three days. The days when I wagged work I would go for long walks past Rivelin Post Office and make for Stannedge Pole, where I would eat my packed up sandwiches and reflect on my existence. The question why I was born kept coming to mind, which if you have asked the question and got a doubtful answer, it is not a good way to have a bag of laughs.

I didn't keep these early days of wagging to myself for very long as I ripped up my wage slip which we got on Thursdays and threw it in the bin in my bedroom. My mother the Sherlock Holmes of the family pieced it together because I had never torn one up before or so my mum said. It showed I was only paid for the two days last week so she wanted to know and also my dad did, what I had done with the other three. I as ever couldn't explain it and felt terrible about the situation but I felt a lot worse about having to go to a job that gave me so much suffering inside. There was no real alternative other than killing myself which was no option at all as that would be giving in and defeatist. Whatever happened and however I felt I was going to get through this minefield of a life that I was looking at and would come through whatever the cost would be.

When I went out with Peter my friend from schooldays we would drink about six pints of bitter, then go on the shorts. In my early teens I was sick so many times it became habit forming and when I was drunk I used to put my fists through windows. I somehow never got cut but the glass one night got its own back, one night when I staggered out of a nightclub I hit a reinforced window. To this day I have never tried such a stupid stunt again. I was that prolific with pukes I can remember hitting Peter's mother with one on a night out. I suppose I must have thought that if I didn't get drunk it was not a good night out. It seems such along time ago my time as a destructive drinker, I think that's what I would call myself because I sometimes would go weeks without any booze. These early days of drinking before I was eighteen were in some ways exciting for that reason because it was against the law. We could easily go to two nightclubs a week and I still couldn't spend all my money, which in relative terms was a lot more than kids get today. Bitter was only 24 pence a pint when I was a lad and I came out with twenty four pound after stoppages a week. That's a little bit more than teenagers get now for doing some crappy government scheme, but then again that's showbiz.

Back to work we must go and on the keeping fit side of the course we were doing weight lifting at Shirecliffe College. It was my turn to lift the bar and I had Rory and Casanova either side of me, to help me if I got into any trouble and the weights were too heavy for me. I lifted the weight above my head and then dropped it onto the Gym floor, it was all my fault but the games tutor didn't see it that way and gave Rory and Cas a bollocking, saying they were miles away from what they were supposed to be doing. The days kept dragging by and an attendance report was sent by the college addressed to my parents but I intercepted and tore it up but this time I put it in a litter bin far from the house. When we were at Salmon Pastures there was an incident when the police were called to deal with throwing things into a work yard from our side of the wall. It was Tom Bowler who did it and when the police came he was in the toilet, where he stayed till they had gone. After many problems the tutors had with our group we got a visit from the Employment Officer at Salmon Pastures with the chief painter's gaffer coming with him. Like I say they got problems a plenty from our group and the visit was to remind us if we didn't buck up we would have our apprenticeships ripped up. They got us to say yes that we would all behave a lot better than we had up to now which wouldn't take much effort as we had been a right bunch of bastards to the tutors and anyone else we had come into contact with.

This has brought up something I hadn't thought about and that is the effect of young teenage lads from whatever their backgrounds being put together for long periods of time and you not getting a volatile situation from them. We were in a way guinea pigs because we were the first group to be given a six month course altogether in painting and we were guinea pigs in another way because of all the troubles our group caused at the college. If my recollections so far are correct I can only think the scheme was a failure or maybe we were just a bad group of misfits. So many of the lads had wanted to be plumbers and brickies but could only get on the painting department of the works. I suppose everyone has a sob story to tell. Another holiday for the college came along so it was back to the gang I had been with before. They were still on the Burngreave Estate and I was still the waiter service for the gang. Barry the charge hand was still chasing women and plenty of blocks had been given two coats of piss; that's undercoat and gloss to you. A lad came on a landing no older than fourteen and gave me a load of magazines; these were not the ones that are on display in newsagents. The magazines were hard porn, the real thing in glorious colour. I took the magazines to the painters' cabin and me and Barry looked through them. During our dinner which we had in the cabin this day the magazines were handed out and various comments were made such as spam fritter, which stayed around for a long time did that one. The magazines were called orgasm or climax, for people with imagination obviously. This wasn't the only time hardcore magazines were handed out; it just depended on what some of the blokes wanted to do in their break times. By the end of the week all the lot of the magazines had gone from the pile that was handed in. They tried to point the finger at me but I didn't take any of it home but it did make you wonder what they got up to with there missus or someone else's. Look what I found at work today, she can do it so you can, is not possible without doing a mischief. I was surrounded by a load of dirty bastards but then again that's the only type any of us are and I will be honest about my own perversions later if only to be fair to a load of perverts.

There was a cradle on the job with us because the work was too high for ladder work. One day I got to work in it for a couple of hours, it was like being on a ride at a fair except the drop would kill you if you fell off. I enjoyed it but would never have volunteered to do it fulltime; it was too much of a risk and for only a few more bob an hour. No I had enough trouble on the ground without adding to it and painting off a beer crate was more my idea about heights than swaying and throwing up my last meal. Because I got a pair of gloves from my dad a load of blokes put in their orders and I tried through my dad to get them a pair but few used gloves to paint houses like I did, so their need was not as great. When I went home after a tiring day at work, I can here the laughter about that one. Just being at work was tiring for me. After a day out in all weathers my face would go a bright red when I got home and I would feel drained. I would change from my work clothes and into my better clothes, feeling a lot cleaner for doing so. When I had finished my evening meal and I wasn't going out for the night I would play some of my records. At the time the Sex Pistols were my favourite group with the Stranglers a close second. The songs by the Sex Pistols would make me laugh which at the time when I was feeling my lowest was a release for me. I would get so down that the music by being so frantic matched my confused mind and many times I would fall asleep listening to the Sex Pistols. There are not too many people who could say that I suppose. When it was time to go to bed I was still capable of getting to sleep until morning when I would be awake before my mother came to get me up.

I was back at College again after their short break and the end of our six months course was not to far away now, which was something to be grateful for. There were some in our group who hated me for some reason and it came out in an incident that happened when we were at Salmon Pastures. We were all allocated with a large door that we had to burn off the paint of and then rub down, prime, undercoat, then finish with a coat of gloss. The doors were finished by all the group members of our class but on one day someone had scratched all the doors except mine. The tutor on this day was Ken Ball and he got us together knowing that I hadn't scratched the doors and telling me something I already knew that someone in the group really hated me. There were quite a few people it could have been but I put it down to the fact that it was someone who just didn't hate me but also feared me. So I wasn't too concerned about the situation and it didn't go any further than this. When we caught the bus to town one night about five of our group paid 2p for the bus ride and we still had ticket conductors at this time which was not the proper fare. The conductor came up the stairs and at every bus stop demanded another 2p off these five and they had to keep paying or he was going to throw them off the bus. He certainly taught them a lesson, which probably didn't sink in as usual. The big day at work was the Thursday because it was pay day. When we were at college a Securicor Van would come in the break time with a gaffer in a taxi to make sure everyone got paid. This was at least a little bit of satisfaction if not a great deal of one. Sometimes when I got paid on a Thursday I would go to town from college and buy a record which I would play all night but this was not usually the case as I would go out boozing on a Thursday night.

The first year of college was over and we had passed all the levels that were set for us to achieve. I didn't go back to Barry's gang this time but joined a gang who worked on the inside of School and Colleges. This was led by Grunty the Cuntie as he was known a right little minded bastard. Because I hated the job but knew I had to stay to build up the circuit no matter how depressed it made me. Grunty would keep saying to me "Why don't you fucking go!" and this did have an effect on me and that was that it gave me something to overcome. In many ways it was an ideal partnership because he wanted me to leave so I wanted to stay even though I hated the job. When he didn't turn up I worked faster and when he came back I would go into my shell again. With the times for bonus not being too good on inside work there were also a couple of other apprentices on the job with me. We didn't become eligible to earn bonus till our third year when we would get some but at a lower rate than the men. The reason for a lot of apprentices on the same job was because the men were given hours because of our inexperience, which went to them earning bonus.

In my time on the schools and elsewhere with Grunty we spent a lot of time in the Norfolk park area of the City, which was a fairway from home. I would sometimes not get home before six and we finished work at half four. Even though there were other apprentices on the job I was still the chief order taker for things from the shops, plus I would mash the tea at the break times to. There was one bloke who was on Grunty's called Malcolm and he was a fairly nice bloke who always wanted me to fetch him some biscuits. The biscuits I kept bringing him were custard creams and he was fed up with them so he told me `whatever you do, don't bring me back any custard creams' and low and behold when I returned from the shops I had bought him custard creams. It must have been a brain lock or something because believe it or not I didn't intentionally bring him back custard creams. But Malcolm was keen to hold up the white flag of peace and didn't order anymore biscuits when I was fetching them. The other major part of the day was the mashing of tea, when we had finished our break it was down to me to wash out the cups. For some reason I kept dropping the mugs and breaking them, I put it down to bad balance as a child and that I was going through a phase where I could have auditioned for a part of the living dead in a Giorgio Romero movie. I was definitely the spot ball but I'm good at acting to type so I played it for all the part was worth and stuff what anyone thought of me.

The Children when we were in the schools would sing "Frigging on the rigging there was fuck all else to do" to us as they passed, especially the part where it says "wasn't fit to shovel shit from one place to another" Maybe they were dropping hints; it appears everyone is a critic these days. This song was on the B side of one of the Sex Pistols' singles. If I give them anymore plugs they will end up being number one again and so many people thought once was enough. On one school we were working on there was a woman who worked at the school who fancied one of the painters. She was always hanging round him even though she was a fair bit older than him. One day they were doing a school play and I was going to mash the tea for the afternoon break and they were doing a religious pageant I think you call them. I had to go through the hall to get to the boiler in the kitchen and by all accounts I could not have timed it any better, just when I opened the door one of the kids said "Our Lord the Archangel Gabriel enters!" so there I was with a hundred kids looking at me coming through the door. Well I did say I was type cast and here was proof of it. The painter going round with a cloud round his head is more than he seems I might think to myself or am I the half wit everyone thinks I am; only time will give up the real answer.

One day our gaffer known as the Monk because of his bald patch on the top of his head came a calling and when he saw me he said "look at those eyes" because they were the eyes of hate and he jumped about leaving the room. Grunty said "He doesn't scare me!" but then again they didn't call Grunty the Cuntie for nothing; in time he would gain the reward that he had reaped. The two other apprentices who were on the job at this time were a pair of creeps because they got on with the job unlike me of cause, who would take up plenty of time just looking out of windows daydreaming. I got into an inert state which I would go into in a big way in my time on the works. It became difficult to move at times due to the inertia that would come over me and it was near impossible to shake it off. I just had to wait for it to pass. I was so unhappy but like I have said because Grunty was such a shithead who wanted me to leave I had least the satisfaction off pissing him off. Its definitely the small things in life that make it worth living and even if I couldn't see a way out of my predicament, I would just have to keep going and hold onto the fact that I was above this and somewhere in the future I would prove that to be the case.

After being with Grunty's little gang I got moved again, this time it was a man called Tony who was the charge hand on the job doing schools and colleges. He was a lot easier to get on with and I think he had a better understanding of what I was going through than most of the charge hands I had in my time on the works. There were only three men on the job and they were not doing the whole school but just some rooms and then they would get moved on. Tony on many occasions said " No man is an island!" which was aimed in my direction because I hardly said anything and was bottling it up inside, which would prove a big mistake in the future but I couldn't really say anything about what I was going through or what I was thinking because the thoughts were too personal. I was in charge of the mashing of tea as ever and went to the shops for any orders the men might want. I didn't mind these chores because it was more time taken up that I didn't have to work. We got moved to Broomgrove Road down Ecclesall Road way in town. The job was a big one and there was already a gang working on the student dwellings that were being painted inside and out. There were little flats for the students with a sink a bed, plus some cupboard space for their stay in Sheffield at the Polytechnic or the University. On this job was my friend Rory who like me hated the job he was in and was always looking for ways to get out of doing work. I was now the chief order taker to about twenty blokes which meant I could take up half an hour taking the orders and another ten minutes to the shops, then another ten minutes to go back. All this meant was that I could take the best part of an hour going about doing a service and nearly an hour from having too do any painting.

Both me and Rory had to enrol at Shirecliffe College for the second year of our course for apprentices in painting. Tony said I could go anytime when it was necessary for the enrolment or that is I think he did. One of the men on Tony's gang was called Gordon and there was a song in the charts by Jilted John who had lost his girlfriend to a lad called Gordon and in the song they sing Gordon is a moron. The Gordon on the job said that all the kids were singing Gordon is a moron as went past. Me and Rory went to enrol for the second year of our course and were accepted.

A change from work was upon me as it was my summer holiday and I went with Peter my friend from my schooldays to Skegness for two weeks. There was supposed to be another lad going with us but he backed out at a late stage. We stayed in a caravan and were taken to Skegness in a van with Peter's parents and Peter's girlfriend at the time Karen who later became Peter's wife. When they went back to Sheffield Peter's mum didn't want to leave us because she thought we couldn't survive on our own. There was a chippy on the site so that was food taken care of and beer in the pubs; it just goes to show that my time in the scouts was not wasted after all. There was also a new fangled thing coming into fashion, the pizza. I can't remember much of the holiday as may be it's too many beers ago. We went to the Disco enough I can recall and I got drunk but don't remember being sick which was something of a luxury when I think back.

With going away with Peter in 1978 I didn't have to go with my parents who went for their holiday on the Isle of Wight, with me left alone in the house which didn't bother me much. My brother had to go with Mum and Dad but he would only be about twelve at the time so it won't have bothered him too much. While they were on the Isle of Wight my dad came back to Sheffield because my granddad died while he was on holiday. He came back to Sheffield with Auntie Elsie and Uncle Jim and my Cousin John from Southampton. The service was held on Cemetery road and his ashes were buried with my grandmother's and Uncle Jack's in the family grave in the Cemetery. Auntie Irene who had been looking after Granddad in his last year at her flat with Uncle Les who was of cause also there as was Colin and Sheila. There were probably some relations I have forgotten, which I apologise for but that's all I can recall about the day now. It was sad to see my granddad die but I was glad his suffering was over and at 90 years old he couldn't really complain. To think when he was born in 1888 Queen Victoria and her bankrupt values were alive. He lived through the Great War, through the Russian Revolution, the birth of the Aeroplane, the Cinema from a flicker to sound and colour, the Second World war, the Stalins, the Roosevelts, the Churchills of this world, he had outlived them all. He was a simple knife maker and was one of many ten a penny knife makers of his time. The birth of the pension which in some ways I don't think he understood, getting money and not having to work for it. But then he had seen out the workhouse and all the indignities that were thrown peoples' way. To watching Star Trek going boldly where no one had gone before on another invention in his lifetime. Maybe he hadn't done to bad after all and its funny but if someone was doing the work of my granddad he would probably be from a middle class background who had a degree, and would be selling his wares for a lot of money because of the time and the skill that would be required to make quality goods in to day's workplace. My granddad may be dead but he is not forgotten.

My dad made his way back to the Isle of Wight after the funeral, with me back on my own again. Getting back to work after my holiday while we were working on the Broomgrove job there was a runner I had seen on the television who was starting to make a name for himself and I saw him on many days going to work practising his training. His name was Seb Coe. The job was still not finished as there was plenty to do. I got back into my stride very quickly or in my case very slowly would be the better description. I was only on the job for a week before I was back for the start of the second year of the course at Shirecliffe College. The second year was thankfully only thirteen weeks long which we would have staggered. What I mean by that is we would go to college one week and then have two weeks back on the job itself. In the second year of the course it was not just council apprentices in the group but from other firms there were also apprentices. I made a good friend in Alan who was working for Hassel Homes I think it was or some thing like that. We would go to the Timbertop pub at dinnertimes and have a few pints, with one of their burgers for dinner. Also there was Terry who I knew who had become a friend and with Rory also in this group I was surrounded by people I liked, so it was already better than the first year. A lot of the idiots from the previous year were in another group now so they were going to the college in weeks when our group were not at the college. Everything had settled down a lot from the first year and a lot of the lads were even engaged or were going to get married for the usual reason but not as binding as in the past. With it only being one week in three it was a lot better to take and was more likeable than the weeks on the job.

One day I was working in a corridor when a teacher from Myers Grove came past me, who was being given a guided tour around the college for some reason. While he passed me he said "Are you a lot better now?" It was Mr Ward my old woodwork teacher who I had not liked and I was taken aback because I had never thought that I would see him again or had wished that I never would. The course work we did I couldn't begin to tell you much about, I was either dreaming, larking about, feeling sorry for myself or getting over the beers I had at dinner time. In the second year we had lessons taken by Ted Fillet or by Mr Claterus. I can recall having an argument with Mr Claterus over colours changing in different light and I kept saying they didn't because they were the colours they were so couldn't be changed by light of a different cast being shown on them. I must have taken up a good half hour over the point and I couldn't give a toss if there was an eclipse due I wouldn't have any of it and if I wasn't having any of it; that was that. On another occasion me and Mr Claterus were talking about stamps because we both were keen collectors and he said there were too many commemorative stamps issued in Britain; I of cause disagreed and took plenty of time out of the lesson which must come to you as a great surprise. The other tutor Ted Fillet was full of himself and a crashing bore who I didn't like. In the class we had with him we covered some theory about something or other and I got so much out of it that I have forgotten completely any of the lessons, which shows I haven't got such a bad memory if I can forget rubbish that I don't want to remember. One of the other tutors was Bob Moody who I don't think I have said much about, which might be a bit unfair because I got on alright with him. In fact some of the class actually got jealous, because of how well we got on; other than that I can't recall much about what we did in his lessons either but in his case it was nothing personal. It was just my way of getting through the time by becoming a statue or a zombie depending on your preference.

When the week had finished I was put In the Painting Depot to help out with the orders for the paint gangs. I didn't mind being in the Depot and I got on with the man who was in charge of the paint shop, even though I didn't get on with the man who was learning to take over the headman's job. There was only one bad thing about it and that was having your dinner in the rest room with the other trades but apart from that it was fine. It got busy when a paint truck came to deliver its load and when it was all accounted for I would have the job of restacking it onto the shelves in the workshop. Fetching putty was the heaviest part of the job as it was in a big drum from which it would be put into smaller tins and then taken out to the job by van gaffers with the paint orders. While I was in the Depot I managed to fill many bottles with turps which I stored at home as it always came in handy. Because I didn't mind being in the Depot and meant passing the Monk's office in the morning, they would sometimes call me back to help out. When my stay at the depot came to an end it was back to college for me.

Now I had a lot of people around me who I liked I didn't mind as much as I had in the first year of going to college. There was plenty of time to talk and have a laugh which sometimes was directed at me. It was said that when I saw a girl nude I had commented" where's the staples in her bellybutton," like they have in men's magazines. A trip to York was in the pipeline, we were supposed to be going to see some painted ceilings in a Church there and look at some of its land marks that people from all over the World come to see but do bare arsed painters who sup turps go to York for such things. The trip was arranged and we would be joining up the groups with us all travelling together by coach to York, so all the apprentices at the college would be going on the day trip. The day came and the coach arrived at Shirecliffe College, with us getting on board. The whole crazy gang of misfits going to York; would there still be a York after this crew had been there. Some of them would certainly be trying to take some of it back with them, if it would fit in their pockets. The trip there was smooth in comparison with going back but having arrived we all went into a Railway Museum, which we all dispersed from and went our merry way around York. Some of the lads were chanting songs going down a street when they were pulled up by some plain clothed C. I. D. who jumped out of there car to tell them to shut up and behave. It was time to try out some of the beer of York, so into the pubs we would go. We all went in separate directions butt eventually we all seemed to end up in the same pub for a couple of pints more before closing time.

The pub we ended up in was a right dump and the landlord complained that we were not taking our glasses back to the bar when we wanted another drink. In Sheffield we do leave our glasses on the table to go for another pint most of the time so we were not doing anything out of the ordinary. There's always someone you meet who wants to be a party pooper that's for sure. When it was time to go back to the coach to go home we made our way to where it was parked. One or two of the painters were really pissed out of there tiny minds and were in quite a state. The tutors led by John Joseph and Ken Ball were not in a good mood because we had not gone on the designated trip for which we had come to York to see. With every one of the apprentices feeling worse for wear we got on the coach. Some of the lads started to sing some chant and were told to shut up by the coach driver and John Joseph. When we had gone a few miles a lot of the lads wanted to have a pee so the coach stopped and we all had a piss. The day had taken its toll on our course leader John Joseph and he was very upset at our behaviour and couldn't understand why we were such a load of ingrates who knew no better than yob behaviour. He came to the back of the coach and gave us a bollocking for what had turned out to be an eventful day. One of the lads claimed he had shagged a lass round the back of some church but he seemed to be too drunk to have performed anything never mind screwing some slag. But then there was going to be many a story built up around this day that's for sure. When we were nearing Sheffield one of the lads capped the day by throwing up in the coach all over himself and over the coach. They would not be taking us on anymore trips that's for sure in the future and in many ways it said a lot about how we felt about our apprenticeship.

We were just a load of mindless morons, the usual for males in their teens these days who couldn't be taken anywhere because of our behaviour and some of the painters not being a full shilling and bordering on being some sort of psychopaths. I was back on Grunty's gang after my stay at college and he was his same loveable shithead self. The good thing about it this time was that Terry my mate was on the job with me; we were doing a school and I was the tea masher and order collector, which I would have been aggrieved to lose the duty of. Grunty put Terry on one staircase and me on another and even though Terry's was a little less work he finished a good day before I did and of course Grunty was going on about it like the moron he was. Terry's work looked like Niagara and he should have had to do it again but I wasn't concerned about the flak I was getting from Grunty; it just made me more determined that I would see my time out and do the job that was only mine to do. I don't honestly believe that ever sunk in with Grunty because he was an ignorant slaphead who couldn't see further than the end of his nose. I went with Grunty's gang for a few months in between the college weeks and one day I thought to myself I will have a change so went into the paints depot to see if they would relocate me. I was put in the paint shop which I didn't mind as the senior man who I got on with was still in charge. I saw Terry on the Thursday night when we were drinking down town and told him what I had done; he said he would try the same thing himself. At that time me Terry and Rory were all firm friends and we would go out together a lot of times over the next few years. It was normal when we went to town into any pub that we would bump into a workmate that one of our three knew; this was the circuit which was being set up in my stay on the council. It would become too many people to recall and a web of threads all over Sheffield which would touch nearly everyone in the area.

When Terry tried on what I had done by reporting to the depot for a change of work place they had a right go at him and he was found a load of shit jobs to do around the depot, to my amusement. I was fine in doing what I was assigned to do in the workshop. Me and Terry looked at some of the gear that was in the storeroom when the headman had gone for a chat about an order that had been made. What caught our eyes while we were looking around were some paint rollers. We both took some and put them in Terry's bag because my rucksack was open to view. When we clocked out at the end of the day we both made our way into the toilets and I went into one toilet and Terry in another next to it. He then slid the roller handle and its covers under the partition wall and started to say "Are you there Wayne!" thinking that I wasn't there and all I could do was burst out laughing. I eventually reassured him that it was me and he didn't have to have a heart attack over our deed. When I was leaving the handle of the roller was sticking out of the rucksack and I nearly poked the eye out of the manager of the paint shop. I quickly just carried the bag in my hands as Monk was looking out of his office window. Getting out of the depot doors was a relief and I walked quickly to get as far away as possible. I'm sure the manager knew as all he had to do was check what had gone out against what was in the shop and it would show they were down two roller handles and about ten rollers. I don't know why I took them really because I hated the job yet they might come in handy at a later stage in my life.

I was moved to another gang and the job was Stannington College about a ten minute walk from our house. The job was led by Clive the only black charge hand at the time. We were working in the college when it was having a holiday. I can remember something Clive said to me one day and that is "You're either the king of the shite or the shite of kings!" a bit of a philosopher was our Clive. There was only Clive plus one more man and us three apprentices. They would buy our dinner for us on a Friday because we didn't earn bonus. There was no big hassle being on Clive's gang, I had joined the gang while it was being moved to Stannington College. When we got to the college I helped get some of the gear off the lorry and it was while I was doing this that Paul one of the apprentices, who had started the same day as me observed that it was the first time he had seen me help somebody. I must have been going through a dizzy spell and forgetting myself for just a moment, I can assure you. It was strange working at Stannington College again because I had before when I was on Tony's gang.

Clive at dinnertime and during the day would rib me by saying I was a virgin and often after talking about another subject he would come back to this topic. At dinnertime we would sometimes go onto the playing fields of the college to play a game of cricket. Clive kept hitting balls in the air in my direction and I kept running around trying to catch them with no sign of me doing so. A cricket ball is very hard and I wasn't going to pull out my fingers by pulling off a catch so I moved in the general direction of the ball but made sure I didn't get to close. In the college when we were working I did a lot of the library of the college and they still had the newspapers delivered everyday even though the college was closed to students at the time. I can remember moving the step ladder away from a piece of work I had been doing round the library windows and Clive bringing me back because I had missed a good couple of foot of the surface I was supposed to be painting. My mind must have been wandering again and I must have thought that I was a faster painter than I really was, which I am sure would have surprised some people. While working on the college I even got to hang some wallpaper even if it was only woodchip. When it was my turn to put on a piece even the time it took me to brush it out was condemned as being too slow by Clive but then again did I ever hear anything else I must have been a tortoise in a former life. Whilst we were doing the gym hall of the college there were some weights which amounted to one hundred pounds and we all had a go at trying to lift them above our heads. Clive was the only one to manage putting the weights above his head and I had a job just picking them up, never mind just putting them above my head. The painting of the gym was the biggest job that we did at the college while we were working on it.

It was time for another week at Shirecliffe College to do the second year of the course, which was getting very near to Christmas by now. Very little of what we did at college was useable in our work setting. The mornings before break always seemed to pass slow and everyone when the break came would make there way to the dining hall. There were machines that gave out sweets when you put the correct change in. Everyone would have to queue up for a drink and you didn't always get a seat. When the break was over it was back to the workshop and whatever we were doing at the time. I must admit I did enjoy the sign writing and the heraldic board that we produced, which I still have because they were done on light weight boards so we could keep them. People in our group seemed a lot more keen to get on with their work than in the first year, with a lot of the hostilities no longer present. In the main we were all looking for a laugh and all the squaring up to each other was a thing of the past. When dinnertime came most of us would make our way to the Timbertop pub, which was just a little walk down Shirecliffe Road. Me and Alan usually drank together and there was another lad called Andrew I think with a face of acne that made him look like a human pizza, who also drank with us. We would order a burger in the pub as soon as we got there and go up the stairs with a pint of beer. Sometimes we didn't go to the Timbertop but went to town instead in Andrews's car and go in a pub in town. We had an hour for our dinner, we were supposed to be back by one a clock and when it was Tuesday it would be chart day so we would listen to radio one to see what was number one on the chart for the next week. After dinner we might go back to the workshop or we may have a theory lesson; it just depended at what stage our work was at. In the main now we would have Ted Fillet to take the theory lessons or Bob Moody, who I liked a lot better than Mr Fillet. The lessons would pass me by and now I was thinking about Christmas. I thought as ever during this period that I was wasting my life away and that this was something I didn't want to do for the rest of my life. In fact when we first started our apprenticeship we were told by our tutors at Shirecliffe college that now was the time to decide whether we wanted to be painters or not. The thing with me was if I left what else would I do that I would enjoy doing for a livelihood and nothing came to mind, so I would have to continue suffering doing my apprenticeship. The college week came to an end with us breaking for Christmas, soon upon us.

I ended up back on Grunty's gang who were as usual working on the inside of a School in the Norfolk Park area of the City. It was very cold on the outside with snow and ice everywhere. I think it was the year the snow gritters went on strike for better money, so the buses couldn't get around on the icy roads. It was a simple matter of having to walk from home to the job at the School, which for me was on the other side of Sheffield. I managed to get to work for quarter past eight and was complimented by Grunty for coming except that I wasn't going to do much work in the day whatever time I got there. It was going to take me a good two hours to get home and I needed all my energy for that trek. I think the strike was only effective for a week because the weather picked up, so the bus service could run again. I was looking forward to Christmas with the holiday coming up but I was walking around in a state of inertia that I was feeling towards the job. When my depression came down on me it was very difficult to throw it off and the consolation of another year being over was not sufficient to raise my spirits. The days passed into weeks and if time didn't fly the last week of college had come.

With it being the last week none of us were to keen to get on with the work that had been set. In the main in the build up to Christmas we had been working on some boards about two foot wide and three foot long. With the end of the week coming and also another year maybe it was time to reflect on the time I had spent at the college since September 1977. I certainly wouldn't have said it had been much of a happy time especially the first year which was a living hell to get through and one to forget other than for Liverpool F. C. I think the only good things to come out of my time were some good friends in Rory, Terry and Alan. There is little else I can recall that was in any way beneficial to me in my life. It was looking back just a case of trying to get through it with as little pain as possible to myself. When Friday came the last day of term, it was piss up time at the Timbertop. We were supposed to go back to the college after dinnertime but I for one was in no fit state to return. I had a couple of burgers which helped mop up some of the beer intake and I was a lot more stable on this occasion than on many an afternoon session. When it was time for the Timbertop to close I caught the bus to Town. One of the lads had put the board that he had completed in the toilets of the workshop and went to collect it and got on the bus with it. He was out of his head because he got on the bus and started swearing at the driver, who didn't take much notice, which was a good thing because the lad was in a mood to smack somebody. When we got to Town we said our goodbyes and went our separate ways.

Back to painting in the school and low and behold Grunty was on holiday so I worked a lot quicker, when he wasn't around. The job was so boring it certainly gave you plenty of time to think and mull over my bad thoughts that I had towards the job and towards myself. I would always get the job of going to the shops even sometimes when I was not the youngest on the job, as my apprenticeship moved on. I probably took more time fetching things than anyone in the history of the works; what a star I was. With it being a school I ended up painting some very large building blocks that the children would play with. When it neared to Christmas the School went on its holidays so it was empty but for us and the caretaker. When we were working on a School light fittings would get broken when moving the scaffolding on its castors, to get at the high ceilings and walls. Also when working in the toilets it was easy to stand on a toilet seat and break it. The caretakers would go mad with us over these breakages but they couldn't be helped. When it was the last day before Christmas holiday the jobs I was given were done in a very quick time, which didn't escape the notice of the men on the job. I have got to admit when it came to the piss up in the afternoon it's a little blurred as to what took place. I can recall we went to Town but after that my mind is a complete blank.

During the Christmas period I got drunk a fair bit and sometimes would be so out of my head that when I got home and went to bed I forgot to go to the toilet so I would have to go while the rooms ceiling was spinning around above me. I didn't always manage to get to the toilet but ended up peeing on the landing. On another occasion I didn't even manage to get out of the bedroom and started to piss on the television and record player which were in the room. One night my mum even put the landing light on and the toilet light on for me but I still pissed up the landing wall, with my dad wanting to hit me so my mother told me the next day. I doubt if I was an unusual teenager and I bet most can tell of similar moments when they got out of there mind, because its all part of growing up and finding out for themselves what its like. Christmas at our house was the usual with my mum and dad falling out about something that didn't really matter but that never stopped them. We would make our seasonal trip to Collin's house and have our tea there and watch something on television. New Years Eve would come along and I can't remember if I was out drinking or at my mum and dad's. I hope I was out drinking. I very much doubt that Christmas 1978 to New Year 1979 was any different to the other years in my life. After New Years Day my thoughts would return to work, which was only a few days away.

In the mornings of a work day I would be awake before my Mother came to get me up. I would be sweating under my armpits and I would be wishing that this is the day my mother doesn't get up. For me there was no such luck and I would usually be on Stannington Road catching the quarter past seven bus to Town depending of course where I was working at the time. Being on the inside in the winter time was nothing to sniff at and in future years I would have been glad to be still working indoors rather than facing the elements of the outside. Another thing that I have not mentioned is that when we reached the end of our second year as an apprentice we were given a percentage of bonus for the work we produced. This made us less viable for jobs inside schools and meant we would be on the outside work on the estates far more. This of cause was still in the future at the start of 1979. I rejoined Grunty's after the holiday festivities with the usual school insides that I did whilst on the job. I would have the toilets to do and one way or another in my life time I have spent so much of my time in school toilets. It must be some sort of an attraction that I can't work out. Thankfully there was college soon to help break up the time. While on Grunty's during this period I made a friend in a man called John who had a very loud voice but was a kind man and he took me to some clubs to play snooker because he was a keen player at the time.

The time at college was going slowly on and I was still not taking anything in. On a Wednesday now we would have a tutor who was called Mr Wilkes, who took us for paper hanging in the afternoon once a week. We would use the walls in the mock house which was in the main workshop, to put up as many pieces of paper as we could or put a piece of paper over a light switch and then cut the paper in a correct fashion so the paper was not torn, with the switch in the middle of the paper. In the main there was no trouble between the painting apprentices now but we did have a running feud with the bricklayers. There were even some attacks by brickies on us and some retaliation by us back but it died down. I would depending on what I felt like sometimes would walk all the way home from Shirecliffe College to Woodend Drive where my Mum and Dad lived. When I was really down I would as I have said before go and get a sick note for three days and not have to go to college or work these days. I didn't just go down Rivelin but also would spend a lot of my time in town. I would go to the main library in town on Surrey Street and make my way up the stairs to the Art Gallery which was on the top floor. I spent hours sitting and looking at the paintings and in the bad weather it was pleasing just to get out of the cold for awhile. The little café in the Library was usually busy so I would wait while there were only a few people inside. I didn't just spend my time indoors as I would walk all over the City Streets thinking how had I got myself in this mess and what could I do to change the situation. I would have a bag of chips or go in a pub for a pint and a sandwich. Sometimes I might go to the Cinema if there was something I wanted to see. The down I would be under at these times was very low and in many ways out of control. I must have looked a right state but I don't think too many people noticed that much. When I went home after a day that I wagged work I would wait for the usual time that I arrived home so as not to raise any alarm in my parents. These days off made little difference to anything except they were my way of asserting myself over the situation and made it seem however little the change that I did have at least on alternative to work.

When it was dinnertime on Grunty's and I had been for the orders there were sometimes not enough men to play a game of crash so I would join but Grunty would be so sad as to cheat to stop me from winning the sad bastard that he was. We would have longer than the half hour we were supposed to have by about twenty minutes. When we used eggshell for the walls and the radiators that were on when we painted them it would make the air thick with paint fumes. Something which I think had an effect in our afternoon break, because on many occasions we would have a laughter session. We would laugh about anything and I am sure the fumes of the paint had something to do with it. I was the one who got to paint the radiators or undercoat and gloss the woodwork. When we moved into another classroom I would help move the furniture to the middle of the room so it was easier to get at the walls. The days passed slowly by as the second year of my apprenticeship went with them. I had a fair few warnings while I was on the council both written and spoken ones but this was a time where I can't recall if I had one to my name. With the oncoming of bonus being paid my time on Grunty's was coming to an end. I can recall one day there was ice on the ground and for one day we joined an estate gang. The gang was led by Barry my first charge hand and because the conditions were so dreadful we stayed in the cabin till the afternoon and then made a big push by using paint as thin as piss to make it look like we had done something in the day. The cold when it hits you on the estates goes straight into your kidneys and it really pisses you off from there. I was fed up with being with Grunty that I wouldn't have minded joining Barry's gang. You can not be anymore desperate than that, I can tell you. I must admit that I don't recall the circumstances for our day on the estates.

We didn't just do the insides of Schools and Colleges but worked on the Town Hall. In the old part of the buildings the rooms were so high to the ceiling you could get vertigo. I recall working with Malcolm in one such room and I don't think I have written that Malcolm was a bit of a Desperate Dan in that his chin could be shaved in the morning yet by half four in the afternoon he needed to shave again due to very notable stubble. I also recall me and Malcolm doing a shop front in the centre of Town because it was council property. In fact in the main I just footed the ladder and watched people go by while Malcolm did the job. The time kept rolling by even if to me it had seemed to stop. It was a matter of getting through the day the best I could.

The college course was going its merry way through the second year and still the best day of the week was when the Securicor van came with our wages on Thursday. The other lads were going strong with their girlfriends or were getting married, while I was pondering the meaning of life and why I had pulled the short straw. Not much difference you might say but then again what do you know. Talking about getting married, my friend Peter would marry in this year and beat his elder brother and sister to the altar. I just tried to keep going even if it was not getting any easier or better as time went by. All I looked forward to at college were the dinner breaks so I could have a few beers and feel just a wee bit better in myself in my predicament. The course held nothing in my thinking and I couldn't believe I was turning up to learn about a subject that I had no interest in what so ever. When college and the second year of the course came to an end I was glad it was over. I was still on Grunty's but not for long because I went into the depot down Attercliffe and because the senior manager was still there I was allowed to stay in the painters' warehouse.

My friend Peter's stag night finally arrived on a Thursday night and I got really canned out of my head. We went round most of the pubs in Town, in a very big group of us. All I can recall is that we went to Faces nightclub and I went to the toilet and when I came back everyone I knew had left for another nightclub. I somehow got home by taxi but I am not sure how. When I awoke in the morning there was sick on my pillow, which was a brown looking colour. My Mother when she saw the mess got me to get out of bed and sent me to work for the day. Fortunately it was a very quiet day at the depot which was fine because I only started to come round at about three in the afternoon. Not being able to face my sandwiches at dinner I ate them on my way home. It said a lot for the job at the depot that some days were very easy indeed. I went out with Peter on the Friday but I didn't have much to drink. When the Saturday night came I went out with other friends round the pubs on West Street in Town. I made my way to the Moseley Arms where the reception was being held in a room upstairs. I was probably the last guest to arrive and can remember having a soft drink with Peter whilst we talked. Peter went through about six jobs on leaving school in a very short space of time whilst I plodded on with the painting apprenticeship in the same span. I wished I could have gone through a host of jobs just to find the job that I would like to do but that was not possible in my journey. There was a path laid down for me and I had to follow it if I liked it or not. Saying goodbye to Peter on his wedding night and wishing him all the best was an end of an era. My best friend at Myers Grove now had a heck of responsibilities of his own to handle. I haven't seen much of Peter since but I always think of him as being one of my true friends that I have met in my lifetime. We certainly had many a laugh in our time and I don't know how I would have got through going to Myers Grove School without him to talk to.

My stay in the depot was only for a couple of weeks and they had me up on the roof putting on some whitener on the windows to retract some of the sunlight off the warehouses. When I was moved on it was to an inside of a school at Pitsmoor and the charge hand was Clive. So I was back on his little gang which had not changed other than for a first year apprentice being on the gang now. It was the usual two coats to the surfaces and the very usual boredom that came with it. Clive was still jibing me about being a virgin but I took not a bit of notice so didn't bite. Thankfully my summer holiday was nearly upon me unfortunately I was going with my parents and my brother to the Isle of Man for two weeks in a boarding house. But on the bright side it would be two weeks away from the smell of paint and the intellectual chit chat that went on between the painters on the council.

We went by coach from Sheffield to Liverpool and after a couple of hours wait we got onto a boat that would take us to the Isle of Man, who were celebrating their Millennium in 1979. The boat journey going was very smooth with the sea being quite calm. When we landed we made our way to the boarding house we had booked. Me and my brother were to share in one of the bedrooms and my mum and dad had another. It was a fairly big house with many rooms unoccupied. One of the events on the Isle of Man is the TT motorbike race but it was not on whilst we were there. Someone who revved up their bike at five in the morning didn't seem to think it mattered there was no TT and carried on as if there were. In the morning for breakfast you could have cereal then a cooked breakfast with toast and a cup of tea to wash it down. The weather was fairly good and the sun was trying hard to come from behind the clouds. So being of the stoutly made stuff we made our way to the beach after changing into our swimwear. We got three deck chairs for me and my parents plus a wind breaker. I even was brave enough to put my feet in the sea but it was very cold not surprisingly. The first couple of days went by and towards the evening we would use the bar in the boarding house before going to bed.

One night I was on my own in the bar as my dad had gone to bed and there was a girl on her own sat in the bar only a few feet away from me and we started chatting and I bought her a drink. She was working in the kitchen of the boarding house and was from Liverpool. When the bar closed we went into the television room where there was a Woody Allen season on so we watched one of his films. Being the sort of person who laughs at about anything I really enjoyed the comedy in the film even if I did send the rest of the holiday goers to bed with my chuckling. I said goodnight to Susan as she was called and made my way to the bedroom where my brother was fast asleep. Over the next couple of nights I spent a lot of time with Susan and even arranged to meet her in the day time when she had finished her chores. I had a crush on her, it was as simple as that and I wanted to be near her all the time. We went to a Hotel bar one evening where there was a group playing a lot of Sixties tunes. One of the more popular bands on the island were Generation X who I passed while walking on the beach front; their lead singer was Billy Idol who would make a big name for himself in America as a solo artist in years to come. I was glad to have some female company which made my holiday as I didn't have to stay with my parents all the time. On a few days there would be all of us together in the day time on the beach before Susan had to go back and help with the evening meal.

Because they were promoting the Millennium on the island they had brought out a coin to celebrate the fact and they were giving them away if you could answer one question, if you had a copy of the Daily Mail. I bought the paper one day and we were on the beach when a man and a Beauty Queen came round to do with the Daily Mail. I said that I had in the main read the back of the paper so the Beauty Queen asked me who was the famous person featured on page 3. I said it was the Pope which was the right answer, so I featured on page 3. I still had my radio for company which was one of the better things, got a coin and also had my picture took with the Beauty Queen, who seemed a little bit on the stuck up type for my tastes. Some of the serving girls were unkind to Susan because she didn't have good clothes. I felt something for her that had never been there before and it was a good feeling. The holiday because I was enjoying it flew by and it was time to leave in what seemed very quick time. I promised to write to Susan and she said that she would also write to me. The last night we had together made me feel very sad and looking back on it there is no doubt in my mind that I wanted to be like everyone else and fall in love and make a fool of myself. The journey back across the sea was no picnic due to rough sea with my mum for one being very unwell on the way back to Liverpool and all the toilets were full of sick. I myself didn't feel to well but that was not down to the weather conditions it was because I had fallen in love and didn't want to part from Susan.

When I retuned to work I was quickly moved on to an estate gang for there was only a little time left of my second year on the council. I was put on the Shiregreen estate on Pryertolla's gang as it was known with a reputation that went before me. In one dinner break Pryertolla said "You don't say much for a trouble causer Wayne!" "Who me?" I replied. There were some men on this job who knew who I was and they gave me encouragement. I was missing Susan and so I arranged to go to Liverpool at the weekend because she had left her job on the Isle of Man. The week only passed very slowly and I was feeling indifferent to my life in Sheffield. When the weekend finally arrived I travelled to Liverpool by train and had to change in Manchester. I arrived in Liverpool at about ten in the evening and Susan was waiting for me at Lime Street Station. There was a long bus journey to the place where she lived in an area called Speke. She was staying at a friend's house that had seven children and a man who was living with her who she had just had a child to. The area was like the Second World War had just finished. There were bars on the upstairs windows to keep people in rather than keep them out. I got on really well with the children and they were a great bunch who I hope got a better deal in later life than what they had been given at the start. There was a Club which me and Susan went to. I think it was a Catholic run club. When I left on the Sunday I didn't want to leave. I phoned her at the club in the week and I returned to Liverpool two weeks after my first visit. The children were really glad to see me which is more than Susan was and by the end of the weekend I knew we had finished. I couldn't have an intimate relationship anyhow so it was just a bit of foolery on my part. The lady with the children rang me a few weeks later and informed me that they had been rehoused. I hope it was a darn sight better than the house in Speke which wouldn't have been to difficult a task to beat. Even cave dwelling man had paintings on the wall which is more than could be said for that house in Speke. It was certainly an eye opener to how the other half live as the saying goes.

The last year of the apprenticeship at the college was soon upon me and I enrolled for the course. In the third year we had to attend one day a week which we all treated like a holiday from work. I was on the Shiregreen estate still and when September came so did the two thirds bonus I think. When I first started on the estates the house you were working on was where you left your ladder and the paint and brushes. But ladders started to be stolen and brushes and paint went missing, so we had to lock all the ladders together and take all our gear back to the paint cabin when we finished for the day. While I was on the Pryertolla gang I worked with Heavy Bill who got his nickname because he was in to heavy metal in a big way and had very long hair. The work we were doing was just the outsides, that were down for a two coat clean up as it was known. The job was very repetitive and luckily I had a radio so I could go into the great beyond while listening to Radio One. It really helped to get through the day listening to songs that could have a different meaning from the one intended depending on what I felt like at the time. On this particular gang there was Tom Bowler's elder brother who liked to fool around but got on with his work. There was Campbell Meatballs who was always a contender for despond of the year and he came out with a right statement one day that I can still recall; it goes something like this "Its all a matter of mind over matter, if you don't mind it don't matter!" What a great sage through the ages Mr Campbell Meatballs was. Some of the others such as Steve and Dirty Mickie were usually very funny at dinnertimes and Steve came out with the classic "I fucked the wife last night and gave her nine inches, I fucked her three times!" Well it's a joke that makes me laugh anyway. There was Gerry a very quietly spoken Irishman who was from Northern Ireland and also Mick who was from Southern Ireland who was a very up and at it type, who was full of stories. Mentioning Irishmen reminds me of a man on the works who was Irish and the thing about him was that he didn't turn up on Fridays. He was given a warning over his conduct and told if he had any more Fridays off without a reason he would be on his way. So the Irishman had no alternative and so started to come in on the Fridays but then he started to not come in on the Mondays, such was life on the council.

In the mornings before work I had toast for breakfast with a cup of tea and a very long face. The whole thing made me very unsociable towards my mum who got me up or anyone else I met in a morning. There was no desire in my whole frame to go to work and the only alternative I had was to hit the sick and I couldn't be on that the whole time. Being on the outside meant I was open to changeable weather. The cold windy wet days I endured whilst being on the council will always be with me. I hated the rain and spent many an hour sitting on the floor in a tenant's porch watching the rain come down in buckets. On days like these you found out who your friends were that's for sure. There was a day on the Pryertolla's gang that was an absolute wash out and one of the van gaffers had been round to say we could go at four but the charge hand didn't bother to come round and tell us. When it was winter and there was ice on the windows, plus incredible draughts that hit you in a biting way, I always wanted to go to the toilet. We never had our own toilet on the job but this was fine when tenant's houses had outside toilets. If this was not the case it was a matter of asking permission to use the tenants inside toilet which was a might embarrassing when you dropped your guts and left a smell that was so bad it resembled a rat having died up your arse. It was just something more we had to put up with on the job, no pun intended, then again maybe it was.

The one day at college was a doddle and we worked in the workshop before dinnertime doing some work on boards that were provided. Sometimes we would use a spray gun to do part of the course but it was mainly done by hand. At dinnertime we would go to the pub. Alan and me would down four pints before making our way back for the afternoon session at college. In the afternoon Ted Fillet took us for a theory lesson which I had a job staying awake in. He would waffle on and my head would get closer to the table as tiredness came over me during the lesson. When the break time came I was glad to have a drink of tea that might just bring me round a little before we went back to the lesson. There's one thing for sure about it and that's he might as well have been talking in Greek for all I knew. The last year at college was one long piss up as far as I was concerned and I can remember a funny and embarrassing happening when me and Alan were in the Timbertop. I put a record on which was John Paul Young's hit called Love is in the Air and when it came on everyone in the pub looked my way and started to laugh. Its moments like that when you want the ground to fall away beneath you so I could disappear from sight.

The job on the Shiregreen estate was still in progress and me and Heavy Bill were still working together on the job. We were snagged on one block we had finished and the van gaffer pointed to a part that had bubbled up and said "it needs bleeding every half hour does that blister!" I was trying to hold my laughter but I just couldn't so burst out laughing. This didn't endear me to the van gaffer but you can't please everyone can you. The estate when we got close to Christmas was nearing completion. The monotony of the job was getting me down and I felt in myself I could do with a change.

When it was the last day of college in 1979 we decided we would make an afternoon of it as it would be the last Christmas we had together at college. We left the college at twelve and caught the bus to town and made our way to the Roebuck pub. Me and Alan plus Andrew were in rounds together and we had three pints before making our way to the Hoffenbraus where they had strippers on at the time. The woman who took her clothes off was about as subtle and graceful as an elephant. It was enough to make a man shiver. We only stayed for one beer and made our way back to the Roebuck for a better drink. From there me and Alan were supping pints to everyone's halves with us ending up in the Golden Ball on Campo Lane for the last drink. I bought myself and Alan a big cigar which I don't think helped my health that much as I was shortly taken ill but I made it to the toilets just in time to throw up. When I went back to the table the pub was empty but Alan was waiting for me when I went outside. The fresh air nearly made me fall over which was not much of a surprise after drinking at least eight pints. The thing is that I just can't take my liquor in the afternoons. It goes straight to my head. Me and Alan walked for awhile and when we went past the Mulberry pub we entered the newsagents that are close by. We started looking at the men's magazines and knocked them off the shelves. There we were out of our heads trying to pick up a load of magazines while the newsagent staff looked on. When I finally got home it was about half four and I went to lay down on my bed but felt sick so got a plastic bin in front of me and started to spew up, which must have lasted a good 15 minutes. I was expecting to see my kidneys and liver emerge it was hurting my chest so much. When I finally got to rest I said "Never again!" which somehow didn't seem to sink in to my way of thinking when another round of drinks were coming my way. I don't think the college were to happy because we still had a class in the afternoon but that was their hard luck story for the day.

I have just remembered that we also had a night class on this day throughout the year of college. Me and Alan after the night class would go for a drink in the Cannon. One night a man came in holding his side and in a moaning voice he asked for some plasters from the bar staff and went straight in to the toilets. The pub was run down and was a well known dive but it was ideal for us seeing as we were in our working clothes.

It was soon the turn of the Pryertolla's gang to have their session of bevies in the afternoon. Its not one that sticks in my mind though so nothing much happened or if it did I don't remember it. With me always writing about the Christmas piss ups I hope you don't get the wrong idea that it was one long trail of piss ups in my time on the works because this was just not the case. I think the reason I have written a fair bit on the Christmas times is because they relieved the tedium of painting which is something that sticks in my mind. I think also it was seeing certain people in a more sociable environment that you could see that some people were actually human who I may have had doubts about before. It was the one time in the year that certain people let there hair down and enjoyed themselves which is something that a lot of the painters I worked with only did do at Christmas times.

The end of 1979 was followed with the birth of 1980 and I wished for a better year and for my life to change for the good. Don't ask me how I saw in the New Year because I have no idea which means I was not sick with an hangover or even worse than that I must have been at home with my parents. Life can be so cruel at times. So after the Christmas holiday it was on with 1980 and the completion of the work we were to do on the Shiregreen estate. When the move came it was to the outside of a school which was very near Concorde Park and I think Concorde was in the school's name. That is it had Concorde in its title, I am just an ex painter you know. I was still working with Heavy Bill but we were all working together really. The job we got was to paint the doors and the frames of some prefab classrooms. But first we had to remove the wire mesh that was protecting the glass from vandalism. The day was freezing cold and I was glad that we had to go inside the classrooms to loosen the screws, so I could have a little moment in the warmth. The painters were laughing at me because they said my face had turned blue at one stage. It was a damn lot warmer on one side of the blocks than it was on the side of the open field because the wind on this side would blow right through you. It was a lousy freezing cold day that made me pissed off with everything, with me asking what had I done to deserve this. The damp wet days on this job were to familiar in my time on the council and I just hated going to work on these days. It was bad enough going to work at anytime but the winter months were a kind of hell all to themselves.

One day the charge hand told us there was a day's work on the inside of a school, which was being done by Grunty's gang. Me and one of the numerous Steve's on the works were chosen for this one day of work. So me and Steve got going leaving the painters' cabin to go to this other school across the field. Grunty was his usual charm less self who only had a veteran painter on his gang with him because all the others had escaped. By seeing him again it brought back memories of the times when he told me to go and I had no alternative but to stay. I so wanted to go but who said my life was to be easy, I had a purpose to perform and no matter what it took I would carry out my side of the bargain. We were shown to some cupboard rooms and we got stuck into it to get it done. When all the walls were coated up we sat behind the door and had a breather. We were both silent for a few minutes which was unusual for this particular Steve and I broke the silence by saying "Grunty is a Cuntie!"

Steve said "Oh Wayne!" and we both started laughing about what I had said. When dinnertime arrived Steve left the job for an appointment with a dentist that he had been trying to see. This of cause left me alone with Grunty and the old hand Jim who had been on the works a very long time. We got through some chit chat but I don't really remember what was said. It was like the day it passed by quickly and I was glad it was over so I could catch the bus home. Just before we parted I said "I will see you!" Grunty gave me a look which made me feel good inside for I had overcome the bastard.

It was back to the great outdoors for me the following day and I can recall saying during my career counselling that I wanted a job on the outside, what a dope. Of cause it was different in summer but that seemed an awfully long time away. In fact I can remember something else that I did with this Steve, who became a shop steward, other than our jaunt to Grunty country and that was painting the outside of a house in the pouring rain. This was the only time in my stay on the works that I painted in the open rain, to get a house finished.

The day at college was heaven sent during this period because it gave me a day off from thinking that I was nearing the end of the World as we know it. The day was one big laugh and we all got on so there was no friction between us. It was strange how so many of the apprentices had changed so much in such a short space of time and that we wouldn't be apprentices for much longer. I was probably the only one who still didn't care about the job and didn't take notice of the theory side of the course, which would be tested in the final exam at the end of the three year course.

I was moved to another gang and this was led by happy Larry and one of my best friends on the council was on the site to and that was Rory. In fact I even got into an argument with happy Larry over talking to Rory. I had taken my ladder to the place where they were being chained up and it was close to the block where Rory was working, so I just went for a harmless chat. When I went back to the cabin to change and go home, Larry tells me he is going to dock me half an hour of my time for not being on my own block. I had heard enough I said to him "You've got a nerve telling me I am not working when all you ever do is get blisters on your arse!" If he had been a younger man I might have hit him but he was an old fart with blood pressure. The next day I was called to the cabin for a chat with a van gaffer, the shop steward who was John one of my mates from earlier days and of course happy Larry. We were in the cabin to talk about why the work I produced was so slow. I mentioned the fact I was the furthest away from where the ladders were locked up at night. The van gaffer was Scrachit who with the help of John and Larry started to play name your time to see who could paint the fastest window and tell me that the times were fair. I had heard all this before somewhere which goes to show how original the conversation on the council was at the time. Then we got on to the argument that me and Larry had the day before. I made it very clear that I would not retract a single word because I had meant what I said, Larry was a lazy bastard; it was as simple as that. I don't recall if I got another warning on this occasion or not but I reckon they were on very shaky foundations if they did. It came as no surprise that I was on the move again the following week.

The job was at Stradbroke and it concerned painting new houses that had just been built. They were nice semi- detached houses but were a big bind when you were working on your own as I was at the start. It was a long way from Woodend Drive to Stradbroke every day and when I went to the shops in my dinner break I thought I saw someone who was on Barry's gang at the start of my apprenticeship. I didn't give it another thought but when I was waiting at the bus stop to go home a car pulled up and it was Dave. He told me the other bloke he had worked with went to Germany to paint and caught sunstroke so came back. It was strange meeting him because it made the time I had started on the works come flooding back to me and it seemed like it was a life time ago all in the same moment. The new house I was on was a real drag and there was the small matter of the final exam only being a month away, plus I still had to go to college once a week which meant I was one day behind the other men all the time. Also I was having driving lessons so my life was hectic at the time and I couldn't care less if I ever finished the house. Another painter joined me to finish the house, and then incredibly I was given another house on another site. I was only on the job two days when the foreman told me I could leave the job. This meant the following day I had to go into the depot for another placement. The painters' gaffer Monk wanted to know why I had been thrown off the job and I told him I didn't know. The rest of the day I spent in the painters' warehouse and the senior manager of the supplies was still in charge but not for much longer. While I was in the supply depot I got the job of stirring some old paint that was going to be used to paint the inside of gutters on an estate. I was moved after a week in the depot back to an estate gang who were working in the Parson Cross area. The charge hand was called Jack who like so many of the charge hands I met on my travels was adverse to doing any work if he could help it. In the words of squeaky Pete "Alright for some!" How true that was and still is.

The final exam was soon upon me in my final year of the college apprenticeship and I had done so much preparation with having four pints at dinnertime and the theory lesson being in the afternoon when I was falling asleep. The fact is I was in top condition for a beer tasting competition, the only trouble with that being there was no beer tasting competition at the end of the course but there was a written exam. The day finally arrived at the end of the course but there was no happy ending as I managed to write my name and I correctly spelled it. The rest of the exam was not as easy because it was about a subject that I knew so little about. It might as well been written in Greek for all I knew, to say I wasn't going to pass the exam was not an understatement. When the exam results came through I had failed the exam and decided to retake it. The reason I retook the exam was because I wanted to be sure in confirming my thoughts that I had spent the best part of three years at college totally wasting my time. Another reason was that I felt guilty in letting my parents down. The worst part was getting the signature of Ted Fillet the man who had taken us in the theory part of the course on the form. I can recall going red in memory of my school days, for I felt embarrassed when asking him to sign the form. I was not the only person who had failed the exam but I bet I was the only one who took the exam for the second time who didn't do any revision. I put my name on the paper yet I can recall little else other than going off into a haze and feeling tired. The exam result when it was announced was in no doubt as I already knew I had not passed but I had learned something and that is if I don't want to do something then I don't do it from now on, no matter what the cost to myself would be. It was heart felt resentment at this thing that hung over me like one big dark cloud but I couldn't shake it off, it compelled me to my destiny but I knew things would not work out to the plan. It would be strange not going to the college anymore as it had been a very big part of my time on the works but I would not miss it as I hated people trying to learn me something of which I couldn't care less about. With the end of college it also signalled the end of the apprenticeship, so now I was expected to be the finished article, which of cause I was, I was totally finished with the job if I got my way.

I was moved on to the Home Improvements and base camp was inside the Stubbin and Brushes' estate. The Home Improvements meant there was a kitchen and bathroom to emulsion and woodwork to undercoat and gloss in all the houses that were improved. The charge hand for the painters was called Les who was a war veteran who nearly brought up the subject every dinnertime. Not surprisingly it had been the most telling moment of his life. He also did some work himself and left us to get on with our work without snooping around all the time. Because there was indoor work as well as outdoor we didn't have to work in the rain, which won me over from the start. The thought of no painting in the rain made me think of Gene Kelly who had he been a council employee would he have done a number called Painting In

The Rain, probably not.

I was no different in my deep thoughts on the Home Improvements even if it was the best part of the job in my time on the council. I still went round as a brain dead zombie most of the time. I was usually a million miles away deep in my thoughts anyway and it was a good thing the job was simple enough and didn't require to much concentration. I wasn't paid to think so left it to those around me. I would walk around as if there was all the time in the World and I certainly made sure there were plenty of opportunities to go on a Wicker walkabout as I called them. When you ran out of gear it was often a fair walk to the base camp and then back again, took up plenty of time also. The job put me in my element to do mostly as I liked. I spent a long time on the Home Improvements site and worked with a series of different partners as in the main it was better to work in pairs on the job. The first partner I had was new to the site like I was but he didn't like the Home Improvements. He put the gaffer's shoe into an emulsion bucket, which played like a tale of the unexpected for a while. Then he did something which was totally unforgivable, he stole some dirty books from the paint cabin; enough was enough. His wish was granted and he got a transfer to an estate gang. My next partner was called Steve which was a fairly common name on the works. He was a right creep when it came to dealing with the charge hand or the occasional van gaffer. When he saw them to talk to he would offer them a cigarette. This particular Steve was harmless really and I can remember spraying him with deodorant in one of the tenant's houses we were doing at the time. It could be said though when it came to arse licking Steve was your man. I was working in the kitchen of a house while Steve was doing a window upstairs, when he shouts to me to come upstairs and see something. When I joined him in the front bedroom of the house he said that the cupboard door had swung open and right before my eyes was a blow up doll that seemed to be dripping. There were no curtains in this bedroom and the houses across the street looked straight into the room, so what the neighbours thought was any ones guess.

The house was lived in by somebody who would have been the village idiot in times gone by. My partner was working in the kitchen one day when the man just happened to knock over some dirty plates which broke when they hit the floor and he said "That will save washing them!" When we were both in the kitchen we took a look at his cutlery, which couldn't have been dirtier if they had been buried in the garden. The man also had a dog that was so dirty it looked like all the workmen had used it as a mat to clean their boots on. It could hardly walk the poor thing and it definitely needed a bath but that could also apply to the man of the house. Both me and Steve worked as fast as we could to get out of the house and we were glad when we had finished it. When looking back on it the man could hardly look after himself and desperately needed some form of help to do daily tasks that most of us take for granted. We both had a laugh over the blow up doll but the situation overall was one of sadness and lack of care.

Steve's sucking up to gaffers was sometimes brought up in the dinnertime conversation and he had his leg pulled and the piss taken out of his creeping behaviour. Other than his sucking up to the gaffers he was alright really. While we were on the inside of a house one day I felt that I couldn't continue doing the job, I couldn't move being in a state of inertia. The depression when it came over inside my head made it difficult to do anything, so painting was out of the question. After working with Steve for another day I got put with another Steve as a workmate. This Steve was known as big mouth because he talked all the time. We were mainly on the outsides, finishing the houses off so they could be booked in as finished. There was some wood that needed knotting and priming on the Longley estate and me and Steve got the job. I had a radio with me so it didn't get to boring but it was repetitive. When we went back to the Stubbin and Brushes we got a lot of the outsides that had not been modernised due to the fact the tenants didn't want to deal with the mess that was part of the job. After doing a fair number of these outsides we got an inside to do. It was the usual kitchen and bathroom emulsioned and all the new wood to be painted. While I was working on a window in the kitchen the women of the house said "He is so sweet!" in reference to me. I just hate being called sweet and she wasn't the first to say it by any means. If I had known that in time I would hear this said hundreds of times I might have changed my mind, it makes me feel sickly just thinking about it.

Anyway back to the grindstone or more like back to the daily drudge. After this house me and big mouth Steve were split up. I got another house to do on my own and the female tenant was a bitch from the start. For some reason she couldn't have her kitchen ceiling painted and had her back up from the very beginning. I had been painting the windows of the house on the first day and I left early because I had done all I was doing for that day. The next day there was a van gaffer on the job who was following up a complaint that had been made by the woman. The van gaffer asked me what was going on and I said I had nothing to say. She did not fill in a form of complaint so there was no real bother but the whole thing was about the kitchen ceiling not being done. The outcome of it was that arse licker Steve was back as my partner to finish the house off and keep me company. The thing about it was that the pink primer bled through the paint in her house and another three houses did the same. The wood had not been kilned dried in the Bramall Lane workshop as it should have been. The wood in these four houses had to be repainted. I got a warning on the site from the man who was the overseer on the job but it was shortly after that I was told it had been squashed.

So creepy Steve was my workmate again. When we went for our dinner back to the base camp compound, the cabin would sometimes be over crowded especially when a quota of houses had to be finished. To make sure the quota was met they brought in more painters to the job. When in this busy period I drew a typhoon on a piece of paper and Des who had been drafted in to help with the big push took the drawing off me to get a better look. He said "The power of the thing!" when he showed it to his workmate. It was definitely an intense drawing and when I got the piece of paper back I turned it into a carrot. Des who had looked at the drawing closely said that he thought that the Carousel from the film Logan's Run should be what happened to me. If you haven't seen the film the Carousel is a way people in the future are murdered when they reach thirty. He also mentioned that two rows of people facing each other and with hammers to the ready and then I was to run between them getting hammered to death. This idea was taken from a western that had recently been shown on television. There can be no doubt he feared me for some reason and didn't grasp what I was up to. The trouble is some people hate what they don't understand and they despise what they can not comprehend. To the other extreme or to the opposite if you like there was Ken the second in command on the job who one day when we were alone in the painters cabin said "I wouldn't do what you're attempting for all the tea in China!" He also mentioned on another occasion that he felt sorry for me, which in all my time on the council he was the only person to do so.

There was a change to how we filled in our sheets which were to tell the firm how much we had done for that week and get the bonus from the hours we had made accordingly. The meeting was held in a cabin on the Longley estate so we had to make our way there from the Stubbin and Brushes compound. It took half an hour to tell us the new arrangements which were basically having certain numbers for the job and the time allowed alongside in a little book. It meant we would be doing our own measuring from now on and if we were caught lying we would be sacked for fraud. Some of the men didn't latch onto the idea so got the painter's union man to go through it again in our cabin on the Stubbin and Brushes site. It was all fairly straight forward and no one had any difficulties with the filling out of the weeks work.

Some of the workmen on the Home Improvements were knocking off some of the female tenants, that is they were having sex with them. One of the roof renovators told me and my workmate that he had been shagging a woman in the kitchen when her husband came back into the house, because his car wouldn't start. He quickly pulled on his overalls and helped the husband start the car. When the husband had gone he went in the house and started shagging the woman again. He also told of a time when they had driven to a place they thought secluded and they had been shagging against a tree when they noticed a man looking at them through a clearing. They made a hasty retreat back to his car and drove off. The roof repairer wasn't the first to have this woman by all accounts she had previously been seeing one of the plumbers. The plumber had even rung her to say her new sex partner was a nice man; he wasn't bothered about her now because he had found another woman who he could see in the afternoons. The fact is there are many lonely people out there whether male or female who need someone at times to break up the boredom and of course its nothing new.

While priming some doors one day the charge hand came up to me with my face nearly touching the floor he said "You look like life's passing you by son!" that was an understatement. My thoughts about being unhappy with my job were well known throughout the firm. I would often go into a depressive daze which could sometimes take weeks to pass by. There I was moving as fast as a snail with a face on and I must have made an unpleasant sight for the tenants to encounter. A job came up on the firm and I got moved to it with someone who I knew from college, it was Tom Bowler. The job was on Middlewood road, there were six terraced houses that had been modernised and it was our job to paint them in and out. There was still some work going on for the plasterers and joiners but there was plenty to go at for us bare arse painters. Because there was only me and Tom we took it easy and would arrive after eight most days. We would have a good half an hour tea break in the mornings. Then get stuck into doing some work before going to the pub at dinnertime. We went in the tap room of the Park and played darts while we supped down our beer. Whoever lost at darts had to pay for the chips from the Chinese across the road which meant I paid for the chips more often than not. The outside was very high and there was a long ladder specially on the job for us to get to the gutters. The van gaffer, Squirrel as he was known, wanted us to use the ladder so he could move it to another job that needed it. When he came he was always asking us why we hadn't used the ladder and it became a running joke. We put it off for weeks and then decided to use the ladder at long last. The ladder couldn't fit on the path but had to be based on the busy road, so we had some road cones to stop the passing cars running into the ladder. If I was presented with a job like that now I doubt if I could do it because the sheer height of it would have me shitting my pants.

The job very slowly but surely was getting done and we were the last workmen on the job. When the job was over Squirrel came to take us away and move us to another job and started to snag the work we had done in the last house to be completed, I went round with him tutting as he said what was wrong with this or that piece of work. He was really worked up by my tutting and was not in a good mood. Both me and Tom put our gear into the van and we were taken to an estate in the Shiregreen area. During the trip Squirrel didn't say a word because he was so peeved at my tutting him. I had arrived on the job at half nine in the morning on this particular day and the first thing Squirrel said to the charge hand was "Dock Clay an hour an a half from his time!" Wow big deal obviously Squirrel couldn't take a joke and was going to be ratty for the rest of the day, the poor dear.

The gang I had joined was Pryertolla's so I knew most of the painters on the gang but I needn't have gotten unpacked as I was moved again back to the Stubbin and Brushes. It was now going into winter time so working on the insides was a good idea if you didn't want to freeze your balls off. One of the events of the year took place but not one of rejoicing with the slaying of John Lennon in America. With me listening to Radio One they were playing a lot of the songs of the Beatles and of John's solo career. There was an hour long tribute played on the Simon Bates show and I can remember the last song was the Long and Winding road, I think it was one that McCartney had written but it fitted the bill. It was a day I will always remember.

Christmas 1980 was coming up quick on the rails and to get you in the mood some of the painters drank many a beer all year round. Some I knew would have four pints at dinnertime and it was said of those that did that they had a hip flask to keep them going through the day. Also some didn't just put turps in the paint but drank it, of course these were exaggerations but some I think were put on a drip feed at night giving their blood hundred percent proof.

The Christmas piss up of 1980 came along and we started in a pub not to far away from the base and had a few pints before catching the bus to town. Steve who was big mouth met some of his friends when we got into town and we made our way to the Bar Rio. The Bar Rio pub at the time was one of the busiest in town, with wall to wall people. To the right as you entered the pub through the main doors was a little bar with no one serving behind it. With our beers in hand we stood very close to the bar and I tried the Martini bottle to see if it was releasing the drink and it was. What with all the beers I had and all the Martinis when I left the pub I thought I was going to fall over. One of Steve's friends was sick in a pint pot but it came out like a piss and was all liquid, when another lad came back from the toilet he picked up this glass and started drinking it to the amusement of our group. I somehow made my way out of the pub and didn't fall flat on my face but I was out of my mind. Walking along Fargate I went down Chapel Walk and went into Vallances who used to have a shop there. They sold records upstairs and that was what I wanted to buy. I asked for John Lennon's Imagine and also for Starting Over at the main desk. There were three teenage lads at the side of me and they said something that I didn't like, so I hit all three of them and left the shop. I went back to the shop to ask if I had hit someone, because I was totally of my head and the girl behind the counter said I had. The whole incident spoiled my Christmas; it wasn't my usual behaviour to go round hitting people for something they had said just because I didn't like it. But it did bring up that now famous line I will never do it again. If only I could believe it maybe it might come true, you never know. After the business in Vallances I kept a very low profile this Christmas and I don't believe I was drunk again during it. So it was a very sombre me who brought in the New Year of 1981.

When I returned after the break I was still on the Home Improvements with the big story doing the rounds was that a workman saw a 14 inch Dildo in a house that you could tell had been used. Its always those heart warming stories that make the news, don't you think. I got a new partner who was called, Wait For It Mick, who like me had joined the firm at the same time but we had never met until now. Looking back it was strange because Mick turned out to be Catherine's brother but that knowledge was kept in the future. On a repaint we were working on, that meant the tenant hadn't had the modernisation done we couldn't help noticing that the only furniture in the living room was a Juke Box and a Pinball machine. Well you have got to admit they had got there priorities right if nothing else. Just a couple of doors down from that house there was a Labrador dog that was so fat it was as big as a lion. It would somehow get to its feet, walk four steps then collapse down again and have a rest. Why the owner hadn't put it on a diet I will never know but it did possess something the other dogs on the estate didn't have and that was it still had four legs. The other dogs only had three legs to get round on. I think the reason for this was the roads had very tight bends with the drivers not having enough time to stop the car quickly because they were going to fast round the bends.

During most days at work I would start thinking why am I here, being so miserable with my lot and my whole self wanting to leave but at the back of my mind I knew I had to stay and stick it out. The numbness I would feel in the time I was on the council will be with me for the rest of my life. I wondered what else I could do if I didn't want to be a painter for the rest of my life and I could never think of any alternatives to try because they all required work. This built up more inner hatred for me to cope with and it made me hate everyone I knew and worst of all my self. I was involved in going through a living hell which if there was a good reason for it I could not see it, even in the far off distance. I just kept picking my self off the floor like a punch drunk boxer who as lost his head. I certainly needed to unwind and going out to have a skinful of beer seemed the best way of achieving this aim.

Being able to stay in bed till nine on a Saturday morning felt great. Not having to be woken by my Mother was a bonus, no sweat under my arms and best of all no work. The weekend was something I longed for during the working week. There was time to do nothing or do anything that took my fancy. I would go to town and look around the shops, where I might buy a record or just browse and buy nothing. If I felt like it I would visit the Fish Market and have a plate of muscles with vinegar on. Depending on what mood I was in I might go to watch Wednesday play if they were at home. When Sunday came and I had been out drinking the night before I would take my time to get out of bed, I needed a shave but let it wait till the evening. I always wished that Monday wouldn't arrive so I would not have to go to work; it was the same with school and even more so with my time on the works.

Just to keep up my spirits I got transferred to an estate and met what was happy Larry's gang again even though he wasn't there because he was on holiday. The estate was on the left before the Five Archers and the weather was cold and damp. When working on these types of houses we would always leave the porches at the back till last in case of rain. It was an in joke on the firm that when it was raining you worked on the dry side of the house. Incredibly before I left the firm wet time could be booked for the first time by painters; wonders never cease. Because I had joined the job late I was still doing my block when the rest of the painters had finished their houses. The painters' cabin was hooked on the back of a lorry and all the men followed it to the new site. I was left on my own to finish the two semi-detached houses. Because I was left on my own I went to the Forty Foot pub that was across a field and drank five pints. When it was chucking out time I made my way home. The next morning I got there a little earlier and started to finish the bits that needed doing. When the block had been completed I had to make a couple of trips to take my gear to the new site up Wordsworth Avenue. My friend Rory was on the job and so was John from my time on Grunty's. When it was time to go home Rory gave both me and John a lift in his dad's red van. I was sat in the front in the passenger seat and John was in the back, sitting the best he could. We came along Penistone road and were on our way to Hillsborough corner when Rory, now outside the Bradfield road flats said to me "Am I alright?" "Yes fine!" I replied. A car nearly went right into the back of us and it scared John shitless. Me and Rory laughed about it when we dropped John off.

With us starting at eight in the morning not all the tenants, whose houses we worked on were awake and ready for us, but it rarely caused to many problems. The break in the morning was supposed to be half past nine but we could move around it somewhat depending on what we were doing. I would put a tea bag in my mug and ask the tenant to boil some water so I could have tea with my breakfast. The tenants would make you a cup of tea most of the time any way. Then again there were times when you wondered how some people got by. I can recall one tenant giving me a cup of tea with a fly in it and even only once a tenant filled up my mug with water from the tap. These though were the exceptions and thankfully not the norm. In the main the tenants were fine and some would give you pieces of cake or a bun to eat with the tea they gave you. One tenant gave me a bottle of home made wine, which sadly had corked when I got around to drinking it. Another tenant I can remember gave me some money but I put it through the letter box when I left the block. We had talked for awhile and I told her how I was so unhappy in my job and that I would like to leave it behind but had no alternative but to continue along my depressed way. She told me of her son who was doing a job he liked and that he couldn't have been more happier about it. For me there was a big dark cloud that followed my head everywhere and only time would ever take it away. Funnily enough on the other part of the same block I was undercoating the side door whilst listening to a tape by Mike Harding. It was about a Budgie and a Turkey and how they got mixed at Christmas because someone had been out of their head blind drunk. The story was reaching its climax when the lad of the house turned it off but straight away his Mother told him to put it back on so I could hear the end of the story. I had been laughing my head off whilst the story had unfolded and the door I painted while I was listening was probably the world record for the slowest undercoated door in the history of the works department, beating many of my previous efforts along the way.

When working on another house on another block I got talking to the tenant who was a keen football fan, who like me supported Sheffield Wednesday. He told me he had recorded a game on video of a recent match against Luton which I had travelled to see myself. He invited me into his house and we watched the video of the match that the Owls won, a rare achievement. The tenants were fine but it's the ones who were not that you tend to remember. I was on the move again this time to the Wincobank estate which was to do with the Home Improvements. I was with Mick again who was Catherine's brother. Our job was to finish off the work, so the houses could be booked in completed. In the main it meant a lot of moving around the estate for little reward. Going back to the tenants there were two families who had a very bad reputation on the estate. One of these families had been moved from a Home Improvement house into a non-modernised house again and you could smell the piss when they opened the door. The head of the house was still dressing up as a Teddy Boy, with one of his sons following suit. Thankfully me and Mick didn't have to work on that house. The other problem family I was told were not in the habit of using the toilet but instead shit into buckets. Their house when they were moved was in such a state that the workmen refused to work on the house before Rent a Kill had been in to kill off the lice. They were put in temporary accommodation while work was being done to their house.

The house was taking a lot of finishing because people were breaking in and stealing the copper tank and anything else they could lay there hands on. The living room floor was concreted three times because the sites standard manager was a bastard. The estate had been started by a private firm who had gone bust leaving many homes unmodernised and the council had to step in to get the job done. By all accounts the standard officer had let any old work pass with his approval when the job was being done by the private firm but now was going by the book and pulling up any work he didn't like the look of. The house with the redone floor cost overall three times of the normal modernisation. The workmen were hoping to see the end of it so they could start making bonus again. Me and Mick whilst on the job took it easy as we knew the score of the work very quickly.

Talking about problem families reminds me of one of the few jobs we did on the inside of a house. It was the usual emulsion in the kitchen and bathroom plus paint all the new woodwork in the house. The tenants had two dogs one was a friendly Alsatian the other a Terrier. We started the job and painted most of the kitchen and bathroom in the first day. When we left to go home we didn't take our painting gear back to the cabin because we thought it would be safe in there house. When we arrived the next morning just after eight, the living room caught both mine and Mick's eye. The tenants had glossed over the primed wood and hadn't brushed away any of the dust that had settled on the wood. It was a total eyesore and we were not going to put it right. We had to go and see the sites Foreman and get him to look at the mess the tenants had made, so he didn't think we had done it. Having sorted it out we got back to painting what had not been touched by the tenants. We put down a gallon of white gloss in the yard behind the house and had just filled our paint kettles when the Alsatian was let out and promptly knocked over the gloss tin but the Alsatian turned out to be the nicest member of the family. When we left for dinner we forgot to close the gate and the little terrier nearly ran off, when we returned after dinner we got a verbal in our ears about closing the gate. The male tenant said we had been told to always close the gate with them already having lost one dog. One of the other workmen when we were talking about the incident afterwards said they were not very nice people and the Alsatian was the best thing in the house. I for on didn't dilly dally on this house because I wanted to be away from there as fast as possible. When we had finished the house and only booked in what we had painted I can remember Mick wanting to go back into the house to make a more in depth list of what we had done but I told him I was not going into that house again and eventually he agreed not to either.

After this inside job it was back to our normal jobs like painting gutters or the washing poles. There were two girls at one house we were doing the gutters of who were listening to David Bowie and they looked like they were from another planet. They looked like they could have been aliens but that didn't stop me from trying to cadge a cup of tea out of them. By this time I was a dab hand at getting cups of tea out of tenants and there was no doubt I would get me and Mick both a cup. Mick thought I was a cheeky bugger but if you don't ask you don't get. The girls were not that friendly even though they did make us a cup of tea. Mick had at this time a Black Capri that had John Player Special on it and it was is pride and joy. We went for little trips in it at dinnertime which usually meant him going home. One day we were having an argument and he flicked my nose and I grabbed him, with both of us ending on the floor wrestling each other. I pulled out my putty knife from my overalls and he accused me of trying to kill him with my putty knife, which made me laugh. The fact is I wasn't very nice to Mick even though he was one of the nicest people I met in my stay on the council. The Hunchback of Notre Dame had just been on television and I was forever saying in a silly voice "Esmerelda" to Mick to make out he was ugly and grotesque. I also made fun of his car which was on its last legs or am I starting to have a go again. Its funny when thinking back because there is a strong family resemblance between Mick and Catherine. May be I should have been born a homosexual because I got to talk more to Mick than I ever did with his sister. But this is very much an after thought and not something I was thinking at the time. My thoughts were ones of much darkness and hate which I bottled up inside me.

To put a smile on my face it was time for my two week holiday in Biarritz a once a time place where only the wealthy used to go. I shared a tent with Rory and Terry my fellow painters in crime. Some other friends were in another tent and altogether there were seven of us but definitely not the magnificent. I enjoyed the holiday but travelling by coach is no way to go from Sheffield to France with a ferry ride in-between. We stank due to the two days of travelling to the holiday camp and the same again on the return. The only other thing wrong with it was that I only had a Sunday to keep me away from work on the Monday. How I wished I could have another two weeks off work or even better not have to go back at all.

When I got back to work I was moved to another job and got a new workmate called Andy. We painted a house where the tenant gave us Rington tea and it was very good tea. So we could go back to this house and have another cup of tea we cheekily made out we were working there. Andy suffered from hay fever and he used the toilet paper at this house to blow his nose. When Andy was waiting for a bus to go home the man who was Rington tea to us accosted him about using all the toilet paper, in front of the bus queue. Andy said "I have never felt so embarrassed in all my life!" Well one things for sure it was a laugh working with Andy if nowt else. The work soon dried up and it was move time for me again, I must have been born under a Wandering Star, its all right I am not going to sing the song. This time I ended up working on some houses in the Norfolk Park area of the City. The charge hand was known as Ernest who had the nickname of Wurzel Gummidge because of his changeable heads like character. This was a running joke with the men guessing what head he had on at the time. The men would say he was wearing his cabbage head or his empty head or even his gaffer's head. One of the men put forward that he must be running at night to help him get to sleep because of his doing nothing all day but sit in the paint cabin and that he probably suffered with insomnia. He was no different from the other charge hands in that he did no work even though he was a lot younger than most of the lazy bastards who were charge hands. In fact it was an historical job because we actually booked a couple of hour's wet time which was a novelty to the painters. We still had to go out and I just stayed in the porch looking at the other men who were painting during the pouring rain. I didn't get to finish my block because I was a wandering once more. The next job was at a depot which was in the Wordsworth road area.

The job was to paint hundreds of rusting gutters, which were going to take up a fair bit of time. I could wear rubber gloves to do the work and got stuck into it for once. Dinnertime soon rolled along and gave a welcome gap to the monotony of the job. There was a big hut at the depot where all the trades took there dinner and there was a boiler provided to make a cup of tea. There was a card game and I was asked if I wanted to play with me nodding my head. All I did was lose from start to finish. When I was going back to my work area I was saying under my breath that they were a load of cheating bastards. One of the men heard what I had said and brought it up in the next dinnertime, he said "Peter the painter thinks we are a load of cheating bastards!" Not to surprisingly I didn't play cards with them again, what a bad loser you might say. Being called Peter the painter was a lot better than some of the names I was called in my time on the council and its a lot more repeatable. The favourite name I was called when I was working briefly with Andy, when he said "You're like Doctor Who you!" When I had finished the gutters on the job I was given some huts to do inside and out. I also had fallout with the site Foreman with one of the painters' gaffers coming on the job to tell me to behave. Who me, I am as good as they come except when I lock horns with an idiot but that could be the story of my time on the council. Some gaffers would look at me gone out because I stood up for myself knowing full well that nobody else would stick up for me. It was not to long before I was on my way again back to a former estate gang I had worked with.

It had a different charge hand but all the men were from the same gang and it was one of the former gang members who was now charge hand. The time was moving into winter now and the weather wasn't to good but in our climate it doesn't have to be nearing winter to be lousy weather as we know. There were plenty of houses to go at and I was close at the time to getting the sack. If I didn't earn bonus on the next block that I did I would get the push even though I only learned this after the event when I earned twenty pounds bonus. That was typical of my time on the works, there were just to many rats on the firm and for that matter to many Cowboys. I worked on a house one day when the tenant brought me a cup of tea and told me that he knew a painter who was on the council. When he said who it was I said I knew him myself, it was Ken from my time on the Home Improvements. It was proof of the circuit coming together and that it was a small world in Sheffield at least.

The estates were where the most painters were on the works in my time on the council at any rate. I looked forward to the dinnertime chat that would sometimes develop over something silly that someone would say. In this gang there were quite a few characters who I reckon I will always recall. There was Ken who had a great sense of delivery in everything he said, that is when he came out with a statement it was usually funny and he could go on telling stories for a very long time. This Ken is not to be confused with the Ken on the Home Improvements. Also there was Mack who would always be saying about his wife "Fill her up with concrete!" There was a story in a paper one day about a man who cut out all the coupons out of the papers and gave them his wife and then paid her the exact amount to buy the food with the coupons. It was just like Mack to do the same thing because it would definitely be in character. On the job there was Charles who was about six foot seven and he had a size complex. He always seemed to think he was clumsy and had a severe inferiority complex that he didn't appear able to shake off. My friend John from my time on Grunty's was also on this gang, he was always chasing some women other than his wife. In fact he actually brought a photograph of the woman he was seeing at the time and it was enough to put you off, she was in the nude and I have seen better looking beach whales. It was a sight to make your eyes sore I can tell you. There was Campbell Meatballs on this gang who was still trying to win despond of the year. There was also Michael the gang leader who didn't seem to bother if he didn't get the charge hand's job fulltime as at the time he was on trial. Then there was me who you know plenty about by now and I was still the quiet one of the group.

The winter months were closing in on us now and when we finished the estate we were going into a school. Some of the men though would rather have stayed outdoors working on the estates right through the winter. The school was only a twenty five minute walk from our house and for me it was a little bit strange because I had attended the Nursery part of the school when I was a child. I could remember queuing up for cod liver oil and later in the day beds would be brought out and we would have a nap. The school was in a poor state and had not been painted for twelve years. The times given for the work were unrealistic and this meant that the bonus would be very low. This made a big difference to the married men's wage packets but I was never interested in bonus anyway so it didn't bother me. We all worked together to get the school painted and also worked in pairs when there were smaller jobs to be tackled. I paired up with John who I had known for over four years in my time on the council. Being the youngest on the job and my reluctance to work well known I was the tea masher and the chip fetcher on the job. This was fine with me and I could do what I wanted most days.

John and me sometimes had an argument over our work practices but it didn't take long to get back together again. A lot of the time I was the basis for many conversations on the job and for that matter whilst I was on the firm I was probably the most talked about employee. Of cause you might say I was being paranoid but you will have to take my version of the story because it's the only one you have got. The weather was now cold, damp and icy. I for one was glad to be indoors during the winter and because there was no bonus on the job I think it made for a better atmosphere between the painters. There was another man who joined our gang who was called Frank. Frank was close to retirement age and had false teeth; he was a gentleman which made him very rare indeed on the council. After a short while he kept saying to me "Wayne is alright but some know the truth!" and you can make of that what you will. Christmas was drawing closer, the job was taking as long as it takes and it would be my last Christmas on the firm, even though I didn't know that at the time. The last day of work before Christmas came a long and because the job was local we went in a pub at Hillsborough called the Shakespeare. My mother was in the pub but I didn't introduce her to any of my workmates. They didn't stay long in the pub with them making there way to town. I decided to go home so didn't get plastered for once on a Christmas do.

The New Year brought in a very special year in my life 1982 would bring at long last change to my predicament even if overall it was still very difficult to get through. On going back to work in January of 1982 I was still in the same position of being an outsider as far as other people were concerned. The Nursery school slowly but surely got its two coats of paint plus plenty of filler. I missed the end of the job because I was taken ill and was off for two weeks. When I returned to work the gang were doing a school at Wisewood, which was very small in comparison to the one we had just left. After the school it was back to the estates for the gang and we were moved to Foxhill. The charge hand was changed to a man who I had met on my first days of work on Barry's gang but he had changed and was not the nice person that he used to be, which is probably something which comes with the job. On a two block I was working on I told the tenant that certain parts of the window frames needed to be burnt off but I didn't bother to burn it off and I got snagged for my work and fell out with the tenant but by this time I could not give a toss about what anyone else thought with me being pissed off and down over my life. The whole world seemed to be on my shoulders and the strain was proving to much. I kept asking myself what am I doing here, I physically and mentally hate the job so why do I keep turning up for it in some half baked belief that it would eventually lead to something which was a million miles away, on the far horizon and that it would prove all worthwhile in the end. There didn't appear to be an answer at the time and I felt more and more removed from other people and that no one understood me or knew what I was going through. If only I could get hit by a speeding bus I wouldn't have to think anymore about anything. My life seemed to be a total waste and all I did was keep going through mind games that got me nowhere at all. The days would sometime drag so much they would feel like an eternity.

I did a block of two semi-detached houses and they took ages to finish, in fact I was on them that long they were going to give me the right to buy. One of these tenants had four big dogs that looked like they could be entered in the Grand National, they were that big. The food was put into two big washing bowls and was a heck of a lot of food to buy I can tell you. The shit was big also but the best thing about doing this particular house was that in no way would it get snagged. It turned out to be my last house on the estate before I got my marching orders once again.

I got put in the priming workshop at Bramall Lane, which I didn't like from the start. The charge hand was a total dickhead and everything was done to a hooter. The break hooter would go and all you had was 15 minutes to make and drink your tea and eat your breakfast. Of cause if you went to the toilet you didn't get a break because of the clock ruling over every movement. With the pun intended. The dinner break was just half an hour and then back to priming again. I helped on the priming machine stacking the wood after it had got a coat off the machine. It was a totally crap job and thankfully on the Friday I got given a message to move from the clockwork depot. At four I left claiming moving time of which they could pay or not but I couldn't care less. I went to visit my Auntie who lived on the top floor of a high rise block of flats known as Annover.

I was moved back to the Home Improvements again this time on the Norwood estate that was getting the full treatment. I also got as my partner Mick who was Catherine's brother don't you know. It was in the main the usual for him and me to get the gutters done and any outsides that needed finishing. The charge hand on the job was not there very often because he had an illness, so Ken his right hand man was taking over the charge hand duties. I got on well with Ken so the job was as good as it ever got even if I was pissed off most of the time. Me and Mick did some oneing of the gutters but we were not the only ones to do so. Mick no longer had his car due to the fact that it had fallen to bits. Mick went on holiday and I was left to do the gutters by my lonesome but I didn't need him to get me a cup of tea from the tenants I could do that perfectly well myself. I can remember Ken coming round one day when I was oneing but he didn't report me.

I had been on the job a few months when it was my turn to go for a holiday. There were six of us and we went to Tenerife, with us staying in a four star hotel called the Atlantis. There was a lovely pool at the hotel and it was a fine holiday and one day I would like to go back.

When I returned to work it was to the Norwood estate and there was plenty of work that needed doing. In 1982 it was the World Cup and England for once had qualified. I was a big Kevin Keegan fan at the time but he had a problem with his back so only played for twenty minutes in what was England's last game of the competition. When it was the days when England played I even left the job early to be able to watch the match at home. Since Keegan stopped playing for England I have not been bothered about it in anything like the way I did when he was playing. It was one of those times when you say it's the end of an era. I did see him play in the 1983-4 season at Hillsborough and for the previous fixture against Newcastle the season before the ground had 18 thousand spectators; the day he played there was over 40 thousand in the ground. The thing that I remember about watching Keegan play was that the ball looked like it was sewn into his instep which was not bad for a player who couldn't play or so some of his critics were quick to tell us. In fact for that matter only Kenny Dalglish was a better player in British football in my time of watching.

I can recall staying for hours in a house with an unmarried mother and had plenty of cups of tea, telling my life story to pass the time. I was working on my own now and knew I would get moved when I had finished the blocks gutters. I got the usual message and was on my bike once more. The job was to paint a new shopping centre that the council had built and it was a clock in, clock out job, which I never liked. I was on my own for the first week and the charge hand for the painters was a real bastard who I think was called Morton or something like that. Another painter was brought to the job to make sure it got finished in time. The new painter on thee job was a fanatical Sheffield

United supporter and you could tell this by the fact that he bragged about United winning the fourth division championship. He also had a bruised eye from a fight that he had at the last match. When the work we were doing was nearly finished I got a job painting a railing. While the painters charge hand started to tell me what there was to do I asked him what else was there to do if it started raining. By saying this the charge hand was taken aback, being used to sheep. The next day he took me into Manor Lane because I had not completely painted the railing that I had done. When I got there I didn't say much but if all the painters who had missed a bit were brought in no job would ever get finished. I was left in a room on my own and the charge hand was talked to by his seniors and he was a changed man. When he drove me and the site shop steward back to the job he was a nervous wreck because of what he had been told. You see the main men at the top knew who I was and what I was attempting to do, so they didn't want to get in my way.

Me and the United fan got moved to a job down Staniforth road. It was a couple of huts to be painted inside and out. The charge hand from now on didn't speak to me but talked through the United fan if he had something to tell me. While we were on the job one afternoon me and the united fan went to a pub and got legless and when we returned back to the job we picked up our gear and left for the day. We got away with it and anyway I couldn't care less if they sacked me or not. One more complaint about me would mean the boot as I was on my last warning, which was like two falls and a submission.

It was coming up to winter now and I got a move to the Canal Wharf where there were some listed buildings. The charge hand had a speech impediment and he wanted me to work off the ladder to do some window frames in this protected building. When I had finished the window frame I started to paint the ground level window, which upset the charge hand because that was the job he wanted to do. If he didn't like it, tough. I was quickly moved to an estate gang at Lodge Moor. It was around that time that I started my O level courses in English, Math, History and Biology. I asked to have permission to have Tuesday and Thursday afternoons off from work and it was granted. I paid for the courses in order to show some willing on my part and to see if I enjoyed the more academic life.

Getting back to the Lodge Moor job, we were painting old peoples flats and maisonettes on the outside and with the staircases if the weather was poor. It was not yet winter but someone had forgotten to tell the weather. It was so cold that it seemed to me that the old folk who lived in these dwellings were put out there to die and with the freezing cold wind it was not going to take long to happen. The tenants in the main were women who were fine when it came to making cups of tea, which always ranked high in my priorities. The painter I have already mentioned called Des was on the job. Me and Rory who had also worked with him called him Richard the fifth between ourselves. I had not earned much bonus in the last couple of months and I knew if I continued it would amount to the last straw and be the reason for my saying goodbye to the job.

I was working on my own on part of a block and I knew it was all coming to an end after five years of heartfelt anguish. Just before the dinnertime on a Friday I think it was, I was informed by the site charge hand to report to Manor Lane Depot after dinner. I had my dinner in the paint cabin and went back to the block I was doing to collect my brushes and paint. I said to Des "I am going to get the sack!" but I don't think he believed me. The Lodge Moor bus service was very sparse and I was waiting at the bus stop for over half an hour before a bus finally rolled up. When I got to town I had to ask which number bus to take if you want to get to Manor Lane. When I at last arrived I was half an hour late. I was directed to an out building for the whereabouts of the people I was due to see. The headman told me I was late and I told him the bus service from Lodge Moor is not up to much. We went into a room; there was the head of the department of the works, the head of the painters, the head of recruitment and the git of a charge hand who was running the Lodge Moor job, who didn't offer to give me a lift to the meeting. In my corner there was the head of the painters union and of course last but certainly not least, there was little old me. The gist of the thing was that I was given the sack for not earning enough bonus. When I was asked if there was anything I would like to say I said "No!" It was very much a walk on part for me and even a walk off part when I was asked to leave the room. I left behind me these great minds of our time who discussed the matter of whether they should have Rich tea biscuits or Digestive with there afternoon drink. They asked me to come back into the magnolia painted room, such an original idea. The Head Chief put his black cap on and I was at last given the boot.

It was a strange feeling getting something you have hoped for over such a long time. I thought the day would never arrive but it was unbelievably here and I think you could say that I was a little bit dazed by it all. I told the union official that I hated the job anyway and that I certainly would not be appealing over my sentence. Because I had been on the firm for five years I was given a stay of execution for a whole five weeks. I suddenly wondered how my parents were going to take the decision of me getting the sack. My mother guessed and stuck by me, my dad was less than pleased and anyway we weren't talking while I had a job, so it wasn't much of a change.

To think that all the days of being inert and feeling like a dope and just some sort of robot who carried out small minded tasks for a load of mindless cretins was to come to an end was hard at first to sink in. I had played the fool and it had been my part to fulfil and I had learned that things are not always what they seem. It would take a long time to be a person again and not just a number who was treated like cattle by a bunch of morons. One thing for it was that after the pain of these five years it was all downhill from here.

To actually wake up without a cold sweat anymore was something to look forward to. We all moved to the Annover estate in Town where my Auntie lived at the top of the high rise flats. She found out I had been given the push through the painters who were working on her block. One dinnertime I went up to see her and Uncle Les who was now very ill. She wondered what I was going to do now and I didn't have a clue other than the O level courses to take up my time.

The last thing that I painted was the garages on part of the estate that are close to the Little Mesters pub. I even earned bonus in my last five weeks on the firm just for the hell of it. I left in a whimper because it snowed on the last two days of the final week, so I didn't go to work on these days. The 17th of December was my last official day on the firm. It had seemed like a life time when looking back over the last five years of my life. The main thing was that I had survived these very trying of times and had primed the circuit which would all fall into place in the future, if I just kept going along. It was the end of one life with the beginning of another, which would take me all the way to meet my destiny. At the time though of my finishing work I was just relieved that it was all over.

4 Return to Education

To return to education was not an easy decision to make considering my unhappiness at school. To say I had hated my time at school would be no exaggeration. The whole situation needed some deep thought but I was at the stage in my life where I needed some alternatives to my being in a job that held no future for me as far as I could see. In some ways it was like being a traitor to my beliefs that education was for a lot of small minded arse lickers. So I did not make my mind up lightly, one of the things in my mind also was that I deserved something better than painting and decorating and there was no longer a reason to stay on the Council as the circuit was completed. I decided still whilst at work that I would do four courses, which I could fit in with doing night classes. I chose to do English, history, maths and biology and paid for the courses myself. The problem with the courses I had chosen was that the history class would mean having to have two afternoons off from work each week. The other classes were Tuesday night - biology, Wednesday night - maths and Thursday night was English with the history class Tuesday and Thursday afternoons. In order to do the history class I went to see one of the main men at Manor Lane Depot to ask for permission to have two afternoons off and still return to my job on the works. The man, whose name I have forgotten, said that he didn't recognise me and that he would have to ring up the chief gaffer of the painting division. He finally got through and I was given permission to have the afternoons off and I know the painter's gaffer used some bad language on the phone because of the main man's reaction on his face.

One thing in the back of my mind was that the history, biology and math classes were to be held at Shirecliffe College, a place I had many bad memories of in my time there as an apprentice. I somehow managed to get over these dark thoughts, which were in the back of my mind. The courses began in September 1982. All the lecturers who took my classes were women. The first class I started was history on Tuesday afternoons. The lecturer was Ms Bishop and we certainly didn't see eye to eye from the start of the class. She always seemed to be wearing black or if not black, very dark clothes, which made her look like she was in mourning. I would make my way from where I was working and smelled of paint when I reached the class and usually I was tired and not in a very good mood when I entered the class. I was the only student who had a job and I felt isolated from the rest of the group. I was not very friendly toward the members of the class after all the effects of my depressions and it could be said that I was cold, ignorant and full of suspicion. It would take a long time for me to thaw out and behave in a more sociable manner towards my fellow students. After the history class, which was on world events in the twentieth century, I made my way home to have my tea. The biology class started at seven in the evening and finished at nine. The reason I chose biology was I got a good grade in my last exam that I took at Myers Grove and felt that it would be an interesting subject to do. At the start of the course, the class was too big for one lecturer, so the class was split up into two groups and I ended up with another lecturer. The lecturer's name was Charlton and after a while she kept asking me if I had found the secret to life because of the doubts that I had inside me, which I had expressed to her during the break time we had. The rest of the group was mainly female who were taking their hopeful exam passes to get a job. My reason for being there was to see if I could enjoy education and whether I had changed inside during my time on the Council.

When I started the course we were still living on Woodend Drive, which is awkward to get to from Shirecliffe College. I got in a routine of running through an estate which was in front of the college and catching a bus to town and from there, a bus home. The following night, Wednesday, it was maths night, which was always something to look forward to. The lecturer was a really nice person who was called Clement. She was fond at explaining the method you use to solve the equations that were being set, except I kept forgetting the order you do the sums by and kept making a pig's ear of the work she set! You could say I didn't like the lesson but I did like the lecturer - a big change from my experience at school. The last but not least of my lecturers was a Ms Emsworth, who took the class for English at Stannington College. It was a very hectic day on Thursdays for me now, I first went to work in the morning, then to my history class in the afternoon and from there I made my way to Stannington College, as the English lesson started at five and finished at seven. It meant I had to have my dinner after the English lesson.

My English was very poor at the start and I had a problem with thinking one thing and writing something else in between the two. It was hard to believe; here I was, twenty-one years old and writing like someone who was only about twelve years old in the work I was turning out at that start of the course. Mrs Emsworth gave us a couple of authors to read who were P G Woodhouse and F Scott Fitzgerald. I must have read over thirty books by P G Woodhouse and I read everything they had in the libraries by F Scott Fitzgerald. Going into libraries did not come easy as I thought that only creeps and ponces used them. In my time early on of going to libraries I wanted to hit people, that is I thought everyone else was being rude and small minded at my expense. It was difficult to come to terms with my bottled up emotions at this time. The reason I think I liked Mrs Emsworth so much was because she was there at the right time when I wanted to learn and was able to point me in the right direction. The other thing that helped me was that she gave me low marks on the work I submitted, which could be rewritten one more time and I took note of her criticism of my work. One of the things that really hit me was how little time it took to do the work that was necessary for the courses compared to the five days a week school days. I think in some ways it backed up my thoughts that school was in part doing a children-watching scheme. But back to Mrs Emsworth, I don't think I could have gotten more out of the English course and more importantly, out of myself, without her help and if she had been one of my school teachers when I was younger I would no doubt have fallen in love with her but I had grown out of such thoughts and liked her mind more than her body. I hope that doesn't make her sound ugly or anything because that was not my intention.

After the English lesson which signaled the end of my academic week I made my way home and hoped some of my friends were going out because I could do with some beers to help unwind, one things for sure I didn't have much trouble with going to sleep at this time in my life. The history lesson at first was held at a school in the city centre, as there was a shortage of space at the college. The class was made up of an assortment of people from different backgrounds. There was an overage student type, a couple of return to education types like myself and mainly ethnic minorities making up the remainder of the group, such as blacks and Asians. I found it very hard to communicate at first in particular in this class because I had just left work with all the bleak thoughts that were going on inside my head. At first I didn't even go for a break with the rest of the class and stayed in the classroom by myself, which I suppose didn't make me too popular not that I cared what anyone else thought. In the main the average student or mature student as they are known would have arguments with the lecturer while the rest of the class were mere spectators. I've got to admit I don't really know what it was why I hated the lecturer Bishop, perhaps it was just one of those things where you meet someone and are immediately repulsed. I didn't get much help from her during the course and in the main, it was down to me if I wanted to gain a good grade, which was fine by me if that's the way it had to be. Thankfully my biology lecturer was a lot easier to get along with and so I thought, was the subject.

Those night lessons that I attended seemed to fly by and be over before you knew it. One of the nights when the other students had gone for a smoke the lecturer and myself talked about life and I said I'd rather watch the ducks in Hillsborough Park than go to work. Well maybe it wasn't so rare to get round to the meaning of life seeing as it was something I was asking myself daily. Why am I here? This can't be the best I can do with my life, I'm surely worth more than this and what is it that makes me different from other people. I don't think I'm better than other people but I do know I am different to other people through the reactions of those around me during my life. Big thoughts with very few answers. I bet Mrs Charlton who took us for biology, was glad to see the back of me when the lesson was over and I can't say I blame her. The homework that was set, I didn't do very well in during the course but I still felt I was capable of getting an 'O' level in the subject. Maths was altogether a different kettle of fish. I'd get so far with using the methods we were taught and then forget part of the process. The lecturer encouraged me by asking me to help with some sums she was doing on the blackboard but I was really a total loss. It was a big mistake to try and put an 'O' level class of maths into one year and the lecturer told us it would be better to do the course over two years. I certainly didn't blame my lecturer for my shortcomings but half way through the course, I lost interest, which made my chances of passing the exam on line with winning the football pools! In other words, no chance and a total waste of time! I really looked forward to my English lesson even more than it finished college until Tuesday. I just liked Mrs Emsworth's company and my English improved greatly during this time. The course was continuous assessment plus some tests of your understanding of English. We had some mock tests and then for real. One of the tests was on Mice and Men by John Steinbeck which I had seen the film of, but had not read the book. The test was fairly straightforward and I think I did well in it and got a good mark. I have since read Of Mice and Men. I wondered how well I would have done with my attitude at school and what Mr Daniels would have thought of me trying my best, unlike when I was in his class. There's no doubt in my mind that making the effort to go back to education was a very enlightening process and because I had made the effort all by myself I could claim what I had learned for myself. It was mine with my own individuality and not someone else's. This was very much a major difference and suddenly education was opening my mind to new horizons, which it had never done before.

The same couldn't be said of the work situation, which was getting worse. I was told to report to Manor Lane Depot for a meeting about whether I still had a job or not but I already knew the answer. I was going to be given the sack. The masters of all they surveyed gave me a stay of execution for five weeks and just before Christmas I had finally gotten away from the job that I had hated for the past five years. This meant I had a lot more time on my hands to do my studies but I could not change the times of the lessons from in the main nighttime to daytime. There was going to be a party, on what turned out to be my last day at work, for the students who were attending Shirecliffe College but I wasn't interested, so I did not go. Maybe I should have done but I made up my mind not to go and that was that. Having so much time after Christmas meant I could do my homework whenever I felt like it. I would go for long walks as I still had a lot to work out in my mind, which was causing my anxiety and depression. But on the good side, I had plenty of time to take up my new hobby of reading books. I also mellowed towards my classmates and became more sociable in class and took more of an interest in what was being said. In the more domestic arena my mother divorced my dad after twenty-six years of marriage. I promised her that I would decorate her new house, which was a three-bedroom terrace near Hillsborough Park. The house was in a right old state, with a couple of old people being the last tenants and they had not kept the house in good condition through illness. The exams for the subjects were now not too far away and I thought that I would get 'O' levels in history and biology but just fail English, and for maths I needed a miracle to get anywhere near an exam result! Having gone back to education with going into further education in mind I felt that I had gained a lot from the courses and didn't feel as bad as I thought I would from my experiences. Even if I didn't get good results education was a different way. I paid for my exams even though I was now unemployed. I got my history 'O' level as I had done at school, but had not really enjoyed my time in Bishop's class, which was a disappointment to me and gave me something to think about. I failed the biology exam that I had thought I was going to pass, this felt like a real setback. My exam result in maths was not recorded, as I didn't turn up for the second part of the exam knowing I was licked. With the English course being a continuous assessment we had to hand in all the pieces of work we had written. The tutor would then choose which pieces to submit which reflected the work we had put in during the course. I thought when I handed in my course work that it would be the last time that I would ever see Mrs Emsworth who I felt I owed a lot to for helping me when I needed it. This though, would not be the case and I would see her in very different circumstances than handing in pieces of work but that was in the future. When I got my results from Stannington College I had got a grade C - a pass, so from the four subjects I had taken exams in, I got two passes and two failures. I didn't collect my 'O' levels though as I was still fighting my feelings from the past that still affected the present. With my course work behind me I had plenty of time on my hands other than the decorating that had to be done inside my mother's house. Both my brother and I moved in with Mum after the separation with my dad taking on a house, which by the sounds of it he rebuilt from the foundations upwards.

I carried on reading during this time in 1983 and would go for walks around the duck pond in Hillsborough Park and sometimes sit on a bench watching the world go by. The house my mum had chosen slowly took shape with my brother getting a very large attic for his bedroom, which I decorated for him. Workmen were needed for plastering, rewiring and for central heating. I ended up being the one who sorted things out with the workmen and got on fairly well with them. Time passed slowly by and I was still stuck in a semi-depressed state, which would go up and down depending on my thoughts. The thing that kept me on the education trail through all this time was reading books, something which previously I had done very little of but now I must have been getting through five books a week and had turned into a bookworm.

Christmas 1983 was soon upon us with me getting drunk which was my contribution to the Christmas festivities. It was now one year since I had last been to work but the dark cloud still hung over my thoughts. The heart of the matter being that I was still unhappy, something I thought by now I would have gotten over and moved on from. But this was not the case, and looking back on it I perhaps should have got in touch with my doctor to see if there was something I could take for my continuing depression. During 1984 I withdrew into myself even more and I certainly didn't think the world was my oyster even though it might smell fishy! The fact is I was still asking myself daily the same question I had been asking longer than I care to remember, that is what am I here for? Is there a purpose to my life or am I just having myself on by creating an imaginary world inside my head? I was far from being in a state where I could seek work again. I was on the edge and fighting for my very existence. I don't even remember what I did other than read, watch some television and occasionally go out for a drink. I was looking for inspiration where there was nothing to be found. From the time of my parent's separation I had not seen my dad and this didn't change in the whole of 1984, a doom-laden year if ever there was one. But for Liverpool F.C. doing the treble it would have been very hard to bear.

The year drew to a close and I felt just a little bit better about myself and felt it was time to burst out of my shell and do something with myself, as my mother's house had taken shape. After Auld Lang Syne I decided to make my move in the year of 1985. I had in mind trying to do an A level course in both history and English but felt there was a gap in my learning, so I needed something to get me into shape and get my mind in gear. I had a look around the library one day when I came across a scheme called Fresh Start. It was a refresher course to help anyone who wanted to apply to get back in the education groove. I went to see them about starting their course and a new one was starting in two weeks time so I had timed my interest very well. The course was held in an old junior school on London Road and all the tutors were women until a male tutor joined them to take the math class. There was a great range of people who were looking for different things from the course. There were pensioners to teenage girls from mixed races. One of the members, a man reminded me of a neighbour from Woodend Drive I knew in my childhood. Another lad interested in art was a keen snooker player. What we did on the course was to see if our writing was okay and to see that we could still do sums, which I was always forgetting such as fractions. The best thing about the whole course was the trip arranged for us to go to the Northern College situated in Barnsley and previously known as Wentworth Castle. The trip was for the weekend but because of some long running dispute the tutor from the centre could not go with us. The transport, which was supposed to take us to the college, did not arrive. So we had to wait for over an hour for transport to come and take us to our destination. When we arrived at the college it was a lot later than had been expected and a meal was ready for us in the dining room so we made our way there immediately as the kitchen staff wanted to go home. The meal was well done, that is cooked but not overcooked, but it couldn't be helped, as we were so late. When we had finished our meal we were given a key whilst our names were being read out. I ended up sharing with an Asian man who was called Laurie. The bedrooms were in a dormitory outside the college, there were toilets and a kitchen for making drinks also in the complex. We were supposed to have a lesson when we arrived but because of the delay it had been cancelled. There was a bar in the cellar of the college and we made our way there at about 8.00 pm. We had a few beers in the bar and there was a picture of Lenin coloured in like an Andy Warhol poster. I can recall one of our group asking who it was, which seemed strange to me at the time but why should someone know Lenin when I bet had he been shown a picture of Marilyn Monroe he would have got it in one! This must point to something, even though I don't know what!

I met a female student in the bar who had also arrived the same day. She told of the previous night when someone had tried to break into the flat she was sleeping in. Thankfully she had managed to stop him breaking in but not surprising was still shaken by the incident. The course she had come to take was due to last a month but she was going to be present in the lectures that had been arranged for us. The group I was with made the big push to go back to our dormitory but I for one didn't feel tired. There were about four of us who made for the television room even though there was nothing in particular on the box, which I suppose is a usual Friday night. One of the women in the group made us a cup of tea and some toast. It was past twelve and the morning of the early hours of Saturday when we retired to our rooms. It's always struck me as strange that in some ways we tend to forget the early hours are another day other than at Christmas time. The room was sparse but everything had been kept clean which is the main thing in these situations. The beds were a fair way apart and after saying goodnight to Laurie I tried to get some sleep. It took me ages to nod off and when the morning came I felt very tired and could have done with going back to sleep again. I went to the bathroom and tried to have a shave without cutting myself which surprise surprise I didn't manage. I cut myself fairly deeply and there was plenty of blood dripping off my towel and toiletries. I made my way to the dining room where a cooked breakfast was waiting or me. After breakfast the group made our way to a classroom that was the other side of the college. The lecture was about nothing in particular and seeming to me to be a total waste of time. When the session was over, it was time for dinner and back to the dining room. Whatever else I might think about the place you certainly couldn't complain about the food service, it was excellent.

On the dining room ceiling there were murals from a long time ago which were highly provocative. We thought that this was the place the past owners had been involved in their love affairs. When I had finished my dinner I went for a walk around some of the estate, it really must have been something in its heyday when the owning parasites governed the area. It was soon time to go back to our classroom, which meant walking through a lounge that it was claimed was the longest in England. The lesson after dinner was on one of my weaker points - poetry. Poetry is something that leaves me cold. The lady tutor who took the class asked me to write about summertime and what it meant to us. My effort was a load of rubbish and I didn't read it out to the rest of the class unlike the others who had done a lot better than me. The lecturer was nice enough about it when I said that poetry did nothing for me and she didn't seem to mind. In fact, she said that it was alright to stand by your beliefs and go against the grain or words to that effect, which I thought was nice of her. When the class was over, we all made our way to the garden around the side of the college. In one part of the garden it appeared to be a wall of flowers that greeted us. It was so colourful and even though it had not been kept up it was still a fantastic sight to behold. One of the group took some photographs of the group in front of the flowers, which must have been as high as eight foot in places. The lecturer was also with us at this time and when she left in her car a few minutes later I can recall she waved at me. It made me think back to my schooldays if only I could have had her as a teacher my time at school would have been better spent. But then again we can't go back, only forward, which isn't such a bad thing.

The rest of the grounds were acres of open green grass surrounded by trees in this part of the garden. Also on the estate there were tennis courts and stables that were now run down. There was a conservatory but it was beyond repair as most of the glass had fallen out and the wood was rotten. The group I was with went to look around more of the estate and I went with them, it made me wonder how a family could have owned so much. The grounds were no doubt, still impressive even after the so called glory years of which I'm sure for the folk who had worked in mines nearby were nothing of the sort. When the scenic tour was over it was time for a wash before dinner and then to the dining hall for the evening meal. When we had finished the meal we made our way back to the college to have a singsong and we were all invited. There were three black girls together in the group I was in and they had brought a tape recorder with them to this sing song which they were asked to turn off. After the singsong, upon reflection, it might have been better if they had kept the tape on. The ex-students went through a lot of folk songs I think you'd call them and I thought to myself what a load of posing prats this lot are!

It was almost two o'clock when they finally decided to leave, all except for two of them. These two kept telling each other that they were working class heroes for their past exploits in the big wide world. I thought more to the point they were working class assholes that ought to be getting a move on so I could get some sleep.

When I finally got into bed I didn't feel like sleeping anyway and neither did the three black girls because one of them called Carmen I think knew who I was. Don't ask me how I know I just felt that in someway she could tell who I was. In the morning I had a wash but did not attempt a shave as I now had a scab from the previous day's shave. I decided I couldn't face a cooked breakfast but I did have a couple of slices of toast. We had a discussion group in the classroom with the man who had the responsibility of running the college; he gave us something written by Bertold Brecht. I'm not sure of the spelling of his name but is a thought provoking piece of work which I found interesting. After the lesson was over the main man gave us a guided tour around the college. He first told us the Wentworth's had sold the property just after world war two for forty thousand pounds. He then told us they had been parasites who, when thirty people had died in a mining accident, were more concerned about some hailstones breaking a few windows in the conservatory than the fate of their workforce. One of the later Wentworths had a statue made of him in Roman garb, which is still standing outside the college today. This was not the sort of tour you get on Blue Peter but was a refreshing change being told the true story and not the lovey-dovey version you usually get. It was time to go to the dining room for one more meal and then to say our goodbyes.

This time we weren't waiting hours for the transport to come and we all got on board to the trip to Sheffield. When the van reached Hillsborough Park I got out of the van and made my way through the park to my mother's house feeling a little bit tired but I had enjoyed the weekend. When I went to the scheme the following week, the scheme for me was nearly over as it was only for eight weeks. I had made up my mind to go on and try and get some 'A' levels. I would say the fresh start helped me brush away the cobwebs and it gave me a little more confidence in myself, which I had not had before. I don't know how the others fared in what they wanted to do and I don't recollect having seen anyone from the course since. They did send me a letter once but I can't remember now whether I answered it or not. My sights were firmly set on doing some 'A levels and I just thought 'Roll on September!'

When it came to enrolling at the college I had decided to do a daytime course in English language and an evening course in history. I think the reason I did the courses this way around was as I was not a fulltime student, in order to claim my benefits I had to stay within so many hours. I enrolled in the English language class at Stannington College and the man who was running the course was John Edwards. The history course I would take was at Granville College where there were two men running the course, Geoff Hammond and Mark Davies. When the English language class began there was no room for us at Stannington College so the class was held at Wisewood School. Also helping John Edwards were Christine, a staunch feminist and Keith, a staunch nobody. The course laid down you did a project of your own choosing plus some writing of stories and finish with an exam on your understanding of English, which had been covered during the course. John Edwards, who was in charge of the course, had been a workman in his early days before becoming a lecturer. He was in his late forties, he had very little hair on his head, his teeth had gone rotten, and he always seemed to be wearing the same clothes, which had chalk marks all over them. In fact, it could be said of him that he had let himself go. The thing that kept him in his job was that he was one of the most intelligent people I have ever come across. If not for this reason I think he would have been shown the door a long time ago. The female lecturer who took the class was called Christine as I have already mentioned. She covered areas such as the media machine and a lot of women issues which she was heavily committed to. Contrary to popular belief, Christine was a fairly attractive woman just like Ms Emsworth had been even though I doubt if she would have liked being told so. Moving on but I can't see why there was Keith who I can't recall what he was talking about in his part of the course. The man was just too dynamic for me to cope with!

Even though both Geoff Hammond and Mark Davies were running the history course, I only had Mark Davis for the first year of the course. With it being an evening course the age group in the first class at the start of the

114

course was very varied. The history course was going to consist of European history from the late 19th century up to the forties of the 20th century, and English history from 1905 to 1939. This was certainly a lot of history to cover in two years, at the end of which we would take a three hour exam to see how much we had learned and have understood the information we had been given. Mark Davies was a normal looking man compared to John Edwards and there was nothing distinguished about him but I got on fairly well with him. At the start of the course it was hard to find a space in the classroom but within a month there were less than half of the original class left. I think the reason for this was that some people thought that on the face of it the history course sounds interesting, but then it hits them that there's a lot of work to do which when it sinks in brings their attempt at the course to a quick finish. The other students who stayed after the first month were mainly females, other than a male nurse and of course, and yours truly!

In my English language class there were lessons on Tuesday and Thursdays. I made two friends, Michael and Jayne who were the same as me as they were ex-Myers Grove pupils. In fact, Jayne was in the same year as me even though I didn't remember her face. Michael was trying to get 'A' levels so he could get to Music College and Jayne was just doing something to get her out of her house. The three of us had many a laugh between us and talked about sex, politics, football and anything else that crossed our minds. There was another lad called Bazz who also joined our group who when we were having a class with Christine said, "I'm a feminist!" "Males can't be feminists!" replied Christine, but Bazz, I'm sure was prepared to have the operation required to become a female! In fact, there were a lot of things I can remember from the lessons we had with Christine. She told us one day that there had been more books on feminism at the start of the twentieth century than there were on socialism! It was an interesting thought that women had been allowed to express themselves all be it a very small part of the female population and that it was eroded in the passing of time quite naturally or was there a more sinister reason for the decline in the written word for this movement. After reading that I bet some of you want a break! Another thing we touched on with Christine was a book by a woman author called "Man Made Language" by Dale Spender. The book implied that language is what we gather our thoughts in and a monopoly of language has been made by the man who ruled and still rule over us, so it would be very difficult to challenge the status quo with the language that had been laid down for us to use. It certainly is a far reaching thought that the very language in use could keep in the same place half the world's population with a few exceptions.

Another thought that the book looked into was do women talk more than men? It is claimed in society that women talk more than men but is this the case? Are women in society judged in the same way as men or is there a different code? What the book tries to say is women are compared to silence and therefore anything they utter is idle chatter and they are over doing it because they have broken the silence. When men and women are together in the book it is claimed that men take the lead and women keep silent, which in most areas in life is the case, also to look at is when men are together and when women are together in separate rooms. There is always someone from my own experience who will rattle on even if what they say is a total load of crap. In the pecking order of speech the book claims if you are higher ranked you get to say more but I would disagree with this claim because most of the rattlers usually have very little in between their ears other than sawdust. I don't know whether this is the case with women. I think though that in the main it was a worthwhile part of the course and that it opens up many questions that are still to be answered. It also gave me a different angle with which to view things. Of course, there was still Keith doing whatever he did, I somehow doubt whether anyone else from my class could tell me either. John Edwards only took us for one lesson a week while Christine was there. I can remember us having a couple of tapes played to us in one of the classes, one was Basil Rathbone of Sherlock Holmes fame talking through a story to us and the other was about animals outwitting a store owner and grabbing a lot of the food stores. We had to write our own story on anything we liked and had to have finished it by the following week.

The history course I was on was going fine and I was starting to get the hang of it when it came to writing essays on parts of history. Come to think of it I've got it wrong; I had both Mark Davies and Geoff Hammond in my first year on alternate weeks. Mark Davies took the English history part of the course and Geoff Hammond covered the European side of the course. Now that's cleared up, you'll have to bear with me on this as it is a few years ago now. Mark Davies liked to do things by handing out sheets on the topic we were covering and Geoff Hammond was more open to having a laugh in his class.

Christmas was soon upon us and I was glad of the break on what had been an interesting start to my courses. I felt very good and I thought to myself this is really what I want to do. I celebrated the New Year in style! And it soon came time to resume my studies. The English language class was still being held at Wisewood School. I had decided what I wanted to do in my project and told John Edwards; I was going to do football and the language that surrounds it. Everyone else in the group had also chosen their project theme. In our classes with Christine, she was forever telling us she didn't want to stay in Sheffield and was obviously unhappy in doing so. She was becoming more self-conscious with every passing week. I must admit that I felt sorry for her but there was nothing I could do about it. I think Keith disappeared, well he didn't really, but he might as well have done. With the passing of Christmas there were only six pupils remaining in the history class, some people just don't have the staying power! I was enjoying the course even though it was getting more difficult to talk to someone at the break times with people leaving all the time, come to think of it maybe I was the reason people were leaving! There's no doubt it was my BO, which was the real culprit! The English history side of the course taken by Mr Davis was on some of the Parliamentary bills which had gone through the House in the early part of the century, and were about as entertaining as watching paint dry without the finish. There was nothing Mr Davis could do about it but it meant that I liked the European side of the course a lot more. There was one girl in the history class whom I became friendly with as she caught the same bus when it was time to go home. Her name was Leslie. She got off the bus at Holme Lane because her Dad was waiting for her in the nearby Malin Bridge pub or so she told me, whilst I got off before at Hillsborough Corner.

I was starting to feel a little down by this time but could not put my finger on why. In the English language class there were two new members who were as obnoxious a couple as you have ever met. It was in John Edwards's class that we were talking about books on people who had been spies or killers for their country. Both Mr Edwards and me said that we thought the books by Len Deighton were accurate and real and bare no resemblance to the James Bond books by Ian Fleming. The tall streak of bacon, the male part of the fab duo claimed that the character Harry Palmer was a glorified hero and was nothing like a real character and claimed the books were not true to life. There was no point in arguing with him so I just let it pass by. On another occasion, I said it would be a good idea to look at the Soviet Union as we do America and look at America the way we do the Soviet Union for arguments sake, and also gain a different prospective. So what does bright eyes come out with? Only that he listens to Radio Moscow, which is neither here nor there but it certainly made me silent. Michael couldn't help bringing it up and had even told his mother the story to comical effect of course. For some reason Michael always liked to return to that one. Then on another occasion it was the turn of the female half to wake up. We were talking about racism and people who we knew who were racist. I mentioned that an uncle of mine was very racist and she says why couldn't you talk him around? As if! She didn't understand that some people have made up their minds and there's no amount of talking to them that is going to change their minds. I thought to myself that these two needed to live some life and then they'd find out for themselves that the real world isn't contained in a book. There's no doubt in all my time on the courses that these two are the sort of people who give students a bad name, talk about blinkered thinkers.

The year kept on disappearing and holidays weren't too far away and I was having the face on in between some laughter, which was badly needed. The history course was down to the last three students who were the male nurse, Leslie and of course me. There seemed a heck of a lot to cover for just one exam at the end of two years of studying, but I was fine about what we were doing, so didn't give the exam, which was a long way off, too much thought. The class Geoff Hammond took was one I looked forward to because it was so interesting; especially about Germany, which I think was Mr Hammond's favourite part of history. From Bismarck to Hitler, which does raise a lot of questions about the society we live in even today. But they're not questions I'm going to ask or answer in this tale. One of the very last lessons that Christine gave was about what was expected of women living in society today. She showed us a cartoon of a woman grossly made up which asked, "Is this the way women want to look or how women are seen by men? She didn't get any takers from the rest of the group and I couldn't really help her this time. On many occasions I was the only one who talked to her and when she said women were inhibited about talking out she pointed me out as the proof of this. The thing is though, what she was trying to get through to the females in the group is something they themselves will have to look for when they are ready and not before. She also brought up the saying that women are the niggers of the world, which I think comes from Yoko Ono. Christine didn't get much of a reaction from this either and seemed a little bit distressed. I think it would read better if it said women are the slaves of the world, which is something few people could deny. Like I say this was about the last lesson I can remember having with Christine but I thought she had raised many a question and brought a different light to a subject that won't go away. What an arse licking creep I'm turning into! Maybe this is the true price of education.

The term was drawing to a close and John Edwards told us we would not have to go to Wisewood School in the second year of the course and we said our goodbyes for the holidays. In the history class there was the male nurse and me who had survived the year and he said that he couldn't go on the second year of the course. Some work was set and I was given a list of some books to read which would aid my understanding of past events. All in all though, I had thought it a satisfactory first year even though the storm clouds of my mind were not too far away. My moods would change very quickly but I didn't heed the beginning of something that was set to change my and other people's lives forever. I just thought roll on next term.

I had arranged to go on holiday in Torquay for two weeks with my friend

Rory where we would meet another friend of ours, Tony. When we arrived he was not there and after waiting half an hour we made our way to find somewhere to stay. After a lot of walking we found a place. The weather was a lot like my mood - misty and over cloudy with no sign of the sun! This was a big mistake; we should have gone abroad and I was not in a well frame of mind. Towards the end of the first week we finally bumped into Tony and his friend who he had gone on holiday with. They were going home having drunk all their money and I didn't feel like staying another week. So Rory and I also decided to go home after one week and in looking back it couldn't be helped. I was starting to go into the final phase of my mission and if that meant breaking friendships then that's how it had to be. The final phase would be total isolation but this was just the build up as there was a fair distance to go yet.

It was soon time to enrol again for the final year, I went to Stannington College first because it was the closest and did what was necessary. I had to get a piece of paper stamped at my signing on place for both the subjects of English language and history. Before I got my piece of paper stamped for history I had to go to Granville College first to enrol and get the piece of paper. It seems to me that I'm making a mountain out of a molehill but then again that's me! The history course that I attended was now in the daytime and I was the sole survivor from the night time class. There would now be two lessons a week with Mark Davis taking the English history part of the course, and Geoff Hammond taking the European part. So no change there. This class also contained Catherine, even though at the start of the final year I didn't think more than what an attractive girl she was. There were also some males in my age group who had worked so we had a lot in common in the history class. In the English language class we moved from Wisewood School to a class in Myers Grove School. In my time at the School this room had been the staff room and here I was back at the place I had held in contempt in my enforced years of attendance. It made me feel strange for a while until I got used to the idea. In the second year there was no Christine and no Keith. Instead there was Arthur who took us for Nouns and Verbs etc, which had never interested me in the past, which was probably the reason I never understood them. Michael, my friend form the first year turned up to do the second year but Jayne didn't. In the main we would now get our tuition from John Edwards who used an old cupboard storeroom for more private chats about how things were progressing in the written pieces of work that were required for marking and going towards our final total. During the time up to Christmas, Mr Edwards seemed to be spending more time talking to Michael and me. I didn't really think about it but I did mention it to Michael once and he thought it was because we had worked, so we were more like him. Overall though, I was (other than my chats with Michael) withdrawing into myself and not going out with my friends.

This didn't bother me, as in the main I was not feeling very sociable.

The history course was going on its merry way; well it wasn't really. There was a mad Sheffield United fan in the group who like myself had worked so we both knew the score on what it was like in the great big world outside college. With one or two of the other students we would have a laugh and usually when we were in Geoff Hammond's class, where discussion was encouraged, we had many a humorous moment. Because the English history part was in the main about written documents it was a bind for all concerned but we had agreed to do the course so we had to get on with it. I was noticing Catherine more and more as the year passed on but it never crossed my head in the build up to Christmas who she was other than another student in the same class as me. All would be revealed in the coming year and if I had known what was to come in 1987 I might not have wanted to leave in 1986. But for the time being, it was 1986 and I would have to deal with that. We had a drink at the end of the year in the history class and as usual, I couldn't take my ale in an afternoon session, so was out of it when it was time to leave the last pub, never again I may have said with the same conviction as the other times I had said it in the past!

In the Christmas break my brother told me of a function that was taking place that my dad wanted me to attend. Since the separation of my parents I had not seen my dad but agreed to go to this dinner and dance. The 'do' was being held at the Northern General Hospital in one of its halls, the reason for this was that one of my cousins who arranged the little get together worked on the ambulances at the hospital. Both my brother and I attended what turned out to be a fair night out. When it was time to leave we went back to my cousin's house for some more booze. I had smoked the pipe of peace with my father and he asked me to visit him at his home. My dad gave my brother and I a lift home and said that he was having a bit of a party at his house over Christmas and that we were invited. Neither my brother or I went to the party but I did get drunk, I poured myself a large vodka in a glass with a hint of lemonade. This didn't hit me as a good idea when I got up the following morning! I had a right head pain.

The New Year came in with both my brother and I having a nosh up after being out drinking. It was now 1987 and would turn out to be the most important year of my life. It was back to learning when the Christmas holiday came to an end and I started the New Year by sleeping less and less but this didn't bother me at the time. In my history class it was becoming visible with the passing weeks that Geoff Hammond was looking under a great strain, which was playing on his mind. There also seemed to be something that was making Mark Davis rather distant in the way he talked to the class.

In the English language class John Edwards was forever talking to Michael and myself and starting to tell some of his life story to us. The weeks by this time were moving quickly and I had changed; I was no longer down all the time but I was on a high instead. I would be spending a lot of time doing the following of a word through the dictionary to see where it would lead. Also, I was starting to think over parts of my life and whether certain events had more significance than I had given them credit. In the other English class we had Arthur and I seemed to spend the lesson having one big argument with him. By the end of February it was clear to me that this was the time to take charge of the situation and the time had come at long last to stand and be counted. In the history class Geoff Hammond was a near nervous wreck and he even said "No one ever wanted me dead before!" in one of his lessons. But it was John Edwards who one day shouted "Shut up Clay" which took me back to my school days, because they had always called me by my surname, this told me it would not be long now. By this time I knew who Catherine was and I wanted her more than I had ever wanted anything or anybody before. I had affected all my lecturers in what I had to say to them and through the chaos I would take charge and move without obstruction to my goal. When March came so did what I had been waiting to hear for over twenty-five years. In a room with just me and John Edwards who kept holding his head as if it was giving him great pain. I think we were discussing the way language had come together when I asked him a question and we moved on to something else which was to do with redemption and I asked him if he would like a second chance and he said "Yes please!" in a very distressed way. I could now go about things in the way I wanted to after all this time of waiting. It was education that had brought me to this moment and it couldn't have worked out better. By just following a path I had met the person who had been waiting from me to arrive, that of course was John Edwards. None of what had happened was just a matter of coincidence it was all planned and it was just a matter of following the Yellow Brick Road to the prize I have been promised. That prize of course, was Catharine, and I didn't care what would happen to me as long as she was there after all the pain, to be with me by my side, as my love. The next step would bring me to the Northern General Hospital and a new challenge of going into hell.

5 Hospital

After the first couple of days in observation I would make my way to the toilet which was just opposite my room. Before I left my room I would put on my wet woollen hat and also my gloves, so I was protecting myself from some imagined radiation sickness that I was going through at the time. I don't recall talking to anyone when I went on these short trips because I moved as fast as I could. Once inside the toilet I would take off my gloves and do what I had to do. At that time I had a deep fascination with water and there was a sink in these particular toilets. In one of my trips I put the plug in the sink and turned both taps on and let it overflow all over the floor. The staff were not too pleased and I moved back into my room. My brother visited me a lot in the early days and I can recall playing cards with him but I upset him because on occasions I didn't know who he was. He brought me sandwiches that my mother had made and I ate them very quickly because I was hungry. While I was still in this observation room my dad came to see me and said, "If it was me son, I would have all the women on the bed!" Here I was out to lunch and feeling like death warmed up and all my dad could think of was sex, I might have felt bad at this time but there was plenty more to come that would make these days seem like a holiday. When it was time to leave the room my dad brought me a dressing gown which was dark blue and had a wolf's head on the breast pocket. When I put it on I felt like a wizard, it was that good and my dad said that I could keep it.

They put me in a bed on ward 54 which had a curtain around it that could be pulled right around the bed. I was alongside a man called Georgie the Dragon Slayer to me. We would be friends in my stay at the hospital. That night I can remember meeting a man who reminded me of an uncle that I have, who gave me a cigarette which I ate. This was the night time and I don't know what I did in the day time, but I was wide awake now, that's for sure. The night staff were Anne and Barbara who I would like in my stay at the hospital. They would handle the tablet distribution. On this night I was playing a game inside my head, I thought that I had lived before in Egyptian times and that I could only follow the commands of women, as it had been in my past life. I required permission to enter the kitchen from Anne and Barbara who were the night staff on this particular night. I was granted permission to the kitchen and set about making a pig of myself. I made myself a drink of hot chocolate and jam sandwiches and when I had drank my chocolate and eaten my sandwiches I made some more of the same. Due to the tablets and the injection I had received my legs were shaking all over the place. This made sleep impossible, so I would sit around the table with Anne and Barbara, who didn't mind my company. The clocks didn't help the situation of passing time as they were all out of order in the entire hospital. The passing of time was slow, the nights seemed to last forever and the days an eternity. But eventually daylight would break through the sky and herald a new morning. The night staff would leave as the day staff arrived and the morning was very much in front of me. After cleaning myself having a wash and a shave, I would make my way to the dining room for breakfast.

Because I was still new to the ways of the hospital and also I suppose to make sure I didn't get up to any mischief I had a carer, as that's what they seemed to be, with me at all times. These carers were young trainee nurses who had to spend some time on the psychiatric wards to pass their various tests. I can remember making a collage on one of my first days at the hospital when I was in a fit state to do something. While I did my collage the carer who was watching me did some knitting to pass the time away. When we went back to ward 54 the girl who had been with me during the morning told the staff that I thought myself clever when finishing the collage that I had done. Which seemed to me rather a silly thing to say, yet if that's the way she saw it, that was that. With the passing of the morning I was informed that coffee would be ready in the dining area for the patients. So I made my way to the dining room because I was very thirsty which was also another side effect of the drugs I was being prescribed. After the coffee break I went for a walk around the hospital something which I was prone to doing in my stay at the Northern General. Walking gave me a freedom that you cannot get being caged up in a building and there was plenty to see. When I had been for my dinner I made my way to the Art Room. I felt like doing some paintings and I did six or seven very abstract paintings. They were abstract because I could not concentrate to paint in any other way. When it was time to leave the workshops I went back to my ward and decided to have a bath before dinner. The bathrooms were situated on the ward so I didn't have far to walk. My dad had brought me shampoo and plenty of other forms of toiletries to use. This I did with relish, especially so in the case of my hair, which I poured all the different gels onto, because of so much gel my hair stuck to my head and looked greasy. It took over a week to wash out before my hair was in its usual state, all curls instead of straight hair. The Matron of the ward always seemed to be laughing at me and she did ask why had I put all that gel on and I could only think that it seemed like a good idea at the time.

In the mornings from Monday to Friday we would gather after breakfast in the television room, where the daytime staff would be waiting for us to decide which activities we would like to do in the rest of the morning. I would choose to go to the Keep Fit class which was usually taken by Sarah who in my time at the hospital, I grew to like a lot. When I was in the class trying to do the exercises Sarah would be laughing at me because of my stiff head movements, due to the drugs I was taking. The drugs made my movements painful and certain movements were impossible for me to make. The lesson lasted for about half an hour and there was always some music to help in setting the mood for the exercises. When the lesson was over we would lay on the flat of our backs and Sarah would pull the blinds down and then turn off the lights and a tape for relaxation would be put on which finished with saying make yourself a cup of tea, to a tea drinker like me I didn't need telling twice. When the tape had finished I could wait and see where Sarah was going to go either to the art room or the workshop, where I could follow her so I could be near her side for the rest of the morning.

Inside the workshop there were a couple of clay wheels for making pots. I had a go and it seemed to be helping my shaking legs, so I spent a fair bit of time trying to make a pot but in the main using it as therapy on my aching legs. When I was not on the wheel, I would be working on making a man out of clay which was not lost on the overseer who mentioned that I was making something out of myself. The figure had a crude face and both his hands raised in defiance at the world. When the break for coffee would come for us patients the staff in the art part of the hospital would have their own tea break for themselves. The coffee break for us patients was always held in the dining room and a unit would be playing records, which were not that loud but helped to create a little bit of a better atmosphere for us to be in. On the ward where I was based there was a lad called Thomas who had just arrived and we became friends while he was in the hospital. When I went to these coffee mornings I would sit beside him and he would be puffing away on his cigarettes like so many of the patients. On one of these days at coffee time I even asked Thomas to give me a cigarette but after just a couple of drags I couldn't do much other than choke so I gave it back to him. It was back to passive smoking for me.

When the break was over I made my way back to the workshop to work on my figure some more till dinner time. In these earlier times the food was just horrible. I can recall painfully how I even licked the plate clean when I had eaten my meal off it, I suppose one of the reasons was that no matter what, I am a survivor to the bitter end if need to be. I know my manner of eating like an animal at meal times didn't go unnoticed and I overheard some who said it was disgusting. The eating was the easy part at meal times at the moment at least, the queuing up was another matter entirely. All the old patients who could hardly walk were brought to the dining room first and were allowed in before us more able bodied patients who formed a very large queue. The waiting at times in my stay at the hospital became too much for me to put up with, so instead of waiting in the queue I would go for a walk around the hospital and when I returned to the dining hall there was no queue in front of me. Very early on in my stay on the psychiatric ward I went for a walk around the entire Northern General Complex. The size of the thing, it was so vast. I thought of how easy it must be to get lost in the grounds of the hospital. One day I did go into a part of the hospital that was for artificial limbs and I asked the receptionist if Catherine was there. Fortunately she didn't take much notice of me and I left of my own accord a few minutes later

.In the first week of my glorious stay at the hospital, I persuaded George, he of the Dragon Slaying, to go with me to a pub. Wearing our clothes we left the hospital grounds and after walking for ten minutes or so we found a pub to go into. The pub was called the Cannon and when inside I bought a couple of pints of bitter. While we were at the pub George told me that he had no family still alive, so had nothing to go back to if, and when he should leave the hospital. After our pint we made our way back to our ward. When we got back we both had red faces, not because of the beer but through sunburn. The tablets and the beer must have interacted in some way to make us more vulnerable to the sun's rays. The nurse who was on duty gave us some sun cream. The nurses couldn't believe at first I had gone to the pub but they made me promise that I would not go there again. When the matron came in for her shift she couldn't believe it either but on the following night she took George to the pub for a pint and left me on the ward. Some guys get all the luck and then there's me. The Matron as ever was laughing at me when she came back; I wondered not for the first time what I had done to be such a scene for amusement. On this night there was a woman who was only in the hospital as it turned out for a couple of days and nights. She asked the staff if we could go to the pub but they refused us permission, so we stayed and talked. She said she had taken drugs and had been very free with her favours and was very much into looking into her murky past to see where she went wrong. I in the main just listened to her, which is probably my strong point, listening to other people's thoughts. She was very down in the dumps the way her life had so far worked out, yet she was a very kind person and I'm sure with just a little effort she could get herself a better life and for that matter I hope she has.

It's strange but until I started writing down some of my memories of my stay in the hospital, I had forgotten meeting the woman and yet now I remember her clearly. By being with this woman who I can not remember the name of,

125

the night passed a lot faster in her company, but it was the drug time again and guess what, yes another queue. I got my usual dose of drugs for my head and a couple of sleeping tablets that were having no effect what-so-ever. After taking my medicine I changed into my pyjamas and put on my dressing gown, how that dressing gown gave me such a lift, it was definitely a new sensation for me to wear something that gave me confidence when I wore it. When I had changed I went back to the woman who had been talking about her life and I listened for a couple of hours to her story. She wanted to go to bed and so did I but I knew that I wouldn't get any sleep between now and morning. I made my way to the bed on the ward and tried to lie down on the top of it. It was no use as my legs were jumping around too much and the night staff, who were not Anne and Barbara, were not as concerned. So I would go into one of the rooms and sit and watch the stars in the sky and wonder how I got myself roped into this and remembered someone who had once said to me "I wouldn't do what you're attempting Wayne, for all the tea in China!" Maybe at this late stage he was going to be proved right. The night passed like a hangover the next day, very slowly. The routine was exercise, then go and do what your creative urge wanted you to do. After dinner time there was a change in our schedule with a quiz for two of the wards in the hospital, ours and somebody else's. We all met together in a room, there was well over thirty of us in the room together when the quiz began, even though some of the patients couldn't handle the situation so left the room. The quiz idea didn't seem such a good one to me as I couldn't concentrate, so the time felt like a drag. When the quiz had finished we all went in to different rooms to discuss something that was in the news a lot at the moment. We were asked to write something down on a piece of paper which was then to be picked up by the carer who was running the group to give us an issue to discuss. The Zeebruger Ferry disaster was the story that was getting the most attention at the time and we were all supposed to put our two-peneth of opinion in on the subject. I just listened and wished I could fall asleep more than anything else in the world. Because I didn't want to take part the whole event seemed to last forever and I was glad when it was afternoon tea time.

In contrast to quizzes and naff discussion groups we did have a therapy session once a week, there would be about six patients and two carers in the room. We would start usually with a game which would get us to move about the room, I can recall we played tiggy with cushions. To not be tigged you had to grab hold of the person closest to you, if you didn't find a partner then you ended up with the cushion. Then we would form a circle with our chairs and then we would say something about ourselves to the group. What plans you had for the future, why you had become ill in the first place, anything that came into your mind at the time. Not just the patients talked about themselves as the carers also told us things about themselves. This group lasted about an hour and I think it was one of the better ideas at the hospital. It got me to admit that I had been ill and I stopped saying I shouldn't be at the hospital because there's nothing wrong with me all the time. I think looking back on it I gained some confidence by talking about my problems and I was able to face my weaknesses where before I had tried to make excuses for them.

When it was over and it was my dad's night for visiting me I started to hope he would take me to his house for tea instead of having to go to the dining room at the hospital, for I had very quickly come to hate the food that was being served up at the hospital because it really was dreadful. If he didn't take me to his house for dinner he would usually bring me some sweets and we would try to talk for about an hour on things that were going on in the world around me. When he left I would go and sit next to George and if I felt hungry I would make myself a jam butty and also have a glass of milk. At one time in my stay one of the staff had to remind me that there were other patients on the ward. As if I could forget. I do remember putting a burger in the toaster and it got stuck so one of the staff had to clean it out. One thing I don't remember doing was the dead fly on the fire blanket but that's what they'd tell me I had been doing. When I did enter the television room for just a few minutes I realised I was not missing anything as the patients kept getting up and changing channels. I decided if I couldn't eat and drink all the supplies on Ward 54; why not go to another ward. That's what I did do and got myself and a hot chocolate drink and a jam butty for my efforts. I would let the patients talk to me and no member of staff ever told me to leave a ward even though I didn't belong there. After visiting a couple of wards before it became bed time I made sure that I certainly couldn't eat any more. One of the staff on ward 54 when I had changed into my pyjamas asked me if I was going to be the first man ever to give birth because of the size of my belly. I really had made a glutton of myself. When it was time for the lights in the bed areas to go off, I knew it was going to be another very long night of pain and not being able to sleep a wink however hard I would try. The sleeping tablets I was given were just a waste of time as I was wide awake through the night. It was a different two-some who were a man and a woman team on the night watch. I didn't get on with them too much so I didn't sit with them and went for a walkabout instead. My head was full of confusion at how I had come to this point and yet at the back of my head I was telling myself that I was in charge, that I had brought on this illness so I could get proper health care to help me through the promise and also to get things that I wanted from all this pain and suffering. The legs shaking and the mouth being dry had seemed bad enough side effects to me, but now the mouth I had was no longer dry, far from it, now it was very wet as I started to dribble down my front. How to keep one's dignity when you return to a childlike happening. It certainly gave me something to think about and I was walking around with paper towels under my chin all the time now. I got so fed up with it that I just let it dribble down my front one night and just couldn't be bothered to hold it back.

It was Anne and Barbara's turn to do the night watch and when Anne looked at me she brought me a paper towel for my dribbling, it was nice to know that someone else cared. These so called side effects of the drugs I was being prescribed were beyond a joke and I did wonder if I should take the drugs when they were being given out on this night. I did swallow them with a couple of sleeping tablets just for a change. Well at least Anne and Barbara didn't mind my company even if I was dribbling like a baby. They provided me with a blanket for my legs. Their boss turned up on this night for a chat with them and after half an hour he was on his way again. While I was made cups of tea to help pass the time. If the night passed slowly at least I had a couple of nice people to pass it with. The patients were gotten up at eight o'clock. I would have done my usual wash and brush before many of them had even got out of their beds. Go down to the dining hall and then back to ward 54 and the usual meeting about quarter past nine.

In the afternoon something different happened, I let one of the patients who claimed she was a hairdresser cut my hair in the small salon that was on the ward. My hair hadn't been that long anyway and now it was really short which meant I wouldn't have to comb it much. I thanked the girl for my haircut and I also thanked my bravery for letting her cut my hair in the first place because she was usually right out of her head. Not everyone would have trusted her with a pair of scissors as she had to be helped into her clothes in the morning and would go running around the place in a very disturbed way. Fortunately for me she was still capable of cutting hair at any rate. It was all the same old routine after this excitement with our afternoon drink in the dining room and meeting Thomas who was rather edgy in his self. When we had our fill of what was on offer it was back to the Art Room for me. When it was over for the day I made my way back to ward 54 still not feeling any better but saying I was alright when asked or that I couldn't hear voices which I always seemed to be asked. I would sit in the corner section of the ward where the big chairs and a table were. To pass the time there was always trivial pursuits, or better still, George to have a talk to. When I had finished my evening meal in the dining room I made my way back to the ward taking a much longer route. When I was back on the ward a man who claimed he had always been in mental institutions hit me and it sent my nervous system into overdrive. My friend Thomas had also been threatened by another patient. We both went for a walk around the hospital telling each other about our problems and how lousy we felt. The man who had threatened Thomas was, it turned out a compulsive liar who had entered himself for observation at the Hospital. Thankfully this was the end of the trouble and it all got sorted out.

With the clocks not working time seemed to lose it's meaning in my stay at the hospital all of it just gelled into an eternity with what seemed no respite. The night dragged on and still there was no sleep in it for me. If you're wondering if there was any record players or cassette players on the ward you would be right, there was, it was just a small matter about the fact that none of them worked.

The next day arrived and with a chance to meet my psychiatrist in the flesh. It was not a meeting I was looking forward to and I told my Dad I didn't want to see him. When he arrived at the Hospital he was in one of the rooms with plenty of chairs in on the ward. He got around to me eventually and I was called into the room which was very cramped for space because of the entourage that came with the chief Psychiatrist in the department. I entered the room with a load of eyes fixed on me. He asked me how was I feeling and I would say I was feeling better even when I felt like shit. His second question was if I heard voices inside my head and I would say I did not hear voices, which was true. These two minute sessions were the way it was and when I complained about my body being in a right state, it was always the same stock answer that it was down to side effects. This was the way of Dr. Lancer the big chief of shrinks in Sheffield Hospitals. I did see another psychiatrist who was called Doctor Troughton and I got on a little bit better with him as he only ever had one assistant with him, which made it seem more intimate than with Dr Lancer. When I first entered Hospital they said I was suffering from Delusions of Grandeur, then that I was a schizophrenic, but eventually they settled for manic depressive. The times with the psychiatrists was I feel superficial. I got more help from the carers who I talked to about my problems and got over my stubbornness to admit that I was ill and did need the help and care I was given in my stay at the Hospital.

The evening visit tonight was by my mother who would bring me fresh pants and socks to wear. I would usually make us a cup of tea on the ward in the kitchen. We would talk about what I had been doing that day and she would tell me how everyone else was going on. After we had drunk our tea we would leave the ward and make for the entrance to the Hospital where there was a bench. We would sit down and finish off our conversation and it would come for my mum to leave me. I always felt low at this point when my relatives left me as I was back up against it on my own. That reminds me of one occasion when both my mum and dad turned up together at the Hospital. It really hurt me and I couldn't believe they would be that stupid. Thankfully one of them left quickly but seeing them together brought back all the rows and the fights they had during their marriage. My dad had asked me if divorcing my mother had hurt me, to which I said no. In fact I didn't want to see them together ever again after all the bitterness they had shared when they were married to each other and they were a lot better apart. My brother would visit me on a Friday so stopping any arguments between my parents. My brother in fact visited me quite a lot in the first few days of my illness but I had a problem remembering who he was, which upset him. He said I even asked him who he was on one occasion. Anyway it was Friday and my brother was visiting me. He'd tell me what he had gotten up to since I last saw him and tell me how many pints he had drunk which made me jealous because wished I could go for some beers myself. But that wasn't possible as I had given my word I wouldn't go to a pub whilst I was at the hospital, so that was that.

When my brother left me it reminded me that it was Saturday tomorrow which would mean something different because the staff who manned the Art Workshop only did so five days a week and not at the weekends. So which ever way you looked at it Saturday was going to be a long day if my dad didn't take me to his house for the day or I would simply have to find something to do with myself. In the design of the hospital there were squares of gardens in between the corridors which had chairs and flowers in them and I decided to walk inside these gardens for something to do as the sun was out and it was a lovely bright day. The cleaning lady said that I was the first person she had ever seen in the gardens. There was a door on the corridor and I went through it to step into one of the gardens. The walk through the gardens was very enjoyable and it took up my morning, which it was to do many times over when I felt like it. The alternative in the afternoon was talk to George or play trivial pursuits such incredible choices; oh it makes you wish you lived just as riveting a life as me doesn't it. The day seemed as long as a week, where was my dad when I needed him. He turned up in the evening dressed up to go dancing at some function or other with Maureen the woman in his life now. We walked about the hospital as I was finding it very uncomfortable to sit down at the time because my legs felt like jelly. My dad had brought me some butter scotch which I chomped instead of just sucking them as you were supposed to do. The hour passed and we said our goodbyes and I went back to my ward.

The rest of the weekend passed in the usual monotonous way and all I could think of was Catherine. Yes Catherine who I had waited so long to meet and now she was so close to being mine. How best to describe her? She had a modern styled short haircut of blonde hair. Her eyes seemed to be so close to crying and her figure was trim and statuess, she stood about five foot five tall. She looked so fresh; it was like she had just come out of the sea yesterday. Catherine liked to listen to dirty jokes and stories and also said that she liked playing trivial pursuits. I started at first just to notice her and think nothing of it, yet I was looking around for her on my way to college before long. It suddenly struck me that she was the girl I had been waiting to meet for the last twenty five years. It was hard to believe but here she was in the flesh and within my reach at long last. The woman who had teased me when I was a child, saying "there's only one lass for our Wayne!" had been proved right. I had never felt an urge for a girl like the one I now had for Catherine. I wanted to be near her all the time as I was drawn like a magnet towards her. Catherine spoke very nicely and appeared to be innocent in a child like way for someone who was eighteen. After the History lesson had finished one day I walked with her to her bus stop which came as a surprise because the bus she waited for was to Stannington, an area I had lived in all my life. So the girl of my dreams was just a matter of an half an hour walk from my mother's. When the bus came I left her to catch her bus and I walked to another bus stop which might seem strange but I wanted to think about what was happening. With us starting our course in September it wasn't too long before Christmas came along. When Christmas did come a lot of the group went for a drink, those who didn't had another class to go to in the afternoon. We made our way to the pubs in town and I got slowly drunk as I never have been one who could drink in the afternoons as it goes straight to my head. Catherine met one of her girlfriends and they both came with the rest of us to the pubs for a drink. We talked the usual as you do in pubs and told jokes but mainly drunk beer. It soon came around the last bell and time to hit the road. I was walking up the stairs of the last pub when I noticed a bus outside which took you to Hillsborough. I just carried on walking and onto the bus without saying goodbye or happy Christmas to anyone. Well I did say afternoon drinking wasn't exactly one of my strong points. With regards to Catherine I was really smitten by her and wanted to spend a lot of time with her. Even though I didn't see Catherine over the Christmas period I thought about her a lot. She was just gorgeous and now the waiting seemed worth it. One day in my stay at the Hospital my dad asked me her name and where she lived as he knew I had made my choice. I gave him the information and stressed don't get it wrong. In fact my always asking where was Catherine was upsetting my whole family and they just said "She doesn't love you Wayne!" when I asked. I kept thinking to myself that the next day would be the day I saw Catherine.

The first couple of weeks of my stay at the hospital were now over and I felt I had to see Catherine. I could no longer take the stock answer I got when I asked about Catherine. "She doesn't love you, Wayne!" So I decided to go and see her myself, no matter what it took I was going to see her today. I got dressed and put all my things into a bag including my dressing gown which my Father had given me and my spectacles. I walked out of the hospital grounds on a very windy day with some showers. There was a wood across the road from the hospital and once inside the wood and hidden from the road I threw away the bag and never to see my dressing gown again. I made my way through the wood and it came out very close to Shirecliffe College. From Shirecliffe road I made my way to Herries road. Walking through the five arches and then shortly later past the Sheffield Wednesday Ground. The cold wind was blowing right through me as I only had a jumper on and could only walk slowly because of the pain in my legs. I made my way to Hillsborough Corner and walked along Taplin Road so could not be spotted if someone was looking for me. I made my way to Stannington Road and went along Myers Grove lane to go on the Robin Hood trail. I was by now desperate to see Catherine and it didn't matter to me that I could hardly walk and it was taking me ages too make my way to her house.

I came out of the Robin Hood Trail to be at the top of Wood Lane. There was a bread van on the road and I bought a kit-kat which I had been doing a lot of in recent times. I ate the kit-kat very quickly and the wind coming down the hill was blowing me back and I could hardly take a breath. I managed to somehow make my way to the shops and the chip shop was open so I had a bag of chips to warm me up a little. It brought back some memories when I would wag work years before and how far I had come since then. There, thankfully was not far to go now and I passed a friend's house on the way to Catherine's. Where she lived was a new estate of stone built houses. I knocked on the door of her house and waited, there was no answer, so I knocked again and still there was no movement in the house. She had to be in because I hadn't come all this way to not see her. There was a man walking a dog who was watching me. I knocked on the door again and this time I could make out that it was Catherine behind the panel of glass. She had been having a bath and was only wearing a bath robe. I told her to open the door for me to come in but she said she was only wearing her bath robe, so I told her to get dressed and asked her if I could drink the bottle of milk that was on the doorstep. She said alright to my question and then went to her room to dress. With her clothes on she opened the door to me and asked me if I wanted a drink. The man who was walking his dog knocked on the door and asked Catherine if everything was alright, she said it was under control and the man went away. With our drinks of tea we went into the dining room and I sat on the floor holding one of Catherine's hands as I told her how much I loved her. The reason I sat on the floor was because my legs ached, the walk had taken a lot out of me. She told me one of the lecturers had said that I was committing suicide. Mark Davies had gotten it all wrong which upset me to here as I was doing nothing of the sort. It turned out to be a strain to talk to Catherine after such a long trek and she seemed confused about what was going on. Also she didn't want me as much as I wanted her. I can remember regretfully calling Catherine a silly cow and she rightly corrected me by saying she wasn't. It seems rather silly now that it took me hours to get to see Catherine and once I was with her all I could muster was abuse. I left her after half an hour of trying to talk to her.

On the next drive up from Catherine there was a show house for people to look around if they were interested in buying one of the houses on the estate. It was only a few minutes before it opened in the afternoon and I played about with the sign in the gardens, thinking it was a flag. A lady came and opened up the house and I entered the house shortly afterwards and I think the woman thought I was one of the workman on site. I made my way to the upstairs looking in the bedrooms and went to the bathroom where I ran the water to have a bath. I took my clothes off and got in the bath, it felt great after the cold and wet weather that we were having outside. When I had finished my bath I put my clothes back on and because of my head burning so much I felt that I didn't need a towel to get dry. I left the house and I don't know what the woman thought about it all but I think it was her who phoned the police. I made my way to a works cabin, where there was a young apprentice who I told I was a painter on the job. The boiler was on so I managed to get a cup of tea and was on my second cup when a police man opened the cabin door. I went with him and got in the police car. He took me home at first and had a chat with my brother. The police man took me back to the hospital and even walked with me to ward 54 where they had been wondering what had happened to me. They got me to promise that I wouldn't go off again and that I wouldn't leave the hospital grounds again. The Matron couldn't believe I had gone so far in my condition but it did give her something more to laugh at. By now she was always walking behind me laughing and saying "I never believed there was such a thing, but I do now and I love him to death!" I can still hear her sometimes when I think back. I certainly gave her a lot of amusement if nothing else. The walk's affect on my body was to make me stiffer in my joints and my legs still had a life of their own. They did tell me the woman in the show house had been frightened out of her wits and the reason I had gone in was because I thought it was part of the deal, I did feel sorry about the woman but in time I'm sure it was a happening that she laughed about. That my escapade had caused a little commotion was an understatement; my dad later called it the worst day of his life.

The following day we both went to the wood to see if we could find my glasses and the dressing gown with the Wolf's head on. All we found was one slipper so all my toiletries had to be replaced. After the first few days of my return from seeing Catherine I had started to grow stubble on my face because I hadn't shaved during these days. The Matron asked me "Are you growing a beard Wayne?" I replied "I haven't got a razor!" The Matron was in to stereotyping obviously and even this made her laugh.

After this adventure it was back to the same routine and I got myself ready for tea time. My dad had called earlier in the day and he was my visitor that night and was glad that I had got back to the Hospital and was safe and alright. All that was going through my head was that I wanted Catherine and nothing else mattered. Only Catherine was worth all this pain and I would gladly get through all of it as quickly as possible just to be close to her. She was the big carrot that was being dangled in front of me and after all this event she would be mine and I would have a life-time companion. Another week passed by and I was going to be let out at the weekend to go to a meal that was for my brother's birthday, he was twenty-one. I still had to take the tablets and fetched them for myself from the dispensary at the Hospital. He told me that one of the nurses should have come to pick up the prescription and that I should not have. I was just happy to be getting out of the Hospital or the weekend. When I got home I found the chairs to be uncomfortable, so I sat on the floor on a blanket. My nerves were on edge for a while and I thought that I might have to go back to the hospital but thankfully it sorted itself out. When the night came it was time to make our way to the restaurant, where I had a steak. I had a job sitting on the chair in the restaurant, as my legs were wanting to move all over the place. When I had finished my meal I borrowed the keys to the house because I couldn't take it any longer and when inside the house I sat on the floor. The rest of the family weren't too long in coming back to the house themselves. The best part of the weekend was that I could sleep in my own bed again, which was a great feeling even though I didn't sleep much and getting away from Hospital smells felt great too. I had my Sunday dinner at my mum's and was taken back to the hospital in the late afternoon. It was back to the old routine and it made me feel low inside.

The food in the Hospital provided after the meals I had had during the weekend was now even more disgusting than it had been previously. I was back to my old tricks the following day, unravelling the hose pipe in case of fire that was in the Hospital and if the staff hadn't caught me I was going to spray the patients. It took five people to wind it back into place and someone was usually watching me again to make sure I didn't get into any more mischief. This didn't quite work though as the next day I had a shower while still wearing my clothes and made plenty of noise while I was in the bathroom, which got the staff to unlock the door to get me out. I didn't have any other clothes to get into, so I changed into my pyjamas. One of the nurses took me to a little washer room and showed me how to ring out my clothes and put them into a dryer. After all the excitement I got better at staying in the television room to pass the night time. When my dad had brought me some sweets I would offer them to the other patients. During one spell of being in the television room there was a black mother and daughter having a slight argument in the doorway of the television room. The daughter said "But he's white", to which her mother said "Yes, Jesus is white, get into the room with him, after all he's done for you!" The mother managed to persuade her daughter and she sat next to me in the room and I asked her to take a sweet which she did. That was the end of that episode, thankfully, but it did make me wonder what kind of world we are living in.

Because I was cut off from seeing Catherine, I concentrated more on Sarah, the leader of the exercise lessons. She would take much pleasure in telling the other members of staff of how funny I looked whilst doing my best to keep up in the exercise class because of my stiffness. Over the weeks we had started to have chats after exercise lesson and I got on really well with Sarah. It wasn't long before I was saying "I love Sarah" all the time. Sarah had her hair in a ponytail and used mascara to paint in her eyebrows. She walked as if she was pregnant at times and wore long skirts to her ankles. Best of all was her sense of humour and I can't recall one day when she had a face on which was certainly different to my own self. When we went to the Art Room after our exercise lesson, Sarah had gotten hold of some eggs. The idea was to put a hole in the egg and then suck the yolk out of the egg with a straw. I did better than most as I sucked out the yolk of my egg but in the process I broke the egg and gave it up as a bad job. I liked being in the company of Sarah and she was my favourite person that I met in my stay at the hospital.

One of our activities in the afternoon with Sarah and another carer one day was to make cakes and buns. But fortunately for me my dad came that afternoon and took me to his house, I was glad because making cakes and buns didn't appeal to me. Not only had he saved me from doing something I didn't want to I would be eating proper food and not the garbage they were dishing out at the hospital. During another afternoon Sarah and me and three other patients went for a walk to Longley Park. When I reached the park I looked down at my feet and I was wearing my slippers. We reached the swings and roundabout in the park and Sarah had a go on the swings while I had a go on the roundabout, the other patients didn't feel up to anything other than watching. We only stayed in the park for about ten minutes before we made our way back going a different way to the route we came. On the way back we walked past a football pitch which was in the hospital grounds. When we were back inside the hospital it was time for the afternoon break, so we went to the dining room for a drink. Because we hadn't been in the Art Room or the workshop there was no point to go to them, so we made our way to Ward 54. The staff were busy chatting away about their marriages and divorces. With so little to occupy us before tea time it was the old favourite, Trivial Pursuits to the rescue. The rest of the day was how I have already described them to be.

When it was visiting time it was the turn of my dad who came alone. I wasn't feeling too well and I was determined to try and get some sleep so I got into my pyjamas early and was already wearing them when my Dad came. He was dressed like a gangster from an old movie, with dark shirt, yellow tie and a jacket to finish the look off. He kept telling me "You're the Guv'nor Son!", "You're the Guv'nor Son!" I said to him "have I done something wrong?" feeling a great deal of pain. He replied "You've done something which we all wish we could have done!" When it was his time to leave he asked me "can I kiss you son?" and when he'd kissed me, he left. I pulled the curtain around my bed so no-one could see me unless they opened them. Time passed by in its own way and the night staff came on the ward; it was the turn of Anne and Barbara. As soon as they came they opened the curtain to check if I was there and both of them said "He looks gorgeous!" I thought it was not only me who needs glasses. I didn't want to see anyone and when the tablets had been handed out, I made my way very quickly back to my bed, with one intent of trying to find some sleep. I managed to rest through the night and felt that sleep wasn't that far away. In the morning I got up around eight like the other patients, went to the bathroom and then for breakfast. For a change I tried mueslei and nearly ended up choking as it got stuck in my throat, which was so much for trying something different.

The exercise class was the usual punishment half hour, with me being more stiff than I had been before. I was beginning to think I would be needing a wheelchair if this continued for much longer as I was having great difficulty when trying to walk. It was also the day that Dr Lancer held court at the hospital. I was the first in the Art Room with Sarah when one of the carers informed me that Dr Lancer wanted to see me. It seemed to take ages to get back to Ward 54 where he was in a room with about another six other shrinks. He asked me how I was and I thought if he can't tell, what chance have I got. I could hardly move and thought that there was a conspiracy against me; they didn't want to make me better. Dr Lancer told one of the nurses that I was to have an injection to rectify my stiff muscles in my legs. I didn't like the idea of having another injection as I was still trying to get over the first one. When I left the room of the Dr, I said "You're trying to make me into a vegetable!" The Matron was right behind me and replied "Carrot or cabbage?" I had to lay face down on a bed while I received an injection just above my bottom, this time the injection was painless. After about ten minutes I got off the bed and could move my legs a lot more freely than before. The pains my body and mind endured throughout my ordeal made me glad that I didn't have a crippling illness and that I would eventually be normal again after it was all over.

Some of my fellow patients deserve a better look than I've given them up to now. When I was hit by a patient I didn't tell you that he claimed he was God

and was punishing me for ripping pages from the bible. When I had first
entered the ward early in my stay I was told later that I had ripped pages from
the bible but I could remember no such event taking place. The man who
claimed he was God was about forty with very little hair remaining on his head
who had a plump face. He had his own dressing gown and he told me he had
been in mental institutions all his life. He had befriended a rather strange
looking patient, who was in his early twenties. He had a beard of whiskers and
his face looked like he had never had a wash all his life; he also had very long
finger nails which must have been an inch long, I called him inside my head
Karl Marx because he resembled him so much but I doubt if Marx was as
grotty. Another patient who was over six feet tall would always be carrying his
ghetto blaster wherever he went and when you entered a room where he was
present he would leave the room straight away. Because of the way he crept
about the Hospital I nicknamed him Max the Knife. One other thing about him
was that he never seemed to talk to anyone. Another patient who was on the
adjoining ward was an old woman who was always grinding her teeth and
what an irritating noise she made from doing so. She was usually walking
about the corridors asking if you could give her ten pence to make a phone
call. I gave her ten pence one time in the hope that she would stop grinding her
teeth; she just put the money in her pocket and carried on grinding. After that I
just tried to avoid her as best I could. The girl who I had let give me a haircut
was usually in a fair old state. She got help from some of the other female
patients to help her get dressed in a morning because the nurses wouldn't help
her any more. She would walk around very fast with her head on one side
saying silly things. Because she behaved very silly most of the time she wasn't
allowed any of the self-help classes. Most of the patients smoked and I reckon
I must have been passive smoking at least twenty a day. A lot of the other
patients were in the Hospital for bad nerves and were not on anything like the
heavy dosage I received in my stay. I can remember one of the day patients
who came to Hospital on certain weekdays for the activities that were arranged
at the Hospital. He would suddenly break out shouting football chants and
didn't seem to have much of a clue at what was going on around him. He
smoked in his own way taking a puff of smoke in his mouth and immediately
blowing the smoke back out again. One of the patients said to me you're in a
better state than him and I had to agree, I was.

I can't recall any of the other day patients probably because they weren't as
noisy as the star out patient. On the next ward there was an alcoholic dosser
who had ended up in the Hospital to try and dry out, or that is what I thought
had happened. Anyway the tablets they put him on made him sway back and
forth and he didn't half look comical as he did so. Many of the other patients
who were on my ward didn't stay too long and I didn't take much notice of
these patients. There was, however, one exception to this; he was someone

who had come of his own accord to the Hospital. He looked fine to me but within one day of taking the tablets that were prescribed to him he looked a right state and it made me wonder about the drugs we were being given. His face had become distorted and he had changed his personality or so it seemed to me. When he left two days later he looked a heck of a lot like he could have done with staying in the Hospital to me. He made me think of one of my problems that I had picked up during my stay, that of dragging my left leg and I wondered if I might limp for the rest of my life. Of course all I ever heard when I complained about pain was that it was just a side-effect to the drugs I was taking. When Matron was around it was just one big joke to her and I can still hear her laughter now. My friend George the Dragon Slayer was about sixty and was rather thin and mumbled when he talked which made it hard sometimes to understand what he was saying all the time. He had grey stubble on his chin, and liked telling the trainee nurses where they could get off.

The other patient who was a friend to me whilst I was in Hospital was Thomas. He was about twenty, with dark black hair, cut short, who wore glasses, which were similar to Michael Caine's in the movies. He smoked a lot and always seemed to be on a knife's edge with the obvious tension he was feeling. The reason he was in Hospital was because he had threatened to kill himself. But he didn't appear to be very down to me and we became friends in his stay on the ward. I remember he had a book about Adrian Mole which he said was funny and I'll have to take his word for that.

On one of my mother's visits, Thomas came over to talk to me and my mother and I thought at the time that I could never have done that to him and that my mother was here to see me not him. Perhaps I was getting touchy and making mountains out of molehills at the time. Thomas and I were taken to the pictures by Sarah one afternoon to see Crocodile Dundee. When we got to the cinema we were very early so we went in to a pub and had a soft drink to pass away the time. The cinema had no heating and it had a musty smell. Sarah commented that the screen was filthy. The film though was very funny and I really enjoyed it and felt that it was just the right sort of film to give you a lift when you were feeling down.   When the film had finished we made our way back to the hospital and I was glad my legs hadn't moved about too much during the film so I could sit reasonably comfortable. The bus journey back to the hospital meant a return back to reality after the high of seeing an entertaining movie. It would soon be time for tea and all the staff on the ward wanted to hear about the picture we had just seen. There's no doubt in my mind that seeing the film had made my day and it definitely lifted my spirits.

Because Thomas was not such a critical patient in his illness he was allowed at the weekend to go back to his father's house. After that he wasn't too long in being released back into the great big world. With Thomas leaving I spent a lot more time with George again. It was really no great change at the hospital as all the clocks were still not working, so time was something that existed outside the hospital. On being allowed to walk anywhere in the hospital complex, it made me feel that I was in some way special, as none of the staff ever stopped me from going to the other wards. On one of the nights a little earlier in my stay if I remember rightly, I went to another ward in another sector of the building and was made a hot chocolate drink, as I listened to what some of the patients had to say about themselves. No one seemed to mind my company as I went on my trek through the wards of the hospital. I can recall one of the female patients on this particular ward wearing a towel on her head and I never did ask her why she did so. Not that I just went around helping fellow patients, sometimes I made a right nuisance of myself. When I got hold of a discarded wheelchair I sat in it and proceeded to take it around most of the hospital, making a lot of noise as I did so. For some reason no one intervened and told me off, so I got away with that one. At the time of my escapade with the wheelchair I was thinking about the film Tommy and that some of my experiences were in some way related in my confused mind. It also suddenly struck me that I would be wheeled out of the hospital when my stay was over by my own nurse who would just happen to be Catherine. Well this was the thoughts that were going through my mind at the time. The wheelchair business was not exactly an isolated of my rather confused thinking at that time. In a bag I was given by one of my relatives, there were three books and also some sweets. I took the plastic bag with me into one of the bathrooms on the ward and ran the water for me to have a bath. When I had finished my bath I pulled the plug out and let the water disappear. Then I put all the hard boiled sweets into my mouth and spat them out into the bath. I picked up the sweets and threw them into the plastic bag, the books inside the bag became sticky and a lot of the pages were stuck to each other. The books because of this were unreadable and due to my confused state I didn't have enough concentration to read them anyway. After this I went around the hospital looking for things I could pull off such as a cover for a bell alarm or a door stop. I can recall a doorstop I removed by kicking it at first and then I managed to twist the screws that were holding it in place. When I had taken off something I put it in the plastic bag with the sweets and the books. On one of my mother's visits I gave her the bag to throw away. When looking inside I think she thought I was mad but she did take the bag with her.

In the evening sometimes there were fresh faces for a couple of hours on the ward. They would usually take the piss when making up my bed by saying they wouldn't do this for just anyone, which of course was not true. But in the main they were very nice people who I could talk to about my problems and there was one who reminded me of a bear who I told of things that had depressed me in my life. The girl carers or nurses who worked the daytime shifts leaving the night time shifts to the more mature staff. The girls were okay but usually wanted to talk about their boyfriends to each other. One of them asked me what I was smiling about one day but did not get an answer; some thoughts are too personal to share. In the main the reason the girls were on the psychiatric ward was to gain experience and it was part of the course to become a nurse. The main matron of the ward was usually laughing at something and I can still remember her walking behind me laughing to herself and pulling on my shirt which I hadn't put inside my trousers. I had lost some weight by this time and my trousers were now too big for me around the waist. The older women who were qualified nurses would talk about their marriage breakdowns or how they were unhappy with their previous relationships. Sometimes when I was feeling low and sat amongst all these women talking about their problems I just had to go for a walk to clear my head. I, for one, didn't want to listen to the nurses' domestic difficulties. This was another reason I can think of why I liked the night shift when it was Anne and Barbara because they liked to talked about lighter things.

On the ward there was a small store room opposite the kitchen, inside there was provisions for the ward. The contents of the store ranged from biscuits to chocolate drinks and sweets. I thought the reason for these provisions was that we were going to have a party on the day I was being released from Hospital. The ward would have decorations and all the patients would have hats on and join in the celebrations. I would be pushed round on a wheelchair by Catherine and that's how it would be when I left the Hospital. The wheelchair was certainly in my thoughts when I look back and I must have been on powerful drugs when I think back to it. Not that the wheelchair was the end of the ceremony as I thought that I was going to run around the Hospital as I had done around Hillsborough Park and give everyone inside the Hospital lift-off.

When I walked in the gardens and sat on the chairs that were in them I would reflect on my life and how I got here. For here I was, idling and wasting away the day with no idiot telling me what to do. My mind's thoughts would return to my time on the council, to my time at school and of playing when I was but a child. The way I had taken my body to school and my head would travel elsewhere and doing the same thing when I became a painter on the works. My head would be full of dreams while my body stood up to be counted by attending school or work. Of all the small minded idiots who I had met during my lifetime and thankfully would never meet again. The way some people never understood what I was attempting to do and in many cases didn't care anyway made me sad inside, of course on the other hand there were people who did understand and who did care about what I was trying to do to balance it up.

These were some of the thoughts that entered my mind in the very tranquil setting of the gardens with no interruptions as no other patient went into the gardens. How often in my life I had been alone yet I rarely noticed it and it didn't seem to bother me too much. I also wondered how better the garden must look in the summer and how come no other patient used them. The most telling thought going through my head was what if I was just a fruit and nutcase who had lost the thread or was I really capable of doing something that was near impossible and just a faint dream. But on weighing up the evidence that was before me, the idea that I had indeed done something that would change my life forever and other people's also, from this time forward was very much supported by people's reactions towards me. These thoughts though could be explained away by medical practice such as when someone is going through Hyper Mania they fear nothing and believe they can do everything and anything they put themselves to. So due to Hyper-Mania my reactions would have seemed normal and the responses to me would also appear to be normal for someone going through a spell of Hyper-Mania. By reaching this stage in my thoughts I became very depressed and my pain in my head was not helped too much by all these ifs and buts. I was just left with doubts with one fact I still hadn't come to terms with, that of being ill and needing treatment for my illness.

While on my walks around the psychiatric hospital I had come across the ward for the elderly. They were beneath ward 54 and seemed to be entirely made up of women. While I was walking through these wards I can recall being silly by turning lights on and lights off which must have made me very popular. These elderly women couldn't half make some noise when it came to meal times, I can tell you. On one of the other wards in the hospital, I think it was known as the night ward because it was always dark, even in the day. I can't recall if I spent much time on this ward and have no idea why it was dark all the time. The ward which was just next door to mine was filled with people who had similar problems to the patients on my ward. On one trip into this ward I played dominoes with an elderly woman and a man who was a good ten years older than me. The reason I can remember we played dominoes was because I won every game while we drank tea. The elderly lady was friendly and liked a laugh. She reminded me of someone I had met previously when I was a child but then again most of the people in the Hospital reminded me of someone I had known before or had seen in my voyage through life. The man who played dominoes with me from the other ward also played me on another day at chess. We started the chess game and after about ten minutes I couldn't concentrate on the game so I went for a walk with a confused head. In the beginning of my stay at the Hospital I had thought that playing a game like chess would release me from the Hospital and that would be that, of course it was just wishful thinking on my part. The windows in the Hospital that looked onto the gardens were very dirty and I drew things on them with my fingers and they were still visible when I left the hospital. On one of my larking around moods I got hold of a fire extinguisher and a bag with newly washed sheets in a corridor. I placed the sheets over the fire extinguisher and built up a pile of before a couple of nurses caught up with me. They helped me put the sheets back in the bag and wondered what I would get up to next. On one of my many travels around the Hospital a door was open to a room that was for meetings by the Doctors, or it looked like it was to me. I went inside the room and started to look through a book about mental illness. After about twenty minutes in the room I was just walking out of the door when one of the specialists came to close the door and he said I shouldn't have been in the room. I couldn't care less about what he had to say, the door was open and it wasn't as if I was stealing something. A door to the outside was just down this corridor from this room, so I made my way and, just for a change, I walked around the Hospital. During my walks around the hospital I noticed a gold bracelet that someone must have thrown out from a window onto the grass. It was a few days before someone picked it up and probably put it in their pocket and walked off with it. Sometimes when I went for a walk it would be pouring down with rain and I didn't have a coat to wear but went outside anyway because the rain seemed to cool down my head. The good thing about all the walking I did was that I could clear my head for a little while at least from its torments.

The following day came along in its good time and I left the present to go back into the past a lot further. Of my poor bowels making me wet the bed, of being able to virtually fall over matchsticks, of nose bleeds and dizzy spells, of my very poor co-ordination especially in my feet making me useless at football, the one game that I wished I could play. The fears I had when I was a child, the way I turned red as a beetroot when asked a question at school. My very slow learning at being able to read and do simple tasks and my deep fear of failure which I became accustomed to. All these things had helped shape my life in a way that I could use in my later life as for my education, it began very much so when I passed twenty and not in my schooldays. Of showing great strength playing bulldog when ripping a new shirt off a friend's back without intending to do so. These were some of the more fleeting moments that were coming to mind. Of a trip I made when I was a scout when we went for a two week holiday in Scotland, where we camped next to a loch. While in Scotland we visited a dam that was producing electricity. When we were at the top of the dam and looking at the water which was far below us from the massive wall of the dam, one of the scout leaders said to me "If I dropped my baby into the dam I would throw you in to save her!" This hit me hard at the time and I took it seriously and obviously still did as I remembered the incident to this day. It made me wonder why he had said such a thing and I still can't think of an answer to it. May be he knew more than he was saying about me and what I was up to, I certainly, in retrospection, think he saw me as some sort of threat. But may be I'm trying to see something more in it than it really was. There was also in my thoughts that I had always been different in some ways to other people even though I had no knowledge of the purpose of my differences as a child or I wasn't totally in the know as to what they meant and would mean in the future. I can remember very vividly in my time at Myers Grove the hatred I had for the discipline the school dished out. They wanted literally to knock sense into us all, in our time at the school which alienated me towards it. Of course some pupils got more out of things being done this way than I certainly did.

When I first went to Myers Grove School I got the impression that I wasn't at playschool any more and that what we did in the lessons was to work. This I'm sure didn't make me particularly receptive to the ways of the school which appeared to me to be massive. I think the size of the school was used as a weapon against us reminding you of how small you are to the education machine. My school work didn't really matter much to me when looking back, as if I had done well at school I would doubt whether I would have become a painter on the council, so wasting my time and the school's was in the long term not too harmful. Still thinking about my school days I had plenty of problems with the games lessons because of my poor coordination skills which caused me quite a few mishaps. One of the most memorable of these mishaps was when I tried to vault a horse in the gym. The teacher had just shown us how to do it and I waited for my turn to have a go. It was just a matter of putting your hands on to the horse and turning your body over so you landed on your feet; well that is how the teacher described it. When it was my turn I knew I was going to be hopeless but that didn't stop me from attempting the vault. I ran fairly fast to the horse and put my hands out in front of me, but instead of my body going into a somersault, I managed to land on my head, which when I got to my feet, was hurting me as was my neck, which I was glad I hadn't broken in my pathetic attempt at the vault. It seemed that any action that required confidence to do I always failed miserably. On another gym lesson the floor had just been polished and we were all without trainers, so it was just our socks against the floor. We were doing a game which meant running as fast as you could. When it came to my turn I ran as fast as I could but landed hard on to my back, which knocked the wind right out of me. When I managed to get up I put my head down between my knees to aid breathing back to normal. The teacher came over and said, "You seem a little bit accident prone, Wayne!"

My thoughts exactly, doing exercises could seriously damage my health. It's certainly more painful moments of one's life that stay with you, that's for sure.

One of the lessons I liked, thinking back other than history was the Art lesson. Art had always been something that had interested me and I still have a painting of William the Conqueror that I did in my time at Malin Bridge. I can remember a drawing to this day of King Richard the Lion heart with Saladin the Moore leader; in the drawing Saladin was showing Richard that his sword could cut a piece of silk whereas Richard, with his much heavier sword, could not. It certainly is strange what you remember and what you forget in your way through life. In my time at Myers Grove, I always enjoyed my Art lessons. The Art teacher I had in my last two years at the school was fine as he didn't bother me too much during the lessons. He did write on one report that he thought I was hibernating, due too the lack of work that I was producing in the lessons. This of course fell on deaf ears as I went about things at my own pace. I never did sort out a theme for my project, in the main this was because I felt there were too many things to experiment with and not enough time to test them all out. Well, that's my story and I'm sticking to it! One of my regrets is that I didn't collect my folder of the work I had done at the last term at the school. With school finishing it was such a relief that it was over for I had never liked going, but the relief of leaving was short lived as now I had to find a job to do. I had no idea of what I wanted to do thinking back over it, and in the May of 1977 when I left school there were jobs, but in the main they were the sort that were known as dead end. One thing for sure at the time was that going back to education was a non starter.

After seeing the career officer I finally chose painting and decorating and applied for a job on the council and my application was accepted, so I got the job. The other apprentices in the main were from other areas of the city which were a lot meaner than the one I had grown up in. I can remember getting my rucksack strap cut by one of them and I stopped him cutting it totally off by saying "Don't cut me off!" I sewed the strap together again with twine and it was in a way symbolic to me being of not cut off before I had begun my task that was before me. The lad who cut the strap half way through changed a lot in time from being aggressive in his early years to being more thoughtful in his twenties. I can remember him talking to me about an album he had just listened to and it never dawned on me before that he had never experienced such a thing and that it was all new to him to have money to spend on himself. Some of the other apprentices had even worse hang-ups and a couple of them even ended up doing some time in prison. The moments I'm reflecting on in my stay in hospital at this time were of the more nasty elements I went through in order to build up the circuit as I have now called it. The days when I felt I couldn't continue going through emotional turmoil in my time on the works were still with me, stored away inside my mind. The very part of just being there was in itself tiring and testing and a permanent bind. Some days I would be having battles inside my head and everything else that was around me became just a blur. There seemed no way through it even to go round it at the time, so I was left with having to face it. I must have appeared to those around me that I was in a daze and that I was cut off from the real world. But then again where is the real world if it isn't inside our head. The lousy days when I was totally miserable, there are so many of them that I had tried to lock them away, but they were trying to break out so I could at last have my peace of mind back. These previous experiences certainly were still vivid in my mind and I wondered at the moment had I got them under control. For these days I was recalling were some of the hardest of my life that I had to go through. Of the painter who said to me on many occasions "No man is an island!", but I was certainly giving it a good try. The way I did cut my self off from all those around me as much for my own survival than for any other reason that I can think of. The way some of the charge-hands had treated me when I was an apprentice came back to my mind, with the daily arguments about me staying on the firm and not knowing how long it was going to take to fulfil my mission. The losing of my reason for being on the firm was easy to do in my time with the way certain people treated me because of their very small minds, which means they were as thick as pig shit and twice as sloppy, as the saying goes. Those who were encouraging towards me in my stay also kept a distance away from me. The daily tirade over my sexual inactivity an in the main being called a virgin more times than I care to remember or the very fact that I couldn't care less what any one thought of me, for I was going to go all the way and have a sort of judgement day. As one of my friends in my time on the works said, "Abuse is like water off a duck's arse to this lad!" how true. These were some of the thoughts that crossed my mind in my stay at the Hospital and many more incidents of what occurred in my time on the works would come through my head. We were having a chat one day in-between getting the paint out of the cabin and going to our place of work that day. One of the painters started saying he didn't like a song on the radio which was thinly disguised as a bonking number that was just about getting a telephone in all the rooms of a house. After condemning this song he started to talk to us about licking his wife out the previous night. If this wasn't hypocrisy, I've never come across it. Strange what stays with you sometimes.

The memories I have of the works are not all bad because of the great laughs we had in my time. But maybe what made the laughter hours stick in my mind was that I was experiencing heavy depression symptoms, which made me need a laugh a lot more to try to get over it. The relief of being sacked even though it caused a great uncertainty in my life was a great one. It was like having weights lifted off my shoulders which had been weighing me down for the last five years. By being sacked by the works department I could never work for them again which was a nice thought. By burning the bridges behind me, so to speak, meant I could only go forward in my trek through life from here. The day that was my last official day on the works was a cold and snowy one so I didn't go in to work that day. It was finally true no more inert days on the council wondering what the heck I am doing here. When it was night time I caught the bus to town and thought that some of my friends would be on it as Friday night was town night. I did meet a friend who also hated his time on the works who had a date so I left him when we got into town. I made my way to a curry house up from the Wicker. I had a curry but was feeling down about the whole situation and after leaving the curry house I walked a couple of hundred yards and puked up. So not feeling too well I made my way back to home and of course I was early. Because I was home early, my mother guessed there was something wrong being a better detective than Sherlock. She said to me "Have you lost your job?"

And I replied "Yes!"

She assured me that it would be alright and that it wasn't the end of the world as we know it. But my abiding memory of that night is that I felt so lousy even though I had hated that job with all my being; it seemed strange to myself that I had such a reaction to this episode. I was feeling sorry for myself and wondering is there life after work because losing the job was unforgivable coming from such a working class background as mine. Or so I felt at the time of what should have been celebration I was on edge with my nerves and certainly was not feeling euphoric in any way. My granddad must have been turning in his grave after all the years he put in. But he never got much back from the system and so I thought that the family was owed and seeing as he was no longer around I would collect some of his share. Definitely an interesting idea if no more than that. The time after work gave me plenty of scope to carry on with my O'levels I had paid for. Other wise I would spend my time reading books, going for walks and brooding over the recent past as it came to me. At this time I was still sleeping with no problems. I spent much time as I have written here, as well, of going over my teenage years because they were traumatic.

The time I drunk the whiskey was looking back on it a cry for help but was it just another part of the plan with experiencing such despair and anguish which would hold me in good stead for later on in my time at the hospital. To go through true alienation of myself to the outside world in my teenage years but still be able to look at myself from a distance was I really this clever or can't I accept my weaknesses. So did I really do it for the cause or was I so fed up with my life that I couldn't communicate my unhappiness to anyone. When in the hospital one of the patients was from a home and he had drunk a bottle of vodka. He was put on my ward for three days observation. He told me that he had done it for just a lark and he didn't seem depressed so maybe he was telling the truth. He was allowed to leave when the three days passed. But meeting him brought back my memories of the stomach pump and my condition afterward. Thinking back to it my dad coming for me early the next day meant I didn't have to see the psychiatrist at the hospital as they wished me to. So I was not labelled by the incident and it didn't enter into any of the theories that were being made at the hospital now. During my teenage days on the council a lot of the other lads didn't understand me but I did make a really good friend who I've already mentioned his name, that was Rory. He felt in many ways the same as me about being a painter and like me he wanted to leave as soon as possible. We both came from the same area of Sheffield which probably made us friends. When I say I wasn't understood by some of the other apprentices, there was also the lecturers who didn't seem to understand me either. Things became a lot better in time, when in the final year just seeing each other once a week and a lot of the apprentices had grown up, college was not such a bind any more. There were supposedly the best years of your life, with you finding yourself, your likes, your dislikes, finding a suitable girl to go out with and in the main just going out and enjoying yourself. All I got from that period of my life was a sense of emptiness that was inside me and also a sense of isolation. The fact that I was different to normal lads of my age group was something I found hard to accept. It wasn't because I was going out of my way to be different but that I knew the weight on my shoulders that I was carrying was a lot more important than my own feelings on the opposite sex. Not that it made it any easier just because I had these chains on, I felt like any healthy teenager and I feel that some of the scars of this time are still with me. Just because I was on a latter day quest didn't make things any easier. In the last year of college I would go out with a friend to The Timbertop, have four pints at dinnertime and then go back to the theory lesson at the college. I spent the rest of the afternoon trying to stay awake and couldn't tell you what had been said during the lesson. It was strange now with some of the lads because quite a few were married and had children it had changed them so much that they were different people from the ones of three years ago. When college had come to an end I for one was glad to see the back of it. I did wonder what had happened to my drinking partner when we were at college until I met him on my last but one job on the works a couple of years later. With the end of the apprenticeship there was now just the painting and the boredom to contend with. I thought back to all the arguments I had had with the gaffers, workmates and tenants. I seemed to have a talent for putting some people's backs up and making them angry. Well that could well be the story of my life one big argument with me taking the world on and not surprisingly forever losing. I decided that I've thought over work for enough time and shall have a change of what is stored inside my head. I think back and come up with the holidays abroad.

Ah yes, holidays abroad, for the first time leaving Britain I and friends made our way to Biarritz once the place for the well to do but obviously now changed. On the way to our campsite we made a stop at Paris for the night. We didn't go sightseeing as we were told that we could go on the way back from our holiday. So we made our way to a local bar for some beers, when we had our fill we went to the tents. When we got back the two friends who were sharing the tent with me waited a couple of minutes and we made our way to the other tent that our group were in. I got hold of a fire extinguisher and sprayed inside of their tent twice; it didn't spout out foam as I had hoped it would but released a powder. Because of the mess they couldn't sleep in the tent so all seven of us slept in the same tent. In many ways the highlight of the holiday in memory at least. This might explain my behaviour in the Hospital of playing with fire extinguishers, with a water hose and doing the dead fly on a fire blanket in the kitchen. Maybe I've watched too many Laurel and Hardy movies. I don't know where the fascination in fire fighting otherwise comes from but I seemed very obsessed with it in my stay at hospital.

The next time we all went on holiday but one, so there was just six of us this time, we went up market and booked into a four star hotel in Tenerife. One thing in particular being in my mind was the food. Every night there was so much to choose from with there being so much meat on the self-service part of the Restaurant in the Hotel plus you could order the night meal as well. It was certainly a world away from what we were being offered at the Northern General Hospital, the food was an absolute disgrace but I bet some git somewhere was saying it's all we can afford. The very fact that decent food would help the recovery of the patients more quickly obviously didn't hold much store with the powers that be.

Going back in my mind to the Hotel in Tenerife, what I would give now to be by the side of the pool drinking a beer in the red hot sun with just the job of gaining a sun tan, to occupy my time. What hard work the thought brings to mind. As my mind travelled back to recall past experiences, to take my mind off the present ones that I was going through, I wondered how important my past had been to my present. Had I trod a different path would I have gone out of my mind anyway in my life at a given time? If I had not been a painter and taken a job in a warehouse would I have been here in the hospital at this time? I somehow don't think so, I had a path to follow and it was just a case of following it to see where it would lead. I remember one man on the works as I have already written stating that he wouldn't have attempted what I was doing for all the tea in China, because he was the only person who ever said that he felt sorry for me in my time on the council. I suppose in someway that's why I remember what he said so clearly. Doubts raged in my head and I wondered if all the pain in my stay at the Hospital would benefit other people or whether it was just a silly flight of fancy on my part. This was the big question that kept recurring, when it was all over would people have gotten something worthwhile out of it all. It was a great mystery that could only be answered in time.

With my mind being in a state I was recalling things that had been said to me in the past, that now held a more significant edge to them. I thought of my year tutor at school saying "I don't want to do this!" when he gave me the slipper across my backside, but he probably said it very often and it didn't seem to be stopping him very much in his back swing action. Then I thought of a thing my driving instructress had said to me one day that "I've never met anyone like you before!" During my life many other people had hinted the same thing with one former work mate saying that I "was like Dr Who"! I liked that one and didn't mind mentioning so. The driving lessons didn't help me pass my test which I have failed five times and given up as a bad job. Now I'm content to be a born-again-pedestrian!

My thoughts move to the television programmes I liked watching in the past, such as The Likely Lads or Steptoe and Son and Faulty Towers, all great comedies which could raise a laugh even now. Going back even further, I was a big fan of The Man from Uncle series and The Saint starring Roger Moore. The Saint was on Sunday and I would have a bath, watch the Saint and then go on to bed. Thinking through all the favourite moments from the movies I have, there is one by John Wayne in the film I think it was called The Greatest Story Ever Told, which is my favourite. He got fourth billing from the credits, but sneeze and you could well miss his part in the film. It's near the end of the film that he gets his moment with Max Von Sydow playing the part of Christ when he is on his cross. John Wayne in silhouette and using a big drawl says: "That surely was Sesame Sam!", well, he doesn't really, but he might as well have done, if anyone was still awake at the time, I bet there wasn't a dry eye in the house but for all the wrong reasons, maybe someone in Hollywood felt it needed a laugh to cheer everyone up at the end. He did for Christianity what he did for the war effort in Vietnam in the film The Green Berets, which of course was very little. The movie in which the only good Indian - oh, sorry I mean Vietnamese, it s just harder to spell - where the only good Vietnamese was a dead one and the American way is the only way for everyone to follow in the world today. Good old John - what a star! It does make you wonder though, whatever happened to the cast director? It's a wonder he didn't have Ronald Reagan as a disciple or Elizabeth Taylor as Mary. The film must have been released with the bumf that this is the true story, never told before in Technicolor with John Wayne plus his Southern drawl playing the centurion as you've never seen him before. When it's John's big moment, an eclipse happens whilst Max Von Sydow is dying on the cross, and John delivers his awe inspiring line. The director of the picture kept telling John to give it more awe in his delivery of his line. So when John said the line again, he took a big breath and started with a big southern drawl "Awe!" Definitely guaranteed not to have a dry eye in the house. This is definitely one of the great moments in movie history. Of course they didn't use the next line of John's script which was "The Hell he was!" a return to type for John there. There was also a third line, which they also cut, which went something like this "That'll be the day!" Good old John, it makes you wonder how they could have made the movie without him. This was one of my amusing thoughts, that is it was amusing to me, which, with humour being what it is, can be a very personal thing. It certainly helped pass the time which is more than can be said of the clocks in the Hospital, but they did show the right time twice a day, which was something I suppose. They never did fix the clocks in my eight week stay at the Hospital for that matter.

The days of thinking through bits of my life didn't really change too much the way the days and nights seemed to drag on, with only the occasional relief from. Of course, there were times when my thoughts were very clouded and fuzzy in the extreme. Thoughts where I would jump out through the window on the ward so at last I was free from it all but to counter such thoughts I reminded myself, that I had got this far and the finishing line was in sight. It would only be a matter of time before I would be on the final straight and Catherine would be mine at long last. My whole life would change for the better, or so I thought, and I wouldn't get so depressed as in the past over my problems. This thought that I would be starting a new beginning was something that came into my head a lot and I would behave more like other members of society and become a lot more sociable. Returning to Earth Control, it's back to things being normal and mundane after my mind travel adventures, back to me feeling like I had been beaten up, back to my head feeling like someone was mushing my brain to a pulp.

Seeing as there was still plenty of time before the main meal of the day, I just for a change, moved my weary body around the Hospital with no intent of doing something mischievous. If I had been stood in the road and a speeding bus had come along I doubt I would have been able to get out of it's way, and for that matter, I might not have minded if I didn't. That's some more of feeling sorry for myself, I bet anyone reading this thinks I'm a right whinger who can't take his medicine. But then again, would you have wanted to if you had been

150

given the chance?

The passing of the days in hospital was the main highlight of my stay there, for there was very little to make me cheer other than Sarah, my new found friend. My mind travelled back to my time before hospital, when I was attaching too much to the song Bad by U2. Especially the part where it said let go these worthless life cords, or something like that! The release of my chains at long last had led to this point, to throw away my cynical thoughts, my clinical thoughts that I had amassed during my quarter of a century of existence. The fear surrounding my being stopped was now gone as I had followed my path to the letter. The feeling of being dead inside myself could also now cease just as my selfish thoughts that no-one else matters as much as me in my life could now be discarded.

My lack of a good relationship with my parents through the years still caused me personal anguish. But by doing what I had justified my existence. My mind would wander thinking through many parts of my life which with all the time in the world at my disposal meant I could go through what ever crossed my mind. I recalled a moment that had happened when I was a pupil at Myers Grove, in, I think my second year at the school. I was making my way to another lesson when I bumped into someone who was a lot bigger than me at the time. It turned out to be the so-called hardest lad at the school, and he was one of the few black children who attended Myers Grove. I think he was called Winston, and we started to stare into each others eyes as is the way of these things. He walked away and I think he did this because I wasn't worth hitting, with him being twice the size of me. Recalling memories of confrontation, I moved on to a time when I was at a work friend's wedding. It involved his brother and it upset me for a long time after. The brother was very jealous over my friend's house that he and his wife were going to move in to, because he did not get so much help when he was married. When he was on the way to the toilet he talked to someone who he knew and I jokingly said "Good, we've got rid of him!" He had heard the remark and when he came back from the toilet he was looking for a fight over what I said, which, when all was said and done was very hard to believe even for this embittered and incredibly thick and jealous man. What a dickhead, I thought to myself as he was offering to go outside for a scrap. At the end of the incident I apologized to the cretin, even though it had upset me and I knew the real reason was to try and spoil the wedding of my friend. When I eventually went to the toilets there was a terrible puke all over the urinal, and it wouldn't have surprised me one little bit that it was done by the jealous and small minded git. Not one of my pleasanter memories. In the main though, I have always somehow in confrontations managed to tone down the situation and have not had to fight.

The thoughts of having changed some peoples lives was a recurring one, and

I kept returning to this because it was the reason I was here whether I liked it or not. The way I had lived my life in the main as some sort of guru hermit meant not one of my friends ever visited me as I had lost contact with them in the run up to the main event which I was now going through. But this didn't make me feel unhappy, on the contrary I was glad that only my family saw me in such a state and I think the isolation in 1987 was all part of the task I had to cut myself off to come out on top of the whole episode and this is what I did, right or wrong.

When not going through my past I was mainly thinking about Catherine and that when I got better I could see her as often as possible. One of the other thoughts about the future was of seeing the painters I had known in my time on the works and the reaction on their faces to what I had done. I was really looking forward to seeing what would happen to them when the effects came through. When just thinking about my situation in hospital my main concern was that no-one thought of me as mad and that I was just another no-hope fruit and nut case. It really played on my mind and this was the reason I did not want to see the psychiatrist. As it turned out though it wasn't a twenty question grilling that I thought it was going to be, and Dr Lancer just gave out all the medication doses. One of the things I could never understand was why he usually had five or six other doctors with him when I saw him at the hospital. He even used to go through naming them, but he might as well have been saying "Pew Pew, Barney Magrew, Cuthbert, Dibble, Grub", of the television programme, except that I can remember the names of fireman from the programme that was part of a children's hour. It certainly didn't make me feel better having an audience to say how I felt at the time, which I would generally say that I was feeling better in myself even though I felt like shit warmed up and could hardly walk, thinking back, it was thinking back just a bad joke. The low that I was going through did not seem to be going away and my position was very much one of plodding on and hoping that it would become easy in a short time and not keep dragging on for an eternity. What had I done wrong to be punished in this way was a recurring theme inside my head. Only someone who had done something bad could feel this way or so I thought as my pain threshold was being pushed to new limits. I still had thoughts of running off and leaving the hospital but I had given my word that I wouldn't run off again so I was stuck.

So back to my memories in which I would go looking for clues or just coincidences in my life's history. Did my granddad the day he gave me a small knife have a greater significance, or was I looking for something that didn't really exist in my past? Why was this happening to me, what had I done other than want to know the answer to why I was born in the first place? I wanted to know the reason why so many times at school and then at work where the question became even more intense. I so wanted the answer to the unanswerable question. When I saw myself in a dream with a woman and three other males was it just something my mind put out there, or was it really a look back in to my past? The way I rose up in a bubble to look down on what was going on below seemed perfectly real and that I indeed had been waiting for my chance to put things right again. The woman was raped and killed in my dream by the three faceless men after they had chopped my head off. They were our children who would abuse and revel in their evilness and put the human race through great misery just to satisfy their desires. My task appeared to be that of somehow stopping them and to try and heal the wound they had created in the human race, a race to nowhere. It meant I had to be patient for my chance to give people a new beginning and thought of the throwing of the paint all around the Art Room where I experienced such a fantastic high and release from my worthless life. It appeared to me to be a worthless life and this made it easier to throw my life line to my past away and bring me right up to the present. The very thought that in the beginning of this story I was from another time seemed perfectly reasonable to me at that time. That there had been a game or a race going on throughout time and I had been around through the ages was taken aboard very easily. That I, my wife and children had arrived from another planet many moons ago seemed to me to be true, which just goes to show how much the mind can distort our thoughts and our perceptions. At my death in this story my wife saved me by pulling me out of a bubble just before I had my head chopped off. I rose above earth knowing I would have to wait to stop the three from carrying out what was their long-term aim. At first they just wanted to amuse themselves and then after they had done everything that there demented minds could muster they knew for them the only way they could leave this planet was to totally destroy it.

With this story going on in my head there was also a line that kept repeating, which was, "Remember the first day - Remember the first day!" Because we had more powers than the inhabitants of the planet it was easy for my children to indulge in their pleasures and cause great misery on a scale which they could not care less about. They introduced into these poor primitive being's minds anything that appealed to them, such as rape, torture, murder and any degrading act that their whims led them to. They also helped the inhabitants to progress in a way that would make it easy for them to leave by the destruction of the planet and life on this planet. The human race was being guided but did not have the intelligence to work out that they were being led into a situation that would result in the total extinction of their race. The three played at being gods and no-one could stop the great cruelty they inflicted on this sorry race. They knew when they finally got bored with this planet they would now be able to leave behind earth to go travelling through the Cosmos again. I could only put my foot through the spokes the once, so I had to wait for my moment while I watched their personal quest for entertainment. They had helped the primitive life forms develop from their various ape forms so they could control and guide them into the direction they would want them to take eventually. They were the rulers of the planet and were able to use thought control over their subjects. The cruelty they were capable of knew no bounds and many things they did were copied by the lesser life forms who were the humans. They had a great time playing god and abusing the power they were born with, which was beyond the human mind's comprehension. It seemed that the only thing that could stand in their way was little old me. This meant I had to be very careful as I only had once chance of halting the destruction of this planet. After all the waiting could I really manage to get into a body and change the direction that the world was being led to? It was time for action and try to stop The Unfab Three from carrying their well made plans.

All the screams I heard in my years of waiting came to me from the planet below me and hit a sensitive nerve in my soul. They would stop at nothing to move the world into a dead end that the humans could no longer control with total destruction being the only outcome. The misery they inflicted to advance scientific research bothered them not one bit. They played through the ages at being kings and gods who had been obeyed and wrought millions of deaths on the natural inhabitants of this planet. It was called progress, but one does ask for whom, and the only answer is for all three evil minds. No atrocity was too great to inflict in order to be able to leave and go star trekking as they had done with my wife and I in the past. I felt I owed a debt to this primitive race who had been taught that trust and dignity were something that could not be allowed to be, and instead in there place they put fear and envy before them so looked at the world in a cheap and small minded way. To try and balance up all the things would not be an easy thing to accomplish, if they learned of my existence before I could do my stuff it would end for us all in failure. I would have to choose wisely the body I entered, and of course, the time. It seemed when I had decided to do my bit the world was close to destroying itself with me still being in nappies when the Cuban Missile Crisis came to centre stage of the world. I might not get my chance to alter the balance, but the whole episode blew over and I was on course yet again. When I was about eleven years old I can recall thinking that the world could be blown up, this was when President Nixon was in Office, and it was said that all he had to do was press a button to start the destruction of the world. I went on a downer over this and thought what is the point in going to school if the world ends tomorrow? I might as well be enjoying myself, than being fed up and miserable attending school.

These thoughts stayed with me a long time and I was full of doom and gloom. It was very difficult for me to get rid of these really deep thoughts, and I wondered also at the time if I would play a part in all this some day in the future. I was certainly here, which was one of the few things that I didn't doubt at the time. Even from this early age I was getting round to my favourite question of over twenty five years of asking what am I doing here, and why was I born. I sure was deep, even from an early age and knew that I was different, but could never quite figure out what it was, yet I never liked being messed about by anyone.

Returning to my mission, it was all down to me to give the maligned human race a shot in the arm. Only I knew the true cost that had been run up by my cruel and evil children. This story was unravelling inside my head and I truly believed at one stage of my stay in hospital that I made contact with the Mother of Creation herself. Even before I got to the hospital I had thought that I was indeed in touch with the Big Momma herself who would reward my efforts if I was successful in carrying out my mission. One of the things in my corner was also that from an early age I was a very bad loser but very much a keen competitor. I got very upset when I did not win in the games I would play with friends and my reputation for being a very poor loser was well known, but I was a very good winner. Well you can't be good at everything. So my mission was to stop the three from carrying out their plan to escape and go travelling through the galaxy again. The plan I had in mind was one that was simple and obtainable if I kept myself together and didn't loose the thought of who I was. The three, if my plan was to succeed, would not know of my existence till it was too late to do anything about it. Even with their vast abilities to push the world to the edge of destruction I could still thwart their plan. The hurt and wounded, because of the systems they lived by, would try in their own way to put me off my plan, but I had hidden my sensitivity so I could not be got at and fortunately I have a big back. Keeping track of the game was not that easy at certain times but because I had made it all into a game it was a lot easier to get through it. The three thought that it was just a matter of time before they would be released by the destruction of the earth. It all revolved around whether I had enough time to pay back what I owed and make people happy and glad to be alive through my power. I had taken on an anchor role, which carried so much responsibility that had not surprisingly led the more negative thoughts in my mind to the conclusion that I must be mad to think that I could make a difference to the scheme of things. I have spent a lifetime running away from responsibility because I already had plenty to handle. I tried in a way to run away from myself and I hoped the day would soon come when I could be like everyone else and face up to weaknesses, fears and use my humour to combat everyday life. Of course though this is a hard story to believe in, that no-one else in the world knew that a bigger game had been taking place right under their noses. By carrying out my task the three would die and disappear forever and that would be the end of the unhappy saga. When I said that I went back to the Mother of Creation, I really meant to say my wife who I put at the beginning of this story, that she said to me, "Mother weeps no more!" This message was for my benefit. The way I hid in the background gave me a stance in life, which let me have more freedom and also a lot less likely to be put under scrutiny. One such part of being invisible in a crowd was when I had long hair at school and no-one mentioned the fact which, with the strictness of the school I went to, was a minor miracle. So in the main I was very anonymous and felt that this was the best way to be and did not draw attention to myself in my time at the school.

The way the plan came together as I had planned it to meant I had stopped the three from leaving and existing any more. This thought of getting to the post first was something that went through my mind when I was throwing the paint around the Art Room, and at last drawing attention to myself. From that moment everything worked itself out very satisfactorily. I felt I had defeated my foes in getting across the winner's line the first and at the same time I had paid back what I owed with the weight of my responsibility being released very soon off my weary shoulders.

This story in my stay at the Hospital to do with a wife and three children came to me in my state of drugged sedation, it was an interesting thought and I did believe I was going to get a replacement for the wife I had lost. I had made a woman who looked remarkably like my wife in appearance at least. She had to have a vitality and look vulnerable with watery eyes and this was of course Catherine. I felt that I wasn't going to go through my ordeal without getting something out of it for myself. This part also took a lot of planning and pulling together, but it came along and looked like a perfect fit to me. Not only was I getting a great weight off my shoulders but I was getting back the woman of my dreams into the bargain, also I was going to get a house built for me for payment for my deed. Things in my life were certainly looking up and the pain I was having at the time didn't seem like much to pay to get to the parts of what I had always wanted. Of course there were other thoughts also coming to mind that my life was one big nightmare and the truth was that I was always running away from reality and going for fantasy in its place. Which of these two thoughts was the more believable, when asking the question things didn't seem too clever for our Wayne, that's for sure. Was it all a game, or was I going out of my head? With me being a depressive wanker who had suffered so many knock backs in my life, that a final straw had broke my mind and I had gone off my trolley in the process. The conclusion, if you can call it that, being a bit of both, maybe there had been a sort of game that only a few knew about, one thing for sure was that I was a depressive wanker. In saying all that I did feel - and I didn't think it had anything to do with the drugs I was on -

that there was something, or some power that had help pull all the things together in such a precise and a meaningful way. Did I once have a wife who I lost in another time who I missed for an eternity? There certainly didn't seem to be any concrete answers, even though with some more of the reactions I got from other people, it seemed clear that something was known and all I did wasn't something that just appeared out of the blue. Some of my work mates seemed to know about my story and, for that matter, so did my dad. The dressing gown that he had been keeping for me was not the only thing he knew that I needed, or wanted for that matter.

He came in the first week of my stay in Hospital when I was in a more coherent state than I had been some of the time. He just came out with "What's her name son?" I told him it was Catherine and I also told him her address. I knew that he did visit her and he also visited one of my History lecturers to find out what he knew about my illness. I was terrible towards my parents and brother when they came to see me because I would always be asking them about Catherine and when could I see her. They would tell me after I asked about Catherine that "She doesn't love you, Wayne!" I never took this as an answer at the time and I know it upset my brother, even though he did give me a different reply one time and that was "She's gorgeous, Wayne!" This confirmed to me that some of my assumptions about what was going on around me were not too far off the mark. This slight intrigue gave me something to think about and after my brother told me Catherine looked gorgeous I felt really good inside.

By paying people back I felt that it was only right that I got something I wanted out of the deal, and there was nothing I wanted more than Catherine. Throughout my stay, I only looked forward to our time together. There was, of course, a small matter of a house that I asked for which I have not received, but as long as I got Catherine I would have been happy to live in a tent with her by my side. So, in the final straight I certainly had some incentive in front of me which made the pain a little bit more bearable. I never mentioned the story of being from another planet to anyone and I kept any thoughts that were on the dodgy side to myself. The last thing I wanted was for my illness to be made into something that seemed more serious than it already was. I did go through a period of believing I was from Egyptian times, in the Cleopatra era. The thought running through my mind was that I had been a right hand man to a Queen. This meant I took orders from women and I played out a game of having to get permission from one of the night staff women to go into the kitchen. When given the nod, I entered the kitchen and it reminded me of a spaceship and sooner than later we would gain lift off. I think I've said this already, but it goes to show how confused and muddled my thoughts were and similar lines of thought came to my mind to repeat my actions. Talking about

157

lift off reminds me of one night when it was Anne and Barbara on night duty and Barbara teased me about when I was going to take us high by running around the hospital as I had done in Hillsborough Park. I certainly was seen as a great amusement to the staff. If I had tried to explain some of my deeper thoughts of what was going on in my mind, I would have no doubt have been laughed at some more. One thing they asked though, in my time at the hospital, was "Are you hearing voices?" Of course I never did, and I wondered what they were going on about as I was asked each day. After having so many uncertainties going through my head all day I really wanted to escape from my body that was aching all over the place and the strain that my mind was going through made it seem I was living in hell. At times, when the pain increased, I went back to thinking that I was being punished again and that my whole life was one big disaster area with me never getting anywhere. After one of these days of going over my past, or having memories of some past existence, I would try to take my mind off any subject that was bothering me and go and watch some television. Going to the television room in the beginning was an ordeal in itself, with my legs forever jumping about all over the place. I don't rightly remember what I watched, it was the usual drivel but I did upset some of the other patients by laughing at some of the programmes even when they were not comedy programmes but were serious dramas. The night staff didn't mind though because they knew where I was, which was something I suppose. This part of going to the television room became part of my routine just as the queue for the tablets was. When I tried to go to bed I would eat some chocolate and drink some shandy which seemed to rest my mind, if nothing else. This might not seem much to you but it helped me at least find some rest during the night. One night there was part of the curtain that could go right around the whole bed torn, and I pulled a strip off. I wrapped the strip of curtain around me in the way gangster had their guns under their arms in the movies. I told the night staff - who were Anne and Barbara on this particular night - that I was playing a game that had me as an agent in The Man from Uncle. I must have been going through my second childhood, what do you mean, I've never finished my first yet? I had made a mess of my bed, and the male nurse who was also on duty this night remade it for me, saying he wouldn't do it for just anyone. It seemed that everyone wanted to take the piss out of me, just for a change. I started to wonder if I had a beacon on top of my head that proclaimed "Mug!" Some of the reactions I got from people certainly made it seem possible and not just some flight of fancy on my part. Having rested, if not exactly getting to sleep, I would be wide awake by the morning, which was something I looked forward to of course with great glee. Sometimes I would look through the window to see the night change to day, and I even saw a little rabbit running around one morning, the excitement was never ending, you might think. It was wash time and clean the teeth time and I attempted to shave myself. I made my way down to the dining room, which thankfully didn't involve queuing for breakfast. In the main, I was interested in the tea more than something to eat. With me being early, there was hardly anyone to share a pot of tea with, so I got one all to myself. After the breakfast, it was back to my ward again, and, just for a change, waiting around for the tablets yet again. Then it would be the exercise class for me on the five days a week that it was open.

In the main, the class was taken by Sarah, but on a few occasions there was a stand in. Trying to stretch my body at that time was no easy step for me to take as my body, as I've said before, was sore and stiff. After the class I went for a walk instead of going to the Art Room. While I walked I started to wonder why, when I was in such a confused state, that the story of me stopping my own children destroying the world had been so clear and had seemed so real when it was nothing but a load of rubbish that I had somehow made up. Something that was to be said to me on my time on the council came to mind, it was said by a man who knew what I was attempting, and he said "They done his woman wrong, and he always pays his debits!" What did he know that I didn't, and if it has no significance then why did he say it and I can still remember it so clearly. Maybe someone knows why I was born with this power and not you, or was it just a matter of drawing the short straw? Is there something I should know and have not been told? The whole thing sounds like a fairy story anyway. The youngish prince battles with the demons of hell and manages to destroy them all and release the people who had feared them. In this Kingdom there is a beautiful Princess who is promised to the man who could slay the demons and not forgetting the castle that the victor is to be given for carrying out the deed. They undoubtedly live happily ever after. How can a real life enhance such a story of events and be reality, for surely such thoughts if deeply embedded can only be by someone looking over the precipice of their sanity. Or were fairy stories true stories in the beginning which were added to along the seeds of time? Could it be others like myself had done deals and been paid for their services? Or was I another person who couldn't take the modern day stress and pressure situations? Someone who would be looking for an answer to life and who couldn't accept the truth about myself so I had created a fantasy world where I could rule and be looked up to by my subjects. Was my love for Catherine just a figment of my imagination, or just a very good looking girl who I had taken a fancy to and didn't know how to say that I loved her. The fact that I had in some way been waiting to meet her was just a story I had told myself to get around my inadequacy and my lack of female company. That my breakdown had been planned by me and in some way I was in control of what was going on around me, was this just another story, to hide me away from the fact that I had been ill and couldn't pull myself together to stop going out of my mind. Had the whole thing been a mental charade to hide my weakness, that was not being able to cope with reality, so I had gone into myself and created a fantasy world to live in, that would protect me from the outside world that was too real for me to live in. This was the counter argument of the thoughts that were going on inside my head, to which thoughts were the more believable. Did I really have some great power that had been given to me and none of my contemporaries, or was I just playing out a delusion that my mind had come up with to protect my insanity. When I was first admitted to the hospital, they had told my family that I was suffering from the delusion of grandeur and that I was hyper manic in my actions. This explained away the high that I had been on when being admitted to the hospital.

After tackling these heavy thoughts and not getting too far with them, I returned to what it was going to be like when I got Catherine by my side after all the histrionics were over. No amount of illness was going to stand in my way from getting the thing I wanted most from this world. This was the recurring good thought that gave me a little clarity, if not total, and made some sense out of the nonsense that daily would fill my thoughts.

The hospital were now letting me go home at the weekends which was something to look forward to, but I was still in poor shape. I had to take my tablet that had been prescribed for me, which were still at a fairly heavy dose. My body was still shaking about and I couldn't sit in chairs at home because at the time they were still uncomfortable. After getting out of bed on Saturday morning I would go downstairs from my bedroom and have a couple of cups of tea. In the main, I would feel tired so I would go back to my room and lay on my bed. This was the way it was, I think my body was trying to catch up with all the sleep I had not had for months. I would get up off my bed in the afternoon and go and watch something on the television, sat on the floor, in the living room. My meal at dinner time was a lot better than the one I would have gotten at the hospital. I didn't go much further when I went out than Hillsborough Park because I felt frail and vulnerable. When I had been out for a walk I usually went back to my bedroom to lay down again. After having my Sunday dinner - which was, and still is my favourite meal of the week - I would be taken back to the hospital. To start again to somehow pass the time as there was plenty of it. At the Monday meeting after we had lined up for our tablets we were reminded by the staff that exercises and the morning sessions were to help get the patients into a better shape and make for a quicker recovery. What it all boiled down to was that some of the patients were not taking part in the activities and so were not gaining the benefits from the workouts. I went from this meeting for the exercise class which was being taken by Sarah. After the attempt of moving my body through many contortions, the relaxation tape was put on which told you breathe out and breath in and to rest. When the tape had finished the class started to leave the room and go to whatever activity they were prepared to have a go at that day. I stayed behind to talk to Sarah and I can recall we talked about movies and she told me the flat she was staying at was being over-run by some cats she had agreed to look after for a friend who had gone on holiday.

When we eventually made our way to the Art Room, which we were alone in, I said something to Sarah which, even now, makes me wince. I said "Do you want to fuck?" She, not surprisingly, didn't reply and I said it again, "Do you want to fuck?"! The next day I apologized for what I said the previous day and hoped it wouldn't spoil our relationship as Sarah, as I have already said, was my favourite person who I met in my stay at the hospital. Thankfully, she forgave me and would still knock me to see if I was alive while I was making my man with his arms in the air out of clay in the workshop.

The days were ticking away and I could see a gradual improvement in myself, which was real, and not something that I was making up. One of the better things we did was to have the session that we took on a Wednesday afternoon, where we talked about ourselves in a group of six patients and two carers. Because we were a small group it made it easier to discuss what was on our minds and talk about the situations that had led to our illnesses. The carers also talked about themselves, to say what their plans were for the future and how they had overcome problems in the past and that we all experience disappointments.

When the session was over we all made our way to the dining room to get a cup of coffee and a biscuit if we were quick enough. One day, very late in my stay at the hospital, I can remember thinking that a man, who asked if he could sit behind me, was the devil himself. When I was in the dining room having coffee he approached me. He had hairs that must have been an inch long on parts of his face and he looked grotty. Why I thought he was the Devil I really don't know the answer, but it certainly put my nerves on edge and after a few minutes of him being beside me I left for the toilet where I locked the door of the loo. Someone came into the toilet and banged on the door and thankfully that was the end of it. It was a reminder to me of how far I had taken my mind to the very edge of sanity and how I had strange thoughts and flights of fancy due to my illness. I told my dad when he visited me that night and he told me I was being silly and of course that's what I was being and quite quickly I didn't hold onto the idea for very long and now it makes me laugh that I could have thought that some poor bugger was the Devil. The man must have thought the way I looked at him and left him after just a few minutes, that I was a right basket case. When I was having my dinner one night in the dining room I overheard a man say "If he pulls this off, he's king!" to the man sitting next to him. I don't know what it was that other people could see when they looked at me that made me stand out in the world. As far as I could see I was just the same person I had always been except for my lack of any movement and the aches and pains that my body was going through. But there was definitely something about my appearance that was drawing attention to me, or I was just being paranoid. I didn't ask anyone about my concern over my appearance that set me out from the rest.

The build up to the evening meal was always the same when the playtime part of the hospital was closed we made our way back to ward 54. It would now appear to be the slowest part of the day when waiting for grub up. I would end up watching the aptly titled programme Countdown. Sometimes I didn't feel like getting into the long queue so I instead went outside for a walk around the hospital. When I returned I would walk straight into the dining room. When all said and done it was not the most appetising food that I have had put in front of me in my life. Instead of the set meal, you could have a choice of a salad if you were quick enough, but who wants to eat something that wouldn't fill a sparrow. At least they couldn't mis-cook the bread and butter. It was not the cook's fault that the budget wouldn't cover us having better food on our plates. The carers would line up at the bottom of the dining room and help the less able to move back to their wards when they had finished their dinners. The older patients made for a noisy crowd, who were always complaining. First they would complain about coming to the dining room, then the food wasn't being brought to them fast enough, then when they got their dinner they didn't like it. You can't please some folk any time it would seem.

When I had finished my dinner, or more realistically I had eaten what I could and left a fair bit on my plate, which was something I had never done in my life, I would make my way back to my ward, sometimes taking the lift. There wasn't much to do now other than playing Trivial Pursuits or watching television. The ward took on a more sweetly sickly smell after dinner and I would, if it was still light outside, go for a walk around the block so to speak. Of course I'm forgetting my daily visit from my family. After the weekend of spending my time at my mother's it was the turn of my dad to come and see me. He sometimes didn't come alone bringing his fiancée Maureen with him and some sweets for me. He brought me some butter scotch sweets which I chomped when I put them in my mouth and never just sucked them as you are supposed to. I don't remember much of what was said, but we didn't always spend our time on my ward but went for walks around the corridors to the main door downstairs. I think I didn't do much of the talking in these visits which was nothing new to me as I've only ever been able to talk to three friends that I have known in my life. It was a good thing to get a visit from one of my parents on alternate days and my brother, who came on Fridays. It broke up the night a little bit and made me not to just remember the things that had shaped my life in a selfish way. One time when my brother visited I can recall that we were walking around the corridors of the Hospital when I could hardly move my legs so we had to go and sit down which was still very uncomfortable for me to put up with. The hardest part of the visits from my family were when they left because I always felt like I wanted to leave myself. But for me this couldn't be the case, I had to go through with it; still I was on more of an even keel. When they had left it was me all on my todd again with just George to talk to, which I didn't mind or go and watch some rubbish on television, for I didn't want to play Trivial Pursuits because I didn't want to have to think about anything. I just wanted to try and make my mind a blank and shut everything off inside and so not feel any pain at all from either my head or my body; well that was the idea at any rate.

When the night staff were not Anne and Barbara there was a woman who was in her fifties and an Asian looking man who smoked a pipe. I can recall saying to the woman that I could not sleep and she said she would make me a cup of tea if I stayed at my bed because she didn't want me to fall over. They were not as likable as Anne and Barbara and they didn't want me to sit at the table with them, so I would go into one of the rooms on the ward that had plenty of chairs to choose from to sit down on. This sort of night I was going through at the time was typical of most of my stay at the Hospital. The only other patient who didn't seem to sleep was someone I called Mick the Knife. He always seemed to move in a slither carrying his radio cassette player around with him all the time. At one time I thought he was a murderer for some silly reason, but he did even in my time at the hospital seem a little odd. These nights would drag so much at times it felt unbearable, but somehow I pulled through. Catherine was never out of my thoughts for too long and when I thought she had been at the hospital I thought I would meet her any day soon. I sometimes thought that I would be released and then in the next thought that they would want to keep me as some sort of guinea pig in order to find out more about me. That was very much in my mind a lot and would television get in on the act with them wanting to film me. Thankfully these unpleasant thoughts were totally out of my fears of not trusting the people around me. When inside the room I was in I thought a lick of paint in the room and throughout the hospital wouldn't come amiss. It was certainly a long time overdue in my time there. Plus none of the equipment worked, and the snooker table had been ripped to shreds. Well, I suppose we weren't there to be happy and contented because I sure wasn't. The night rolled on and the damp that came from the dew when things were starting to become a little lighter was a rather mystical happening, or that's how it seemed to me. I would go down to the ground level and just look around me at a sort of shining little stars effect that it looked like on the grounds of the hospital. It looked like someone had been out with buckets of glitter which they had thrown all around the grass and weeds. There I would be in my pyjamas and dressing gown taking it all in, thinking to myself what a great sight that I had overlooked in the past. The hospital was so quiet at the time with there being so little movement from the other patients. After looking outside, I made my way back to my ward. There was still plenty of time till the other patients got up so I could take my time in the bathroom doing the usual of brushing my teeth, having a wash and trying to shave so I did not cut myself, which is something that I mostly do not seem capable of doing. I went around the ward many times pulling the towels off the metal ring that they were wrapped round, which must have made me popular with the other patients, this was also part of my mornings most of the time. Well it kept me busy. The boring monotony of it all, doing the same things again and again, day after day and night after night. There must be better ways of making a living, but it seems someone forgot to tell me what they are. If only I could have been born with the ability to be a footballer, but I suppose we have to accept the gifts we are given, and I should be thankful that I was given such an unusual gift. There had been times in the past when I had thought to myself, I'll show them that they were wrong about me and did not know the full story of what I was attempting. I have written about the fact that I had many doubts about whether I was sane but I also had doubts about whether I could get through it all because it was literally mind blowing in both senses of the word. That I who had been a bare arse painter, had seen off everyone on the final straight to go into a world that I imagine very few people who have ever lived on this planet have been through was an uplifting feeling even when I was suffering in pain. How many of the people who had known me through my life had took one look at me and thought "there goes a dopey lazy bastard who you don't want to know if you can help it"? Here I was having the piss taken out of me admittedly, but most definitely being looked up to by the nurses and carers who surrounded me. There's no doubt about it, it's a funny old world.

The next day, before dinner I was told to go with a male nurse to the entrance of the hospital. So I changed my new slippers for shoes and we both made our way to the entrance, or exit in our case. There was a cab waiting for us when we go there and we both climbed into the back seats in the cab. We were so the male nurse now told me to go to the Hallamshire hospital where I was going to have a brain scan, which was a routine measure. The nurse said we were waiting for another patient to come with us who also needed a brain scan. I then said "He's not coming!", and after about five minutes of waiting we started the journey without the other patient. When we were still in the hospital grounds the taxi driver said "I'd do anything for him", referring to me I think, or was it just another case of paranoia? The traffic in town was as busy as ever and at times it might have been better if we had walked. Even so, we seemed to be soon at the Hallamshire Hospital and getting out of the cab. The hospital was very busy with many people about. Me and the nurse waited for a lift to take us to the floor where the brain scanning equipment was. Once on the right floor, a lady was waiting for us and I was led into a dark room which I don't think, if I remember correctly, had any windows. I was shown the chair that I was to sit on while the lady Doctor put probes about my head which all joined up to make a net sort of effect. The nurse, I think, just opened the door a little to see if I was alright and closed it again. There was in the dark a flash of light, or so I thought, and that was that except for my complaint of my head hurting while the Doctor put the probes on me and now took them quickly off my head. There was a curly line on the x-ray print and the Doctor said that it was the normal pattern for someone who is still sane. Thank goodness for that. I felt afterwards at least I hadn't damaged my brain even though it felt like my head was going to explode at times during my ordeal. The Doctor or technician for that matter told the nurse who had come with me the good news. When we got down into the hospital foyer again the taxi was not there so we had some time to kill. I started arranging some of the furniture because I thought it was not laid out straight enough. The taxi was at the foyer entrance after about ten minutes and we made our way back to the Northern General. This was good news, and when my mum came that evening, being her turn, she was glad when I told her the news. We walked outside on this night and sat on a bench overlooking lots of grass and it was a bit warmer now coming up to summer. When my Mother left me, I went back to my ward and watched some television, until it was tablet time, after which I changed into my pyjamas and tried to sleep in my bed.

The following day I was in the workshop building my man still out of clay, with Sarah for company. The workshop supervisor was talking about some of the models previous patients had made and then told us about a model he had just finished. There was a locked cage at the back of the room with a padlock on the door. He unlocked the door and brought out his model of a woman on a rock, which was nude and it looked fantastic. I told him that I thought it was great and then he said "It's not as good as you though son!" I thought about what he had said to me and I thought it was conformation that Catherine had been at the Hospital. I had felt I could sense her presence, not necessarily at the same time as me but that she had been to the Hospital at some time over the last few days. Of course it could well have been my imagination working overtime, yet why had the workshop supervisor said "It's not as good as you though son!" to me. Maybe I'll never know an answer but I was convinced that Catherine had been close by. At one stage, I felt I had found her room on another ward in the hospital, yet I could not prove it because she wasn't there at the time I was. I was always the same when I was at a loose end, I would revert to thinking about Catherine and how it would be after Hospital. Not just Catherine, the house as well which I had asked to be built for my services. Just think, here I am with my daydreaming and knowing my luck something isn't going to work out even after everything as so far, something is bound to go wrong somewhere. Well back to trying to make my man and getting through the day with my favourite person at the hospital, Sarah. She was always good at giving me a nudge and laughing at my exercising my very stiff body to the pop music beat.

On a day I remember very late on in my stay at the hospital I was in the workshop when I decided that I didn't want to do any pot modelling and I didn't want to do any painting either. So I went to join a small group in the yard which was near the dining hall in the hospital. The group were listening to music and were supposed to be dancing, or at least trying to dance to the music. No one before I got there had tried to dance. I felt like I wanted to have a go and with the help of an older woman I started to dance with my partner to the sound of the music. The woman was wearing a very long coat and I hadn't seen her before, so I thought that she was probably an out patient. When the music finished, both me and the woman sat down. No one got up for the next piece of music that was played but then the woman who I had danced with got up and danced with the carer this time round the yard. The reason that I think she was an out patient also is that I saw the woman waiting for a bus one day wearing the same long coat which I think she lived in. In fact I think that to get the coat off her back would have taken surgery. The music lesson fizzled out and I made for my ward and to my bed where I flung myself to rest and if really lucky get some sleep. Whilst I was lying on my bed and not feeling sociable Thomas came for a day visit on the ward but I stayed on my bed and ignored him. This was I think as sure as I am, my last week of my time at the hospital, which I wish I had known. I can recall the man in the next bed to mine getting a visit from a vicar which was something I was glad had not happened to me. I would not have been pleased to see someone from the church and would not have given such a person the time of day. When I got up off the bed and about to go into the television room an old man cried out to me "But I don't believe!", "Neither do I !", I replied. That'll teach him for not going BUPA. But you only ever get this done on the NHS because after all such a thing is for all and not just for the few who can pay a lot more than the usual Joe and Jill average, so now you know.

The weekend drew near and I was looking forward to spending it away from the hospital. One of the doctors asked me to go into a room and said that he was going to take some blood from my right arm; this seemed a little odd as I had been a blood donor and they always took the blood from my left arm. I rolled up my shirt and using needles to extract the blood the doctor started. The blood that had come out first was blue, then it was yellow when he used another needle to extract the blood. I can't remember if other colours came out, but it all seemed to fit into the colours of the rainbow. Of course you might think it was a hallucination on my part, but I know it was for real. The blood as I read the situation would now be injected into Catherine so I could have an equal by my side. It was all over in a few minutes and the right arm where the blood was taken from would hurt from time to time for a couple of years. With my blood in Catherine's body she could be prepared for me when I left the hospital and everything would be fine between us.

With it being Friday I was picked up and taken to my mother's for the weekend with my tablets in hand of course. I still had great difficulty trying to sit down on the chairs at my mother's and I would just sit down on the floor if it got unbearable. There wasn't that much to do at my mother's, but it was nice to be home and sleep in my own bed again. The best thing at my mother's was the Sunday roast dinner, my favourite meal of the week. When I went back to the hospital on Sunday night I had no idea it would be my last night at the hospital. The morning came and after breakfast the same doctor who had extracted my blood took my blood pressure and said that I could leave at long last the hospital. I managed to get a black bag from the cleaning lady to put my stuff in and I made my way to the bus stop after saying some goodbyes. I was running trying to catch the bus I wanted and ran straight into a bollard and got a very big bruise for my troubles. I made it home eventually and was very glad to do so. Of course I would still have to take tablets and see Dr Lancer every two weeks to check on my progress. I don't think it had sunk in how much had been taken from me but I was soon going to find out, that's for sure. The hospital part was over though and I was glad about that at least.

6 Post Hospital

After being released on the Monday all I could think of was seeing Catherine on the Tuesday. I did not sleep well but there was nothing original about that. When it was half past six, Tuesday morning, I got out of my bed, dressed and went downstairs to make a pot of tea and had a couple of slices of toast. On the bus going to town I wondered if I would see Catherine before she reached college. I didn't, and she wasn't in the history class when I arrived but when I felt she wasn't going to turn up she entered the classroom. Geoff Hammond took the class so it was on European History but I took little notice of the lesson. It was time to have our morning break so we all made our way to the large dining room at the college. Catherine sat on another lad's knee next to me as we took over a couple of tables and in between them was Geoff Hammond who asked me "Are you alright?" To which I replied, "Yes!" I asked Catherine how she was keeping and she sort of mumbled that she was fine. I don't know what the rest of the class thought was going on and for that matter I don't care either. The rest of the lesson after the break passed me by and I can recall writing down very little in my folder. Catherine was staying at the college for dinner because she had another lesson in the afternoon to attend. I made my way home and went to my bed and rested till teatime; it might have seemed that it took only a little effort on my part but the day had taken so much out of me. The fact is it was only the start of realising how much had been taken out of me by my ordeal. After tea, I got changed and told my mum that I was going to Catherine's house. The bus couldn't arrive quickly enough to take me up to the top of Stannington. When I knocked on Catherine's door her mother answered and I asked her if I could talk to Catherine. She looked great, wearing a pair of jeans and a denim shirt when she came out and she wasn't wearing any shoes. I said to her "Mind your feet!" as we sat down on a small wall at the side of her house because there were many small stones around on the pavement. I asked her if she was feeling all right. She said she was and brought up a matter that had been bothering her. She said "I don't like the way Graham keeps putting me on his knee". I told her "He's only a gorilla and he doesn't mean you any harm!" I was very big at the time with seeing everyone in their particular group of being an ape. I asked her to come out with me but she said that some other lad was already coming to see her. I felt very deflated and thought "This isn't the way it's going to be is it? I haven't gone to hell and back for no reward have I?" as I walked away from Catherine's. I went in the Hare and Hounds Pub and had a pint even though I wasn't supposed to drink with the tablets I was taking. At that moment in time I felt really down and I was glad that the pub was empty. When I finished my beer I walked all the way down the hill to go back to my mother's. I didn't go to college again that term so I missed the 'A' level exams that were not too far away. When I went to see my own Doctor - a lady doctor called Livingstone - she couldn't believe that I had even tried to go back to college. It was the first time I could remember us meeting but she had met me before at the Northern General Hospital on the Friday I was admitted because she had to be present when they put me on Section 28 of the Mental Health Act. Of course, I didn't remember our previous meeting even though she certainly did. I had not stopped seeing the psychiatrist, Doctor Lancer just because I was no longer at hospital; I had to see him every two weeks at the Hallamshire Hospital to check my progress. My mother would also come with me because obviously she was still very concerned about my condition, which wasn't as good as I believed it was. The tablets I was taking would slowly be reduced over a period of time and I still hated taking them.

With me not hitting if off with Catherine at the first attempt, which I only thought of as a minor setback to the overall plan, I started to visit my sister's house who only lived the other side of Hillsborough Park from my Mother's. My sister had a video recorder, whereas my mother didn't, even though it was me who had said that a video was not necessary! The video was a Betamax model, which if you know anything about videos was not the model to buy, but the video shop near my sister's catered for Betamax and VHS. There were plenty of films I hadn't seen so it was something new to me and I was hooked on the idea. We would have baked potatoes for our supper, which were ready in a matter of minutes as they were cooked in the microwave. When it was time for me to go home I was very nervous and wary of meeting anyone. This fear didn't last long but was a reminder to myself of how ill I was and had been. I visited my sister a couple of nights a week and looked forward to seeing films that had passed me by at the cinema. On getting back to my Mother's with no problems but in my imagination I went straight to bed feeling very tired even though I was now a very light sleeper. I thought to myself if I can't sleep I can rest; and that's just what I did. In the days I would sometimes visit my dad's who when he was not at work would be doing something to his house, as DIY was very much his hobby. He was usually to be found on the front of the house at this time breaking up bricks and stones as if he was on a chain gang! I just about had the energy to watch all this activity going on before me. He would tell me some stories about people that I didn't know before he told me. Sometimes the taxi driver who lived across the road called Danny would come over for a chinwag with my Dad during the day. It was good weather because I can recall not wearing a shirt and the bruise I had from running into a bollard the day I left hospital was a blue and black colour and very noticeable, not surprisingly! It was certainly a leisurely day for me and when Maureen came (my dad's lover) she would make us our tea. When it was time to leave my dad would give me a lift back to my mother's. I still had problems with sitting in some of my mother's chairs and so I would sit on a sleeping bag against the cellar door when watching television.

I must admit some of the things that I am going to write may have happened in 1988 and not in 1987. The thing is that it was a time that got condensed together and I cannot be certain as to the year that some events took place but can only say that these events did take place, which at the end of the day is the important point. I was walking through Hillsborough Park one night when it was still very bright when a man about my age came up to me and knew my name. He started to talk about people I had known years before but I couldn't think who he was. To me he was just a stranger as far as my memory was concerned. The man was in charge of a group of lads playing football and he asked me if I wanted to join them. I told him I had been ill and that I was going to my sister's so I moved on and when I arrived at my sister's, told her the whole story. I have never seen him again to this day and it's very irritating when someone knows you but you cannot place them.

I really enjoyed my visits to my sister's, whom before my illness, I had not seen much of since she got married, because I had not gone to see her. On a few occasions my brother also turned up to watch a video with us regulars. The dog, Chip, was always glad to see anyone and always made a big fuss when you entered the house. I can recall the video packing up one evening and somehow my brother and sister got it to work again, which was a good job because the video we had rented was Raiders of the Lost Ark.

I think in what I've written in this chapter already, that we were a strong family unit, in our way and I was very aware at this time how it was so important that I got as much support that was going. When I got up in a morning all I could think about was going back to bed because I felt so drained. It was something that was very hard to come to terms with and was going to continue for a longer time than I could have imagined. The fact is, because I self induced my illness in order to get admitted into hospital in the first place, I thought I could control everything, and once I left hospital the whole episode would be over and I could forget that it ever took place. This might have been what I thought inside my head but was sadly a million miles away from the truth. The events that I had performed had taken everything; I was just a discarded shell of a person. I never gave it much thought that to do what I did would require me giving away all my strength both mentally and physically. The gulf between the person I had been before to what was left after could not have been anymore telling. To destroy a nervous system in order to gain redemption for John Edwards seemed rather a big price to have to pay and I could never have known the aftermath to come because if I had I might have well chosen a different path through life. But this is one big if, I did destroy my nervous system and I have to live with the consequence of my actions, as everyone has to do in life. In the main, I didn't want to be in an area where there was a lot of people about so I would just go for walks in Hillsborough Park and sit and watch the ducks like I had done years previously when I was at work and wagging it, and in times when I was unemployed. I would go on a lot about Catherine and my mum and brother were fed up with hearing about her. My brother even told me he wanted to leave because of the whole thing that had happened in the last few months. My sister was planning to move to Norfolk to live, but this did not have anything to do with me. When they flitted, my brother and mother went down to Norfolk to help them with moving their possessions into their new home. They also got help from some of their friends. When I say I helped them move, I was not in much of a state to lift things and when the sofa was put inside their new home I was very quickly sat on it. For me, it was a simple matter of hanging in there as I had very little energy in me. Some people who I have known would say I never had any energy when they knew me either but then I was conserving my energy for the day when it would be far more useful. The place my sister and brother-in-law moved to in Norfolk was very much a place where you needed a car to get about in. My sister managed to get a transfer from the TSB in Sheffield where she had worked to a branch in Diss so she would have no problems with having to find a job. My brother-in-law also had a paint-spraying job at a garage lined up so they were fine in the work department. We stayed for a few days down there before making our way home.

I visited my dad's and he was in front of his house breaking up bricks as usual for the foundations to cement a large part of the front garden. On top of that would be paving stones to make a patio. Jokingly, he told me when he had finished it he was going to have fairground lights, plus some chairs and a table, with music playing in the background. The real reason he wanted the front patio was if he got permission to build a path from the road he could then park the car on the front of the house instead of parking on the busy road. With my sister gone I had little to do at night other than watch some television or go to my bed to rest. I had lost contact with most of my friends and I started to go out with my brother and his friends, which my brother didn't like, so it didn't last long. The visits to see Doctor Lancer were still going on and I needed to see a specialist about my left leg. I had been dragging my leg since leaving the hospital and I had put a hole in my shoe through its extra workload. The specialist took about five minutes of doing some tests and told me that it would clear up in time and that it was nothing to worry about. This was at least some good news in the midst of the realisation of the damage that had been done to me in carrying out my destiny.

I was in my mum's bedroom looking out of the window one night when I saw a shape that looked familiar to me. It looked like Catherine rolling dice sitting on the kerb. When I say shape, I do so because it looked more like a hologram than a real person. There was also a male with her but I couldn't make him out so I don't know who he was. I thought that this must be some sort of ritual that had to be carried out so Catherine and I could be together. It made me feel good inside that I had done something that would give me what I wanted after going through my experience, because Catherine was what I wanted from my ordeal. A few days later I was looking out of the same window when Catherine appeared again and did the same thing, sitting on the kerb. Even if she wouldn't go out with me she couldn't, it would seem defy the forces that had been released. I never told anyone what I had witnessed because I didn't want anyone to think I was going mad and suffering with hallucinations.

When I went to see my dad, usually I just watched him do some work, but he did rope me in to help with a fence he was putting up in the back garden. He kitted me out with a pair of overalls to put over my clothes. It was my job to hold the posts in the hole while he made them secure with bricks at their base. He then poured cement into the hole. While I was holding the posts, my legs were swaying backwards and forwards all the time. My legs were still a long way from being normal and I must have upset the part of the nervous system that deals with the legs, amongst other things. The swaying I was going through reminded me of one of the patients at the hospital who was a dosser off the streets. He had been put on medication and he was on the mixed ward, the way he moved the bottom half of his body was really comical and he looked like he was having a shag! It made me laugh at the time so I must have a cruel streak in me to have laughed at him and yet here I was in the same boat going forwards and backwards.

My dad would ask me if I was all right and I would always reply that I was and he would then say, "I wish you were, Son!" In fact, for that matter, when the psychiatrist asked me how I was, I usually replied that I was fine, even though I was a long way from being healthy again. I was still going to see the psychiatrist every two weeks and he told me he could still see the hold the tablets had over me in my face. The months were ticking by and I was thinking of continuing with my 'A' levels so I had something to do with my time. Before that came on the prominent horizon, I got in touch with a group who would try to help you get your bearings back. We went swimming and one time we even went to Matlock in a big van. It was not perhaps for me as the other members of the group were from a different age group and I was the youngest person in the group. One man I was talking to told me his mother had just passed away and was really down about it so much so he wanted to top himself. He was a right bag of laughs - I don't think! When we didn't go for trips we would go to a little room on the back of a nun's house. I rarely said anything on these days as I felt out of place, and in a way, it was depressing. We would always meet on a Monday and there was always a cup of tea on the go, which was probably the only good thing about it. There was a social services man and also a woman who I don't think was full time. He was someone I could talk to now and again and I have seen him since as the office he works from is very near my mother's house.

I was still in a bit of a state at this time and I had lost contact with my friends so it was not too easy to go out once my sister had moved. At the time I didn't feel right in myself so I wasn't too keen to go out on my own. It meant I either spent a lot of time laying on my bed or watching the television over these months. In fact, I felt drained of energy most of the time and it took a long time to sink in that it was going to take a long time for me to be anywhere like normal again. I was keen to go back to college so I could finish the course I had begun over two years ago, and it would give me something to get out of bed for. When I went to enroll again for the English language class, it was still John Edwards who was the main man. I went to the hall where the enrolling was taking place at Stannington College and John Edwards saw me and came up to me. He said, "If it gets too much for you just tell me!" I enrolled for the English language class again and then made for Granville College to enroll again for History. Both Mark Davies and Geoff Hammond were there. I talked a little bit to Mark Davies and got the enrollment out of the way. I had to get a stamp from Peel House on two pieces of paper to verify the fact that I was unemployed and so didn't have to pay for the courses. In fact, it was not very simple because I was on a sickness benefit and it had to be changed to income support in order for me to get the paper stamped. Even though I was not well enough to work at this time, I was still to be put on the dole so I got my courses for free. The courses would begin again in September. I managed to get off taking tablets in August and I thought that it was all over but within a month I was back on them again feeling as bad as before.

My brother did leave and for a time he lived with my sister in Norfolk, to try to find work, which he did do and he's not returned as yet.

It was during the month I was off tablets that I started to go on a binge. I would go for long walks in many directions of the city, stopping in pubs to have a drink or buying a sandwich if I felt hungry. I can recall one day starting off in town at a pub called The Cow, then making my way back to

Hillsborough by going into pubs on the way. When I went into a pub, people would know my name and it made me wonder if I had a beacon on my head. Of course, you could say that I was suffering with a paranoia attack, which is very common in people who have suffered with mental illness. The women would say, "He's so sweet!" or "Isn't he sweet!" If I heard that once I heard it one hundred times! It was strange being recognised wherever you went and I think these and other events took place in 1988, so seeing as I'm not finished with 1987 I will return to these events when I think they took place!

The English class that I returned to had no survivors from the class I had been in, other than myself, of course! I still hadn't finished my project at this time so I still had plenty to do and there was a fair bit that I had forgotten or had not done in my previous time on the course. The history class had one survivor from the group; Jason, who I knew and was the person who gave me Catherine's address the day I first went to see her. Mark Davies was our tutor and in a change from before, he would take us for both the English history part of the course, and the European history part. I think the reason for this was quite clear; Geoff Hammond did not want me in his class because of the effect I had on him when I was getting ready to induce my illness. I had upset his metabolism so much that he probably hated my guts so he had got Mark Davies to take over his part of the course, so he could avoid me. I can recall Mark Davies saying, "You still look depressed in your face!" and I thought to myself so would you if you'd gone through what I have done, but then again, there's very few people who could have gotten through what I had to. That reminds me of one of the visits from my dad when he said, "We never thought you'd get through it all, Son!" whilst I was still in hospital. I can't really say that I was getting much from the course as I had done before but it was good to have something to go to and get me out meeting people again, even though I tended to be on the loner side of things again. There was no one in the daytime course in the English class who I knew but on the nighttime course there was Michael who I could talk to at break times. He was not on my course because he had passed but was working on getting another 'A' level so he could go to the music school he so wanted to join. He knew something about what had taken place with me but I don't think he knew the whole story. I saw him for the first few months but then he stopped coming and I think someone told me he had got a job working for BT. I don't know if he ever got to music school for which he had taken the courses in the first place.

It was strange one night in John Edwards's class because I got the feeling that he was talking just to me in the class. He talked a bit about his childhood, which had no bearing on the course and so he talked about knowing a man when he was a child, which had obviously had an effect on him. I think for some unknown reason he was talking about my granddad. Whether John

Edwards had known my granddad or not I don't know, but he seemed to realise that something was coming his way in the near future from what I had done after he said "Yes please!" and he was right because there was a force coming that would change his and many other people's lives forever. I didn't really exert myself and didn't bother to think much about the courses. In the main, when I did think about something, it was usually Catherine who filled my thoughts. I was also interested in getting my house and I asked my dad on one of my visits and he said, "You've got to wait five years yet!" In the main, like I've already said, Catherine was what I had worked for and I had kept my part of the bargain.

In the English class there was no one who I felt I could talk to other than John Edwards and he seemed to be very busy. I just tried to do my best and get the project and stories finished as best I could under the circumstances. There was still Arthur on the course also who took us for an hour a week. In the main I was just a spectator who rarely had anything to say in class during the term. In the history class, there was Jason, who had failed the exam so he was trying again by doing the course for another year. I didn't feel as isolated in my history class but I took little part in any discussions that might arise from the subject we were dealing with at the time. During one break time, Jason talked about a girl who had been in our class the previous term who had been taken ill so she did not finish her exams, but passed the course because the tutors backed up her term work. The girl in question was, of course, Catherine. When I heard Jason tell one of the other class members it seemed to me to back up my thoughts over the blood that was extracted from my right arm, which had made her ill and it most definitely had been injected into Catherine as I had guessed it had. When college had finished for the day, I made my way home and usually went for a nap when I got home because I was still feeling very tired most of the time. All through the two courses I did no revision in either subject because I was not going to risk a relapse and I didn't think in the same way I had before the illness. Now I felt I had gone far enough through the education system and that I had achieved my true aim in going back to learning. I had no need to go any further and also I didn't feel up to going up a step more in learning. I had reached the plateau that was in front of me for twenty-five years and it was now over.

Not surprisingly, I was just going at my own pace and not the courses. I was more interested in survival so just went along for the ride. Christmas was soon upon us and even though I was given some work to do by Mark Davies during the holiday, I had no intention of doing it. It was the usual Christmas; eating enough so my belly nearly exploded and drinking too much spirits to give me a hangover for a week! This particular Christmas I felt happy to be alive and grateful for the way my family had helped me during my darkest hour. It certainly had been an eventful year in my life and the one I had been waiting for all my life to rid me of my burden, so I could be free at last from my responsibility. I had experienced the greatest high in my life even if the illness that followed had somewhat overshadowed the event. I will always remember those few hours of being free from all the shackles that hold us in during our lives and going to the very edge of my sanity in order to carry out my wishes. 1987 will forever be a year I recall because it had such a big part to play in my life but I was glad when it was all over. 1988 I hoped, would be less full of earth shattering events as far as I was concerned and more full of laughter. I had seen most parts of the family during Christmas and those who no longer lived in Sheffield returned home.

The new term began and I thought the best result I can look forward to would be a 'Z' in both English and history! I was still spending much of my time laid on my bed and if it hadn't been for college I doubt if I would ever have gone out other than for walks, which I did do sometimes. On days when there was no college for me all I could think of after having breakfast was going back to bed because I felt tired. The tablets I was taking contributed to this effect of making me feel washed out most of the time and giving me a dry throat. I didn't have any major side effects like the ones in hospital but because I was still on a high dosage, it was very hard to concentrate on anything for long periods of time. This meant I switched off during the classes I attended and I was just a shell of a person. If I hadn't turned up at all it would have been the same effect of not knowing what was going on and not being able to understand what was being discussed. In fact, I did go through a bad patch when I thought I would have to go back to hospital again but this thankfully was not necessary in my case. I still wondered what was going on in the lecturer's minds in both John Edwards and Mark Davies case. Did John Edwards now believe that he was gong to gain redemption or did he think I was just someone who had gone off balance and made it appear that there was this great reason for doing so? It was Mark Davies who had told my former class that I was attempting suicide because that is what Catherine told me when I visited her while I was still at hospital. What was now going on in his mind especially with regards to the health of Geoff Hammond, who no longer wanted to be anywhere near me. Where he got that I was going to commit suicide from I will never know. I tried to explain to him what was going on yet it looked like I might as well have saved my breath. It was strange that only John Edwards, out of the three, understood what I was trying to do because he was in such a state, the poor sod.

When not at college or laid on my bed, I would be in my mum's front room playing my records; in particular, the U2 album "The Unforgettable Fire" and the track "Bad". I bought a record called "People have the Power" by Patti Smith and played it time and time again. One night while playing the Patti Smith record my mother shouted at me to say the neighbours must be going bonkers with me playing it so often. I kept playing the track "Bad" because of Catherine and I wondered when we would be together because it didn't seem straightforward but I was sure she had been at the hospital when I was and we were still going to meet sooner or later. I knew she would be mine; it was just a matter of time for it to all come together. I was regaining some of my confidence with dealing with people and no longer held any fear of being attacked which I had at first when I left hospital, which I think you could put down to the fact I was in a very weak situation and could have been pushed over by a twig. I was starting to eat quite a lot and slowly started to put on weight. In time, I would be eating far too much but this was the build up that I was going through. The classes were going along and so was I, even though on some occasions, they might as well have been talking Dutch for all the information I was taking in, I really had a hard job following the lessons but kept on going anyway.

My mother mentioned to me that she thought it was time for me to leave home. She had been under a strain when I was in hospital and had not been well. The whole event had taken a lot out of her and she felt, quite rightly, that she had carried me for long enough. I had put my name down for a flat from the Council a fair few years before but I didn't bother to ask in the first part of the year. I would get round to it but in my own time and not at anyone else's.

My thoughts would return from time to time to Catherine and the day when we would get together, which I hoped would not be too long away. If I had her I was sure that I would get better in next to no time. I was still down to see Doctor Lancer and I would keep going to the Hallamshire Hospital for our little meetings and keep on taking the tablets I was being prescribed by my own doctor. The main thing about my health at this time was that I was stable but still prone to being tired in the afternoon.

The months of the last term were coming upon me but I was taking every precaution not to get stressed over the exams that were going to be in front of me in a short time. I enquired about going on and taking a degree in history at the Sheffield Polytechnic. There was a short interview and I was told that they would be in touch if I were successful in getting a place. It was obvious to a blind man on a bolting horse that I was not going to pass with the English or history exams. In the history exam you had to write four essays in only three hours and it took me usually well over an hour to do two sides of an A4 sheet, so not only had I done no revision, I also couldn't write fast enough either. The English exam didn't seem to go too bad but I still knew what I had written was by no means good enough. There was some satisfaction to be gained from finishing the course, which is something I didn't manage the year before. When I got my results there was no big surprise. I had achieved two 'N' grades in both subjects. I did get notification from Sheffield Polytechnic telling me there was a place for me on their degree course but after reading what it said I didn't need much time to throw it into the bin. There was too little of me left and what I had I was going to hold onto. For me the education trip had ended when John Edwards said "Yes please!" a year earlier. There was no real motive for me continuing but most of all I had done what I set out to do and it was now over and done with. Having finished with education and not feeling too badly, I was going to be out a lot more spending some money I had saved from my days as a painter on the Council.

There was three hundred pounds all in five pound notes in a box that I had put away for a rainy day and now it was that rainy day. In the previous months I had hardly been out but that was going to change now I had plenty of time on my hands. I walked all over Sheffield, going into pubs along my way. I would hear someone say "It's Wayne Clay!" or "He's so sweet!" every time I entered a pub. People who I had never met before knew my name, which put me at a disadvantage due to the fact I didn't know theirs. In the daytime I might start having a walk back from town to Hillsborough via the pubs. In every one I entered it was the same reaction and someone always knew my name. Sometimes I was going into a pub for the very first time in my life but they still knew who I was. Of course, this could be put down to paranoia, or the fact that there were a lot of people out there who didn't have much to talk about. After a day of walking around pubs and eating to excess, I would return home, go for a rest and have my tea when my mum came home. Sometimes, I would still feel very hungry after having my evening meal so I would go out and have a burger before I went into a pub. In the main, I stayed in the Hillsborough pubs and I liked going into the Freemasons because they had a jukebox video installed. It was in the Freemasons that I met Tony who I hadn't seen for a very long time. I can remember him touching my head and calling me boss. The rest of the patrons looked on. I went in the Crown on Penistone Road many times and stayed in there on many occasions. The men from the local bakery were in there most evenings having a few pints in their break time. They told funny stories and didn't mind me sitting with them. Also when they saw me, they always asked if I had got my key to my house yet. I had not but it was always a good night in the Crown when these men were present and I enjoyed being with them. It was around this time that people started to look like wobbly jelly to me. The effects of what I had done were becoming increasingly more evident. When I entered supermarkets the bottles seemed to rattle as I walked around them and when I was in pubs in the afternoon the music for the jukebox became distorted with a big bass sound coming through.

One day I was walking, I think beyond the back of Stannington when I saw a pond. I made my way down a steep embankment and took a closer look; there were loads of very big fish swimming around in this very big pond. There was a pathway to a cottage, which was much lower than the pond. I was just looking at the fish for about five minutes when a man came out of the cottage and said "This is private land!" So I turned away and started to make my way up the steep grass embankment. The man was coming up to the pond and I said, "I was only looking at the fish!" Behind the man were two Alsatian dogs and a boy. I stood there on the embankment to get a look at the people and the lad said "But he's not afraid of anything, Dad!" To which his dad replied, "No, that's Wayne Clay, he's given us back our dignity, Son!" So I was even known in the outback! It was not great bravery on my part because my legs were still a long way from being without pain so I couldn't walk fast even if I had wanted to. I don't really know why seeing the dogs had no effect on me, maybe I was going through one of my couldn't care less periods. It still struck me as strange though that even somebody who looked cut off from the outside world should know my name. I probably went and had cake and chips when I got back to civilization because I was on a get fat and stuff it diet. From being eleven and a half on being released for hospital I jumped up at my fattest to weighing in at, wait for it, fifteen stones. I was known as fat bastard from now on even if I was the only one who knew my nickname. I think in some way it was a reaction to the crap food they served up in the Northern General Hospital. I could now go and eat anything I liked because it was there and I couldn't care the slightest about how I looked with a potbelly. On one occasion when I was in the Crown I thought that Catherine was also in the pub collecting money but maybe my imagination was getting the better of me. When leaving the Crown one night I passed two men and one of them bent his back as if in some way afraid of me and on another occasion, the same thing happened, this time he got so low he could have picked things up off the floor. I do not know to this day who he was but he sure acted strange when he saw me. The weather was changeable as ever and I was wearing my long checked raincoat, a cloth cap and carrying an umbrella. I was coming out of the Blue Ball one night when some of my brother's friends were just going in and when they saw me they burst out laughing because of what I was wearing.

One day I went down London Road and went into a couple of shops to buy sandwiches and then I walked so I could go on Ecclesall Road on the way back to town. It just felt great to walk around so many different areas of Sheffield in the daytime. I would pop into one of the pubs in town and then when it was becoming the late afternoon, I would make my way back to my Mum's. After having my dinner at my Mum's one night, I caught the bus up to

Stannington and wondered if I would meet Catherine on one of my visits but there never seemed to be any sign of her. It was like she did not exist and I found it strange that I have never bumped into Mick, her brother even once. The people up Stannington didn't mind at first but that was to change in a couple of week's time.

While I was on my walkabout in the daytime, I would sometimes go through a falling step as I called it and it seemed that I had walked down a step that was not there. I can recall walking along the Robin Hood route into the wood around the back of it and made my way to Loxley Road and went into the Admiral Rodney. It was nearly dinnertime and I had a meal in the Rodney and a couple of pints. It didn't seem to matter where I went because there was always someone who seemed to know my name. On this day, it was raining and I had mud all over my shoes, which didn't matter that much because I needed a new pair of shoes anyway. With the wobbly jelly effect as I called it, on the wane it was now that I saw people as gorillas, orangutans or chimps, even though when I had visited Catherine I had said that one of the class was a gorilla, that was because I knew him and those I knew were already seeable by me. This time it was everyone and there were plenty of men who reminded me of the way my dad walks. I had the key to see the human jungle for what it is. It was quite incredible that I could have affected so many lives by what I had released. The sheer number of people was mind-boggling and I had a sense of having done something that was worthwhile. All those years of dreading the next day of just managing to hold onto the thread, the disappointments and the failures for just a few moments somehow seemed to fit into place. During all the turmoil in my life I had lost sight of my dream but it was all there waiting in front of me now.

My clothes were not very wearable now and in particular, I had put a fair bit of weight on around my waist, which meant I could do with some new trousers. My dad took Maureen and I shopping in Leeds and eventually, after walking around most of it, I ended up with two new pairs of cords. We had our dinner in a greasy Joe café that was all right if you like that sort of thing. I can remember they were tight when it came to giving you a piece of artic roll for your seconds but on the plus side, you got a big mug of tea. This was not the end of getting new clothes, I unbelievably actually bought some for myself. You might be wondering what's unbelievable about that, well I'll tell you; I very rarely ever buy my own clothes. For instance, when I go out I will have paid for the coat I am wearing but then when you point out the rest of what I am wearing, it was usually bought by one of my relatives. There is socks and pants, for a start that I never buy, the shirt, the cords, the jumper and the shoes, all paid for by my family; all I have to do is wear them. I've never been one for being trendy and the more I look around me today I can see that there is a lot of people in the same boat wearing clothes that don't match up because they have to, due to the fact they cannot afford to go out and buy the clothes they would like to wear. Even if I could afford to buy some clothes for myself I still only very rarely do so. But with a hot rush of blood I bought a sweatshirt, which said on the front 'Think Pink', well why should the Greens have all the fun! The sweatshirt was to do with some project going on in America and I liked it so I bought it. I also bought a light jacket for summer, which had 'Wipeout' on one of the sleeves, and 'Bondi Beach' on the back. From the night throwing the paint around in the school I still had the red jumper that I could wear. My mother paid for some shirts so I would be fine up to Christmas in the clothes department.

Sometimes I would walk to my Dad's going up Herries Road to where he lived on Moonshine Lane. The cars that went past me as I walked on the pavement would hoot their horns when they recognised me. My dad must have known I was coming with all the hooting that was going on when I got closer to his house. I tried to deny that it was happening and tried to put it out of my mind. On another day, I walked along Wadsley and turned right just before the White Horse pub. When I climbed the steep hill there was the Magnet pub on the left facing Moonshine Lane. I felt like having a drink so I went into the lounge room. It was empty and so I got served easily and went to sit in a corner of the room. Whilst I was walking to my seat I heard one of the two barmaids say, "He's so sweet!" Of course, by now I was used to hearing this comment so I took no notice and didn't give it a second thought. After having my pint I made my way to my dad's who was working as usual on part of his house.

I was not taking my clothes off when I went to bed and just lay on top of the sheets. There were a lot of my belongings that I got from boxes and put under the top sheet of my bed. The five-pound notes that were in a little moneybag were also put under the sheet by me so I knew where it was. In the morning my Mum looked around my bedroom and I thought she was going to confiscate my readies, so when she had gone to work I filled three plastic bags with some of my favourite possessions. When I had all that I wanted I decided to take the bags to a friend's house, so I caught the bus to Stannington and made my way to Rory's house. When I went up to the house I thought that Rory might be in, but when I knocked on the door, his Mother opened the door telling me Rory was not in. She asked me "Have you been a good boy?" to which I replied "Yes I have" Rory's mother worked at the Doctors as a receptionist so she knew I had been ill and we had talked to each other on my visits to the Doctors. I told her I would come back to see Rory and told her I was going to a sports club that Rory was a member of, but I was not. So I made my way down the hill to the fitness club and when I got there I think they were expecting me and that Rory's mother had rung ahead of me. I asked to go in the member's side and I was allowed through. It was not yet time to sell alcoholic drinks so I made do with a soft drink. The squash courts were right in front of my view and two men were using one court. When one of the men saw me he started calling me "A fucking bastard" and repeating the same thing over and over again. The man's face was full of hate for me and the man he was playing started to swear at me too. You see that not everyone was given a change for the better in my releasing the force. This man must have been one of those who got a shock but he had chosen his own destiny and could not blame me for the punishment that he was now enduring. My dad, on one of my visits to his house, summed it up when he said, "It's the way you sliced it I always liked, Son" It was a quote that would stick in my mind for a very long time to come. I waited for Rory to come to the club but he didn't turn up and I was feeling hungry so I decided to go home for my dinner.

When it was eight o'clock I went out and caught the bus to Stannington Village. I decided to go for a drink and stayed in the pub until closing time, when I left I started laughing in a giggling sort of way and the patrons in the pub were like long grass in a windy storm the way they moved around. I was still attacking their nervous systems or so I thought at the time, especially when I saw the torment on their faces. I made my way to Rory's and his dad answered when I knocked on the door. Rory was now in and Rory's dad left us so we could talk. I tried to explain why I had brought the plastic bags to his house. It was my mother's snooping that had forced my hand, with her threatening my readies and that's what I told Rory. I also tried to explain some of the things that had been going on and I told him about Catherine who was the sister of Mick who we had both worked with on our time on the council. When I told him they only lived just down the road from his house on the Acorn Estate, it surprised him because he didn't know they had moved there. I told him that Catherine was mine but I didn't tell him the whole story. We had a cup of tea and I even got a sandwich whilst we chewed the fat. In one of the plastic bags there was a black jacket that was a gift I wanted to be delivered to Catherine's house in the morning. It was a style that had a lot in common with Mick's car when I worked with him and it was just another part of the jigsaw puzzle that had been my life. I showed Rory the house so he knew where to deliver the jacket; it was strange but as we got closer to Catherine's house the temperature seemed to be dropping all the time, so we went back to Rory's house. Rory gave me a lift to my mum's house and I went inside with two plastic bags after a full day.

The next phase had begun. I could see a mist that was coming down from the sky. The mist of discovery is what I named it and when it came down it had the effect of making people's eyes water or you may prefer that it made people cry. I never did ask if anyone else could see the mist come down in waves but I could certainly see it, that's for sure. When I was around Hillsborough corner I met a neighbour who had lived across from us when we lived on Woodend Drive. He was carrying two bags of shopping and his eyes were bright red. When we recognized each other he said "Remember me to your dad" I said, "I would." Seeing him with two red circles for eyes made me laugh because he looked so comical. When I went to my dad's I told him I had met our old neighbour and my dad said, "What's this with people crying all over the place?" to which I replied "What's wrong with people crying. It will make them feel better". There was no answer to that and we changed the subject to one of my dad's favourites - that of getting a job. Here I was in no state to even get through the day without feeling crap and he already wants me back at work. It was just the same in hospital when he said "If I was you Son I'd have them all on the bed!" I was out of my mind staring insanity in the face on the edge of a precipice and all my dad can think about is getting my leg over. Some people just have no idea what I've gone through especially if they have minds that work like my dad's.

One day, when it was damp and occasionally raining, I put on my Bondi Beach coat, with its little hood to cover your head. I put the hood over my head and my mum said "Don't have your hood on, you'll scare them to death!" I didn't understand why having my hood up would cause problems but I did as my mother wished and kept my hood down from my head. It was my day for visiting Doctor Livingstone at Hillsborough. I told her, while I was laughing about what my dad had said, "It's the way you sliced it I always liked, Son!" To which she said "Your Dad's a bit of a comedian, Wayne!" I was still also going every two weeks to see my psychiatrist Doctor Lancer at the Hallamshire Hospital.

When the evenings arrived I was going up to Stannington virtually every night in the hope of bumping into Catherine in one of the pubs. The pubs would get very busy late on in the night and listening to what other people had to say made me laugh which put the people who were around me into a nervous state. It didn't happen in just pubs either; I could be waiting at a bus stop and overhear what some old biddy had to say and starting laughing out loud which would go right through people. It got so severe that it was passed on to my dad and he asked me what was causing it, and I said, "It was what you said about the way you sliced it! I've been laughing about it ever since!" He said, "I wish I'd never said it to you now if it's going to cause this much hassle!" The patrons of the Rose and Crown were especially fed up with my antics and they would be glad if I didn't go into their pub for a while. Or that's what I sensed from the previous night when the landlord of the pub said, "He's off again!" when I was laughing on my way out of the pub. I was going to go up to Stannington again the following night when I bumped into a couple of friends who I knew so I stayed around Hillsborough instead, on this occasion. I didn't drink too many beers on these outings because they did not entirely agree with the tablets that I was on. The distortion that had happened before to the jukeboxes was no longer happening and that was something to be thankful for at any rate. There were still plenty of people who were going through the changes and I met some of my ex-school chums one night who were pretty high on what was taking place.

My Mother told me that Peter, my friend from school, had popped in to see her and asked how I was. It was a fair while after that I got in touch and arranged to meet him on a Sunday evening. I was very fat that the time with all the food I had got through in recent times it was not that surprising that I had a pot belly! I went to his house and one of his daughters (I think the youngest) kept saying, "Is that Wayne?" Well perhaps I was not quite what some people expected or I was just one big paranoid fruit and nut case who had one heck of an imagination. I said goodbye to Karen, Peter's wife and we both made our way to a pub up the road. I did bring up the subject of all the tattoos that were all over Peter's arms and asked him "Do you have problems remembering your name?!" There were plenty with Peter in between them. I can recall many years before we had gone together to get his first tattoo and he got an infection with yellow puss coming out of his arm. To say the least I don't think I'll ever be getting a tattoo for myself, as that time with Peter was enough to put anyone off this idea.

Most of Peter's family came into the pub we were in but they didn't stay long. We talked about some of our former schoolmates and I don't think that I was much good company with me losing track most of the time of what we were talking about. It was still great to see Peter again and I was full up long before closing time. I walked home and it took me a while to get home. When I got home my mother told me Peter had rung her to check that I had got home all right and he thought that I was fat, which was a fair comment with the shape I was in at that time.

After one boozing session I had around Hillsborough, finishing off in The Crown on Penistone Road, I decided to go for a curry at an Indian restaurant, which was just at the bottom of where my mother lived on Hawksley Avenue. I ordered whatever because I don't remember what I ordered but I do remember it was more than some poor sods get in a week. When I was near the end of shoveling it in, a fellow patron on his way out said, "I bet myself that you couldn't eat all that?" It just shows you that things are not always as

184

they appear and in this case he obviously didn't take into account my potbelly! I bumped into one of my former workmates who was still painting for the Council; it was John who I had worked with for a fair while in my stay on the firm. We exchanged hellos and he said to his wife, while I was still passing one night "But they treat that lad like shit!" He had been one of the many who didn't know what I was attempting and I doubt very much if someone had told him that he would have believed it. I felt like saying to him that things are not what they always seem to be and that I was prepared to wait my time before certain people got what they had been asking for. Don't get me wrong; I don't hate anyone from my time on the works other than myself. The stupidity some people showed me was down to them and I had nothing to do with choosing their destinies, they chose that for themselves.

I was not going up as often to the top of Stannington but one night when I was in the Rose and Crown there were three girls who were together in front of the window in the lounge. One of them kept jumping on her seat to attract my attention and said, "I want him!" Maybe there were some perks to this job after all, but I had only one woman on my mind and that was, of course, Catherine. It was nice though to feel wanted for a change and also that I was not scaring the patrons away from the pub anymore. On another night, when I was in the same lounge, four girls came in and just for a change they said, "He's so sweet!" The originality of the comment was too much to bear. For the rest of my life I hope I don't hear that phrase again. When I went into the post office at Hillsborough, I was waiting in the queue and started to notice that the people behind the glass were laughing. Some of them were my brother's friends who had laughed at the way I had dressed. When I cashed my Giro I was glad to get out of the place. It seemed now that I was the joker in the pack but I've got a broad back and I haven't gotten where I am today by not being able to take a joke, so the saying goes.

I went for a check up at the dentist and there was one of my mother's friends with the receptionist. I was given my report card and went to sit in the waiting room. I picked up a magazine and started to read an article, it was interesting because it was a magazine for women and it was strange what interested the opposite sex if the magazine was anything to go by. Eventually, I went back to reception and it turned out I had been waiting for two hours and my mother's friend was laughing, there's no doubt in my mind she had been one of a chorus of women who had said in my childhood "There's only one woman for our Wayne!" Well it probably made her day to try and get me going but I took it all in my stride. The check up lasted all of five minutes and I was on my way again. There was another incident when I was going to see my Doctor for the usual prescription concerning one of the receptionists; she said to me "Are you the one who makes it rain?" I replied, "No, I make it snow!" There's nothing like telling them. Putting my name down at the desk could sometimes be just the start of another ordeal. They knew I was there but when I got to the waiting area for Doctor Livingstone it wasn't going to mean much because all the chairs were occupied. When a patient finally got to see the doctor everyone would move along in the seats, it was a sort of musical chairs without the music! To get to see the doctor you would have to wait an hour because I arrived a quarter of an hour before my appointment and then it was a good forty five minutes after the appointment time that I got my way to see the doctor. At this time I was also on top of my tablets, getting an injection into an area just above my bum to help my nervous system to get back to being at least stable. I was still having problems with trying to get to sleep, which had now escaped me for over a year and a half. The real reason I couldn't get deep sleep was because I was lying down during the day feeling very tired and drained of energy. I was very lethargic all the time and it was very difficult not to go back up to my bed after breakfast. The only way I could stay off the bed was to go for long walks, which I have already described previously, that is, some of the walks I went on.

I was still into playing U2 and Kate Bush a lot of the time and I had this idea in my head that a game would start and my friends and me would begin a binge. It would commence and continue until Saturday came along and I would marry Catherine and all the reception would go back to the house that had been erected for what I had done. That's what my imagination was telling me at any rate. It was becoming unbearable not seeing Catherine and I felt if I made one big effort she would be mine but I also realised that I had to wait.

When I switched the radio on to listen to Radio One, they were guessing who it could be. On one show they even said that the person was from a northern city and had given him a nickname, which was Willie the Plonka. I was a regular listener of Annie Nightingale's Sunday Request show, where people were writing in to say who they thought it was from the world of popular music. The people who wrote in even gave a reason for their selection, which Annie read out to the listeners. I stopped listening to the radio and just played my records instead. The whole thing would pass over very quickly because it was just one of those flavour of the month fads that come and go with a blink of the eye.

I was starting to come to terms with what had been going on and there was enough evidence to suggest that I wasn't mad, which was rather comforting if nothing else.

One day I was on the bus from town and who caught the bus when we reached the Kelvin Flats stops, non other than John Edwards. It was the first time I had seen him since the day of my exam for English language. He paid the bus driver and came up to where I was sitting and sat beside me. He looked like he'd just come off a right bender but it was his turn to pay the piper, what he was going through was what he said "Yes please" to when I got the signal he gave me to go into my act. I don't know if he was going up to the college but he looked like death warmed up and like he'd been throwing his guts up. I asked him if he was the father to a friend I had known at school and he said no. The last thing he said to me was "Take a holiday, Son" So I did! I had been thinking over going away for a change of scenery and decided to go abroad, either to France or Spain. On the throw of a coin I ended up in Mallorca in the off-season. I booked a coach to Manchester Airport, which was very cold and, apart from one other passenger, was empty. I booked in my suitcase and began a night of waiting because it just so happened that the plane I was waiting for was four hours behind schedule. We finally got off and we arrived at the hotel by coach from the airport and were given our keys to our rooms. It wasn't too warm by this time of year, but when put by the side of British weather we had arrived in a heat wave. There was the usual talk about what was happening with a free drink. The hotel was fine but it was only a two star hotel and I think some of the other guests hadn't quite taken that into account. The only way they did potatoes at this hotel was to make chips out of them every night but there were plenty of food places to eat out nearby. The pubs had a lot of videos in them showing Fawlty Towers or Dave Allen or the latest films. I must confess that I don't remember much about the holiday what with taking tablets and drinking too much its no surprise that my memory cells got a little pickled! I did make some friends in three old ladies at the hotel and also on the beach with some other elder stateswoman. There were not too many young females about, but I spent a lot of time in my hotel room with a bottle of vodka that I bought. Sometimes when I was wide-awake at five in the morning, I would get dressed and go for a walk around the immediate area. Some of the bars were still open when I went past but I was just out for the view. There is always something special about seeing the dark of night into the light of day and with a sea view to look over, you can do no better wherever you are in the world. I enjoyed my holiday all the same and towards the end I caught a cold. On the way back on the plane I had a severe headache and didn't feel too clever. One of the old ladies had too many cigarettes than you are allowed to bring back, so I carried one of her bags through customs while my case was pushed along on a trolley, which also was carrying the ladies' suitcases. My dad and Maureen were waiting for me at the airport and we went and had a late chip supper in Manchester. I was relieved when I was home and I still wonder how I didn't get lost because I can recall so little of the time I was in Mallorca. I brought back the usual presents such as decorative plates and a painting for myself. It was funny when I bought the painting because I'd no sooner left the shop than the shopkeeper put exactly the same scene back on the clip. I did bring something back for Catherine; I got her a bottle of Chanel Number 5, a little ashtray and some adult comics, which I placed in front of her door. Even when I had been away Catherine was always somewhere in my thoughts. The holiday had, perhaps not been such a good idea as I came back in a state and threw up my dinner. I was pacing my bedroom and my mum called for a doctor and thankfully I was over the worst part. Even though he said something strange about "Someone your age it's quite natural" it made me feel like I was one hundred and ten years old! Well, trying to get away from it all had not proved too successful for me and I was glad that I had gone away on my own because I would not have been much company for anyone who had gone with me.

My mum was reminding me that she thought it was time for me to find a place of my own and I agreed with the idea. I had put my name down for a flat in the early eighties. I got an appointment to see someone in the housing department. The housing office was just at the end of the street where my mother lived, so I had no problems with traveling. They took my name at the reception and I sat down to wait for my name to be called. A lady came out of the cubicles and I followed her into the tiny room. She told me that I could qualify for a flat in a good area with the length of time my name had been on the housing list. The only problem with this was that I was demanding that I got a house but what I meant was that I wanted my house. This demand for my house brought out a lot of bad language from me, which I regretted afterwards. I just wouldn't accept the fact that this lady had nothing to do with my house if it even existed. I went on swearing, and we didn't get anywhere with my application. After being so rude to the housing lady I let the issue of my getting a flat rest awhile.

One night I got it into my head to go and see Catherine. I had been drinking around Hillsborough and I had gone home. At about twelve o'clock I made up my mind to see her. There was no bus due so I started walking to her house. The Stannington Hill is a very steep one and it took me a long time to get up it and reach the village. It was after one o'clock in the morning when I reached Catherine's house. It had never dawned on me that they might have all gone to bed by this time, but fortunately lights were still on in the house. Through the pane of glass I could see Catherine sat on the floor so I knew she was still up. When I knocked on the door Catherine's mother answered my knocking and told me that Catherine wasn't seeing anyone at this hour. Then this ugly kid came to the door, who it turns out was Catherine's boyfriend and I told him to "Fuck Off" Eventually Catherine came to the door and said "Have you got something to say to me?" I replied "Yes, put you coat on and come with me"

That's not exactly what I said but its close enough without me having to write down all the swear words. We seemed to all be at a stalemate and soon Catherine's dad and her two brothers were woken and came to the door. I moved further back and they all came outside wearing their dressing gowns over their pyjamas. They stood in a line and said, "She's not coming" it was really comical by now and I started laughing, because of the silliness of the scene in front of me. It was the first time I had seen Mick for over five years but we were not on friendly terms on this occasion. They told me after the performance of the three stooges that they would phone the police. I thought to myself "Big Deal" Catherine was mine and I wanted her for myself and not some ugly git who couldn't fight his way out of a paper bag was going to spoil my plans. Don't hold your breath, but after about half an hour a police car pulled up outside the house and a policeman went inside the house for a chat about what was going on. When he came out, he called me over to him and we both got into his car. He gave me a lift to my mother's and before I got out of the car he said to me "Get yourself a job, Wayne" Even the police were into my dad's favourite line; it must have been a conspiracy. That was the third time I had gone to see Catherine but I was not getting the message of the fact that she didn't want to know me and that I actually didn't mean anything to her. After all those years of just hanging on in there, it was a hard fact to come to terms with.

With my health being slightly better I started to look around the job centre to see if there was a course I could go on to improve my job prospects. In December 1988 I got on an employment-training scheme, which was to do with retail. We all went to the Sheffield Commerce Centre at the bottom of Sheffield Moor in the first week. In the class or group that I was in, there was a wide range of different courses that people were taking. The man who went through things like safety at work or certain regulations that we had to know was full of himself. He told us there was this brainy lad who kept dressing up like a punk and was having problems in getting a job until he wore a suit to an interview one day and was taken on. Somehow I don't believe if I wore a suit that it would make the slightest difference to my job prospects and also if there was ever an intelligent life form on this planet it must have been very lonely. We were shown some videos on how to go about an interview and what not to do. There was one film about getting a job at Marks and Spencer and the real interviews were filmed with the people's consent. One lad talked about UFOs and that it was of great interest to him. The female interviewer seemed very interested or she was just having him on and taking the piss. Another man who went for an interview for the job, claimed he has served in the Falklands but it turned out he was shifty Sid type, who was a compulsive liar. The closest he got to the Falklands by all accounts was Leeds, where he was based in the stores. There was also another video, which was about two men who were out of work, played by the same actor. It was to show that with a positive outlook you could be more able to find a job against a very sloppy attitude by the slob of the two men. It was a fairly comical short story that made me laugh, but that's not much of a recommendation, because I laugh at nearly everything. The old nutshell about race was brought up, that it didn't matter if people were blue with yellow spots on. So if you turn up looking like Coco the Clown you would get the job easily. People who come out with stupid statements either cant comprehend the situation and are total shit for brains or are just not interested in social unfairness but if you turn up with a blue face and yellow spots, remember you'll get the job even if is isn't a Circus you want to join! We did some short tests to get us thinking but overall I didn't enjoy the first week. The following week we were to go to a centre that was down Attercliffe and was used for the more academic side of the courses. I was already feeling down and I definitely had the face on. They told us that they doubted whether they could place us in a job situation before Christmas so we would have to keep reporting to this centre. I felt that it would be best for me to get straight into a work situation. There was a job at a snooker hall in town and I volunteered to give it a try. I lasted out for a whole week but there was no way I could continue because of the massive low that was coming over me. My parents thought I was just backing out and that I didn't want to do any work, if only this had been the case. A depression was taking over me and I was finding it very hard to cope with the effects that it had over me. I so much wanted to be like other people and ably take each day as it comes and not go into an inertia attack like the ones I had suffered in my painting days on the council.

The Christmas holidays were upon us anyway so I had a break to try and think things through. It was the usual Christmas of having a turkey and ending up having it for the following week. I'm sure that turkey is not such a bad meat but because of the overindulgence at Christmas, I reckon most people get fed up with it and don't have any again until the following Christmas. I got the usual aftershave lotion and a pair of socks, and probably did get totally plastered at least once. When it was time to go back to my retail course I had to go in to see them and I got another position at a fitness club that was only a twenty minute walk from my mother's house. I ended up being a glorified plate washer. The chef in the kitchen was also called Wayne so I used my middle name of Donald, which in the main was shortened to Don. There was another chef called Ruby who helped out in the week. The day started at 9.30 in the morning and finished at 2.30 in the afternoon, with the evening shift beginning at 6.30 until 9.30. In the morning there might be some plates from the previous night to do so that's what I would do when I got there. The salad of tomatoes, lettuce, cucumber and cress had to be done for use in the dinnertime period. Fresh bread would be brought in everyday and the bread that wasn't used the previous day was thrown away. In the main, there was little to do in the mornings until dinnertime arose. The public bar of the complex would attract students from the nearby college. The orders for burgers or chip butties would be passed on to the kitchen and done as quickly as possible. Someone from the member's side might order a meal and I would get the job of taking it through if it was just one plate. Ruby and Wayne could carry four plates at once but I knew with my balance that it would be impossible for me to do the same. There were also some trainee chefs from college who were present in the kitchen so it was a fairly busy place at times. Once the dinnertime was over it was time to clean and stack the plates back in their cupboards. Before we left at 2.30 the floor was mopped down so it was clean and hygienic for when we came back at 6.30. I never felt like going back in the evening but it was getting me out of the house and that was the main thing. In the evenings we were rarely busy but when we were there was a lot to be done before 9.30. For some reason, in the member's side they would start ordering at 9.25 when we were all ready to leave and poor old Wayne would have to get the order ready before he could leave for the night. Another of the difficulties was in trying to find who had ordered what and everyone would be saying it was for them if no one claimed it. I know one thing from my experience and that is I'm not cut out to serve people and that I would never go back to such a situation. At 9.30 we were free for the rest of the night and I walked very quickly to get home. I was still suffering with drowsiness and sometimes I would be in bed for 10.30.

I made another appointment with the Housing Office and got my mum to go with me because I was so embarrassed about my previous behaviour. It was the same lady as before, and my mother told her I had not been well. The lady told us I could get a flat in Stannington with my name being on the list for so long. It was all arranged for me to move in when I collected the keys to the flat. The flat was in a good state but I went through the lounge and bedroom with a coat of emulsion on the ceilings and walls. My dad had given both my sister and brother some money and he gave me the same. We went to a carpet seller and got a carpet for the lounge and the bedroom. I paid fifty pounds for a settee and took a couple of old chairs from my Mum's and also bought a small fridge and small cooker. I didn't take everything that was mine from my mother's. Even though I had now left my mother's she still did my washing for me.

I was still going to the fitness club and I was always taking bites out of the food. When I had to go to the big fridge and there was a massive apple pie I would be eating portions as I got what I was supposed to be taking back to the kitchen. One of the funniest events occurred when there was a function one evening and there was a sirloin steak on a plate that I thought had been sent back to the kitchen, so I picked it up and took a big bite out of it. Wayne, the Chef had cooked it for himself and he said, "Who's been eating my steak?" and I said "Me!" The outcome was that I got out a bread cake and had a sirloin steak sandwich for my supper. Ruby said "Don's got expensive taste!"

When there was a function on it was chaotic in the kitchen with all the servers asking Wayne questions and putting pressure on him. I know that I couldn't have coped with it all and for the money he was on; there was never any chance that I would take up being a cook. One of the functions was for a men's night where there were strippers and a comedian, plus a boxing match on satellite television shown on a big screen. We didn't get finished before two o'clock in the morning and I hated the whole thing. The best things about the place were Ruby and Wayne, because I didn't like the manager much but from what I could gather, very few people did. Ruby told us one day how she got roped into the business. She went to help out at the Fiesta Nightclub that put on many household acts in the seventies. From her first night she ended up staying for years and becoming one of the main employees. She told us about Cliff Richard making all his entourage give the kitchen staff a round of applause for how they had look after them during the week. She said she got Michael Jackson's signature while he was still a member of the Jackson Five. It seemed strange to think that after her time at the Fiesta she had come to be part time at a fitness club. She did mention the Manager who ran away from his debts and that was the end of the Fiesta. Some nights a man called Frank would come for his dinner and Ruby would make it for him. I think he helped around the place and drove the Rolls Royce for weddings that were held at the club. The taxi driver who lives across the road from my dad came to the club one day because someone was trying to drum up business for a new taxi that had been made. Talk about small world!

I still had to go to see the psychiatrist, Doctor Lancer at the Hallamshire Hospital every two weeks but I was in fair shape towards the end of 1989. Sometimes I would just go in to his office when it was my turn to be seen and hardly say anything but on other occasions I would tell him if I had been through a bad week. I certainly had realised that there was no quick cure that would make me better by now and that it might be something that might take up a lifetime to mend. The final visit I made to Doctor Lancer, after two weeks of being off the tablets, I can clearly remember what he said, "If it was me I wouldn't want to see a psychiatrist!" With that I left the room and I have never seen him since, even though I have heard that he has now retired.

With me being off drugs, but still very sleepy, I started to miss days from going to the fitness club. I had taken on a retail course and all I had ended up doing was cleaning plates or cleaning down the snooker tables. If I had not been in a state at the start of the course I would have held out for a chance of working in a shop but that was not to be. I felt that I had a lot more going for me than cleaning pots and felt that I had done enough. The good thing about having my own place to live was that my mum wasn't there to get me out of bed, so I could turn over and stay in bed for as long as I liked. My appearances at the club were becoming less frequent and I just decided one day that I was not going to go anymore. I lost a stone in weight while I was working in the kitchen, which you can take to mean anything you like. It was certainly an eye opener to see what goes on in the name of cooking. From the deep freeze to the microwave is the way of the modern chef in all his glory. My dad came to see me about my leaving the course with another month to run, but I knew myself that I had made the right decision to leave. When you're on a training scheme you get a whole ten pounds more, which is for your dinner and travel expenses. A whole ten pounds which, as we all know, doesn't go too far these days, it's a wonder they can spare it. I informed my signing on place that I had left the Employment Training venture that I had been on. For some reason, known only to them, I did not get any money for the best part of two months and I finally decided that I would not sign on one week because I had not been given any money. My name was immediately taken off the list and it meant filling in some big forms again but I got my money. The day I went in to resign, my mother rang up to check on me and explain what had been going on. The money came in handy because Christmas was on its way again and my savings had been steadily going down to zero. One night when I had just been having an early drink in the Freemasons, a man asked me where Crookes Working Men's Club was. I tried to direct him, then I said, "I'll show you" So I got in the car, with an act who was a professional comedian. If anyone knows me, geography was never one of my strengths and not surprisingly, we got lost. The comedian started to ask people where the Club was and he said "You're all bloody comedians around here!" Eventually, after about half an hours detour we found the missing club. There were a couple of singers on when we arrived and he was late so he made his way to behind the stage. The club was not very busy and I kept going for burgers or a portion of chips washed down with a pint of bitter. The girl who was serving at the food counter kept telling me she couldn't change a tenner so I had to fiddle about giving her some change. The comedian came on and he was all right but the rest of the audience didn't seem to be laughing much. To die on stage must be a terrible feeling especially when the patrons are more interested in the Bingo than your jokes. I suppose he wasn't the first and I'm sure he won't be the last.

If I had little idea in finding Crookes Club going home turned out to be a right nightmare. I somehow got lost in streets that all looked the same to me and I was beginning to think that someone had moved Hillsborough Corner. There was a man taking two dogs for a walk and as I was totally lost I asked him for some directions and so on my way to Hillsborough Corner I was bound. The last bus had gone so it was a walk up the Stannington Hill for me. This is what you get when you try to help somebody I thought to myself as I made my way to the flat and the warmth of my own bed.

In the New Year I joined a job club who try to help you find work and give you paper, envelopes and stamps for free. I didn't get on with the woman who was running the class and I was soon thrown out of the job club. It made me very depressed and I didn't need a reminder that I was out of work. In many ways I was still ill from my experiences of working for the council and it was not an easy thing to shake off. People were always commenting on that I looked so down and only time will help me get to a more stable position in my life. In 1990 I was called in for a six-month chat about my job prospects and I told the lady who I saw that I wouldn't mind giving a job in the security business a go. She arranged an interview for me and wrote the time down on a piece of paper. When I turned up, the man who was gong to give me an interview was not there because the time of the interview was not written down correctly on the piece of paper. I never heard from them again and I don't know if it's the right kind of job for me to do anyway. With me not working I've had plenty of time on my hands and have spent many an hour painting in my flat; that is picture painting of the more artistic side of things. If there was a film on at the cinema that I wanted to see, I could go when there's a pound off the usual price. Even in 1990 I was still feeling like I had been drained of energy and maybe I had when I think back to my illness that I induced. The energy of the power I released was bound to take an awful lot out of me when I think back to it. I always thought that before the event that I could conserve energy and I needed all that was going during it. The thing is I didn't give it much thought, jumping in headfirst when I saw the prize of Catherine in front of me. I ended up taking tablets again and not feeling too well, which didn't help my job prospects any, and made any plans that I might have go up in smoke. One of the bad habits that I've picked up since hospital is that I now smoke cigars and I enjoy doing so. The reason I don't smoke anything other than cigars is that cigarettes taste horrible unlike a cigar. The year passed by with little happening in my life until I heard my dad talking to one of my cousins, he said "She doesn't want him" I knew who they were talking about immediately, that Catherine didn't want me had finally come through. The game was over and there would be no happy ending.

The blood I had willingly given was so I could have an equal by my side during my life. I would have settled for her and never looked at another woman ever again as the love I had for her would never cease. The way she looked, how she was such a wet one who had just come out of the sea but yesterday. Her watery star clustered eyes, which would bring out the protector in any man. Her body was so beautiful in its strength and the vitality it oozed forth into your path. She was unique and worth the wait and going through hell for. She was the woman in a billion who I had found in the place where I had been looking for her. It was difficult to not think about Catherine seeing as I had been waiting to meet her all my life. That I had come so close to fulfilling my dreams and here I was in sight of carrying off an amazing hat trick. Paying off the debt I owed, having a house built for me, and thirdly, and most definitely the best, getting the woman of my dreams after such a long wait. Of being released from my promise and claiming my prize at last but was it all just a dream or a nightmare? Had I been suffering from a curse or had I been blessed with a gift? It was definitely a matter of opinion, which one was the true label? I know in myself that I thought of it as a curse because it had got in the way of my sex life but even more importantly, it had marked out a big slice of my life to complete the task. To you it may seem more like a gift I was given, which in some ways it was, to be able to change people's lives for the better was something which I'm sure many people would have like to have done. But would you have been so willing if you had led the life that was necessary in order to complete the promise? I have my doubts about you and already some of you are saying to yourselves I'm not sure about this. I wonder what happened to those of you who said "I wish I could have done what you did, Wayne". Before we've even started some people are dropping out of the race. It makes me wonder how many of those people around me could have lasted a day or a week. Would they have been able to cope with being alone, of not having feminine companionship? I see another load have just left the queue; suddenly it looks like there is not going to be too many people for starter's orders. The ones who were full of "I wish!" etc are slowly but surely dropping out of the contest before it has even begun. It would seem that it takes more than good intentions that were so forthcoming after the event, to even begin the course. It's time for starter's orders; there certainly isn't too many lining up and now the big questions are being asked by the competitors; have I the ability to see it through to the end and more importantly, have I the strength and skill to go right through the course and then perform a form of magic at the crunch, that will make all the difference to those around you. I look around me, there's only me at the starting blocks, which is sad because I have been through it once and I have no intention of ever going through it again. The thought is that never again will I be putting myself into such an awkward position, with very little option but to bite the bullet and get on with it. Those, who on my emergence suddenly wished they could have done what I had done, were pretty thin on the ground when I was going through a depressive hell. Looking at it form where I'm standing at the present time, I think it was a heck of a lot to ask of anyone; to take on the whole world that surrounds you and then to be treated as some sort of disease is very hard to take. To be forever misunderstood by people, with them failing to understand very little of what I said to them. It all appeared at times to be just getting through the hour, the day, the night, the week, the month and then the year, to get me in the position of being able to shed my promise. To finally get rid of the heavy weights that I had carried since birth was something that I had so longed for. Not having to ask daily why am I here and what purpose, if any, my life had, to just being able to be thankful that I was still alive.

Being rejected by Catherine was a very big blow, that I had been through so much to be with her and then for her not to want me was a severe setback in my life. As far I know she has the blood extracted from my right arm running through her veins, which makes her unique on this planet.

She never gave me a chance to see whether she liked me or not and I wasn't given the time of day when I think back. To have wasted so long to meet Catherine and find her just at the right moment in my life, when the scene was set for my entrance, could not have been timed any better. After so many years here before me was a vision of loveliness, who was on this earth just for me or so I thought. Didn't the workshop overseer say to me in hospital that his creation out of clay was not anywhere as good as my handiwork? I thought to myself that I would have the rest of my lifetime to spend with Catherine. The plans of mice and men as the saying goes…. I had come through my time in hell and my reward for this was nothing. The one thing that had kept me going in my time in hospital right through my illness was that Catherine would be there at the end of it to meet me and be my other half. Maybe if I had known beforehand what a cotton wool headed spoilt bitch Catherine was, I could have made another choice at the time. But then again I was promised the woman of my choosing and I chose Catherine. I had kept my promise in the bargain but it seems I was more of a fool than the last of the true romantics. How I wanted to be near her and hold her close to me yet she had no feelings for me in return. In my childhood, did not the women say, "There's only one girl for our Wayne!" Well I had made my choice and still no girl. Who can I blame? Certainly not myself, so I could blame Catherine but I suppose something had to go wrong in a plan that was so close to a fairy tale. That everything else had jelled together in a way that made it seem that it was all meant to be. If only I could have been allowed more of a chance to express myself to her, I'm sure it could have made a difference to me even if not to Catherine. She didn't make any effort to see me as far as I know at anytime even though she was being prepared to be my bride. Why couldn't she have come to see me just the once to put her case forward, it would have all been better than finding out from someone else. Of course, having to wait so long, it never crossed my mind that I was going to be rejected when all the other parts of the puzzle had come together in such a tight fit. What had I done wrong to lose out in the very sight of the finishing line. Was it just another test of my resolve? She surely couldn't be so empty not to face me and tell me that she didn't want me. It would have been a lot better and I could have handled the situation a lot easier. Sure you might say there's plenty more fish in the sea, but do the other fish have my blood from my right arm pumping through their veins? No other person has that blood that I gave in their body and she has turned her back on me for someone else. I hope she will be happy with what she has done. It took me a long time to come to terms with the rejection, why should I bother going on, why not stand in front of a speeding bus, but then I thought why should I be distraught over a selfish small minded bitch. It's not going to be easy to find someone to spend my life with yet I will manage to find someone after all, I'm used to disappointment in my life, so I am very adept at picking myself up off the floor. You could say I learned a very good lesson out of the Catherine affair and that is in future I'll get any deals I do in writing, stating what I get from the transaction. This will ensure I don't come a cropper again, leaving me bitter inside, whatever I might say to the contrary.

A new year came upon me, 1991, and I came off medication and started another job club during the year. It was a woman who was in charge of the job club. She was very patronising and I didn't like her from the start because above all else she was ignorant and stupid. I somehow managed to go for a few weeks. The other people at the centre kept telling me that I looked down and pissed off, which was definitely the case. It all reminded me of my unhappy period of working for the council and I believe I have a serious problem to overcome with regards to my attitude of gaining work. I think I have a mental block because of all the pain I suffered while being on the council. It isn't because I don't want to work, but I feel that if I even managed to get a job I would not be able to keep it for too long before I got a reaction from my head. In some ways it goes back to my time in hospital where I finally realized that I have been ill, just because I brought the breaking of my nervous system down on myself didn't mean I could control all the bottled up feelings I had stored up. There was a depression posing a threat to my health so I jacked it in. I went for walks again and did some paintings to pass the time. I would visit my mother's during the week and go to my fathers on a Monday for his legendary beans on toast. My sister had come back to

Sheffield and my mother let them stay at her house while they waited to get a council house. They now had a son called Richard and a daughter on the way. They moved out during the year to a council house in Beighton, which was the other side of the city.

Even though I knew Catherine didn't want me I still thought a lot about her. I would walk around Catherine's house hoping to catch a glimpse of her. The door had been changed on the house to a more solid door. The strange thing about it is that I couldn't feel the presence of Catherine in the way I had done before. I still don't know how I've never bumped into Mick, Catherine's brother, who I worked with while at the council. I did see her other brother in Hillsborough a few times but I didn't really know him so I never spoke to him. On going often to walk around Catherine's house I would smoke cigars as I walked and thought that one day I would meet her walking the dog. With me not picking up her presence as I had previously, I began to wonder if she no longer lived in Sheffield. I had not seen Catherine since the night I got a lift home in a police car so maybe she had left the city. I know one thing, I still wanted to see her again, but in time I hoped I would never meet her again.

I was moved from my flat while it was being modernised to another block close by. After the improvements were finished I moved back into my flat which was now a lot warmer. I certainly have no complaints about the flat other than I don't want to have to stay in it all day. Most of my neighbours when I first moved in have left the flats to go elsewhere. I got in touch with a group offering to teach computer know-how to beginners like me, who knew nothing about them. After enquiries they got in touch to tell me of a test that you had to do in order to get on the scheme. On the day of the test I had a terrible head cold and was in no fit state to do any thinking. Not surprisingly, I didn't pass the test but the lady I had an interview with did mention another scheme that was being run later in the year, and I told her that I would be interested in having a go on that course. I went straight home and went to bed to die! Well that's how it felt at the time. So I had failed another exam to join the list. There's no doubt about it, I'm definitely a genius when it comes to doing exams, especially when it comes to failing them, I'm in a class of my own. My sister had started a part time job and she was leaving her two brats at a crèche where I would collect them and take them to my mother's house. I would have them for just over an hour, but one day the crèche was closed so I had to baby-sit for five hours. The two munchkins were a total pain in the bum and they drove me up the wall. I just couldn't take it and it did my nerves no good whatsoever and I was glad to see them go after such a nerve racking session. I take my washing down to my mum's usually on a Friday then go for a walk around Hillsborough. I was gone from my mother's house for less than an hour. When I returned someone had kicked the door in and the back part of the door was on the floor. It took a while for it to sink in and I went into the front lounge where the video was but it was no longer there. After about five minutes of disbelief I phoned the police and told them there had been a break in. I looked through the telephone book to find out the number where my mother works so I could ring her and let her know what had happened. I rang my mother and told her that the video had been stolen and I couldn't tell if anything else was missing. The police seemed to be taking an awfully long time in coming so I rang again. A man and a woman came and I thought they were selling insurance but when they came around to the back door the man showed his badge. They came in and I told them that the video had been stolen and only my mother would know if anything else was missing. I was asked if I had a job, my shoe size and whether I'd had a haircut in the last month. No doubt about it they certainly are keen even when it does take them fifty minutes to answer a call. The man said when looking at the door that had been kicked open "It looks like they got in through here!" Good grief, Sherlock Holmes is not dead but is working for the police in South Yorkshire. To deduce that the door had a big footprint on it and then the burglar had entered the house after kicking the lock off left me totally breathless in amazement. With people of this caliber on the tails of the criminal element in society, we have nothing to fear for these police are on the ball. I was glad when they had left; it was taxing keeping up. They did mention that a man would come to take fingerprints. My mother just missed the police and after having a good look around realised there was a watch missing too. The theft had an effect on me, which took over my life for a month. Even though my mother had bought the video for my brother and me it was virtually mine and was like losing a friend. I ended up buying an ex-rental that was not as good as the stolen video but at least I could watch a film when I wanted to again. The police did not recover the stolen video.

The firm who were offering computer courses got in touch with me and told me that there was a place for me if I wanted it. I got in touch with them and said that I would like to go on the course. The first week of the course was the week before Christmas 1991, which meant us having a holiday straight after the first week. I was now suffering with a head pain but I thought it was nothing. The effect of my major cold on top of looking after my sister's kids and the stealing of the video from my mother's house had been piling up against my nervous system. After Christmas, and feeling like I was going through one big hangover all the time, I started the year by going to the computer course but I was having a job following what we were supposed to do because my head was full of confusion. When the first week of the new term was over, I realised I could not continue with my head in such a state. I caught the bus to town on the Monday but when I got there the pain seemed to be getting fiercer. I caught the bus back to Hillsborough and made for the doctor's surgery. When it was my turn to be seen I knocked on the door and entered. My doctor, Livingstone could not even remember my name, which just goes to show how many patients doctors see in the course of their work. I told her it was like someone inside my head squeezing my brain and making my thoughts a muddle. It was a build up of events that had taken its toll but it appeared that the computer course was to blame but I don't believe that because I enjoyed my time on the course. When I told her about the computer course she seemed surprised that I had undertaken such a course without getting in touch with her first. She put me back on medication and I knew that only tablets would take away the pain. My legs turned pink and the hairs on my legs all went dark black, this was the side effect of taking the tablets. The pain was still there and I had to get in touch with the dole office to tell them I was now on the sick and not able to work. When it all got sorted out I did not have to sign on anymore and my cheque would be sent to me or so it was explained. They kept not sending me the cheque so I had to go to West Street office every week to get the cheque I was due. Sometimes the waiting room was full and with me not feeling well it was not doing my nerves any good. Thankfully, after having to go and collect my Giro, it got sorted out after five weeks. When I told the doctor about the difficulties I was having she wondered how I would have gone on if I ended up back in hospital again, with them not sending the cheque through. The drugs took the best part of three weeks to take hold and I was very glad when the head pains ceased. The tablets made me quite sleepy and I would usually go to bed in the afternoon. I must admit that the whole situation worried me a great deal because it was the first time that the head pains had come back to haunt me since hospital. I had been having problems with depression and with my nerves since hospital but the head pains I endured in my time at the Northern General Hospital had not reappeared until now. It sent shock waves into my thoughts, would I ever be free from all that took place in 1987 and the years are passing quickly even when you're not having fun. The massive burn out I went through inside my head looks like it will be with me in some form for the rest of my life and I will have to come to terms with it all.

I certainly used up a lot of imagination in the chapter on my time in hospital. I don't believe that I stopped the world from being destroyed but there were some other things that I didn't mention. The tune about bears having a picnic went through my head a lot in my time in hospital and it all seemed to make a strange sense. I also thought that from what was being said on the television, which people were being shown their numbers in relation to a new order for people to live by. The whole thing had been worked out for them and they would now live more fulfilled lives than they had done before. This reminds me of how out of my head I was for a long time in my stay in hospital and that I used my imagination to shelter me from the turmoil that my brain was going through. By having a good imagination I managed to hold on to my dreams. I always believed in the dream that I could help change things for the better for myself and the people around me. I was also a very bad loser as a child and I think my single mindedness helped me very much to get through my ordeal. Daydreaming was something I did a lot of while I was at school to get me through the day. I never believed that one day I would have a supernatural power to release that would change other people's lives and mine forever. I never thought that I was better than other people but I had a strong sense that I was different to others, which made me the odd one out. There was a lot to put up with during my childhood, such as loose bowels, nose bleeds, falling over matchsticks, sometimes just falling because my head went dizzy, all these things that I had to go through to get to my destiny. Except I didn't know that at the time, so I was usually jealous of people with a far greater balance than myself but I grew out of a longing to be someone else, that made me come to terms with my accidental nature. While on the works I also daydreamed and sometimes I would get angry about the way I was treated and I thought of the day when I would pay them back with interest if they deserved it. Of course, you might think that this is just something else I have made up to protect myself from reality but I can assure you it is all true. During my life many people said to me "Cheer up, it might never happen" and I thought to myself what if it did happen, what would they say then? Maybe because of the way things had to be I always thought that I was missing out in my life and this affected my personality, which made me different to other people. There certainly aren't any concrete answers to my thoughts from past time to the present of now in my thinking.

I had to see the doctor every month to see how I was getting on and also to get a sick note that I could send off to the dole office on West Street. After the first few months of being on the tablets, I became more stable and started to feel better in myself, there were still days when I didn't feel too well but in the main, I was feeling better than I had done for a long time. After being on the sick and getting Income Support I was sent a form to fill in which would get me put on Invalidity Benefit. For some reason Invalidity Benefit pays more than Income Support but I have certain other things to pay for unlike when I was on Income Support and it was all paid for me. I now get a book with a cheque to cash every week and when it runs out another book is sent to the post office to be collected by me. With plenty of time on my hands the suggestion by my dad that I could write a book about my experiences in my life seemed to have a lot of appeal. The main problem was to get motivated to begin in the first place. I talked into a microphone and played back what I had said on tape. It was not particularly any good but it helped me to start and that was the main thing. I wrote about four sides of A4 paper and would have in the past called that a book as far as I was concerned. It wasn't very well written but I had made a start. The months passed by and I wrote very little and kept taking the tablets that were prescribed to me. By Christmas of 1992 I had been on tablets for nearly the whole of the year. I kept putting off doing some writing and I was very half-hearted about the whole thing. With Christmas coming up it gave me another excuse for not producing any written work. My brother and his wife and newborn baby came up from Colchester for Christmas and stayed at my mother's. I was glad they came because it made it more of a Christmas for my mother. My dad and Maureen went to my dad's sister, Auntie Elsie who lives in Southampton, for the New Year. My New Year resolution for 1993 was easy to choose; I chose that I would get stuck into writing about my life with all its' trials and tribulations that I have had to contend with up to now. The more I wrote the better I felt about it all. It gave me a chance to get parts of my life off my chest and come to terms with the new me. I know for me that it was not going to be an easy thing to do but that it would be beneficial in getting over some of the more telling scars that my journey through life had given me. There are some thoughts that have arisen from me thinking about my life that I would like to write down so you yourselves may be able to think through and gain something from the ideas. When I was a child was I really taken around the houses so people knew who I was or is it just a figment of my imagination? When I was a child did I sense fear from adults around me or is it down to one great hallucination? Maybe I haven't gone back far enough, I've mentioned that there was something different about my birth but does it go even further back to even before my conception? Am I the bearer of a prophecy? So I was expected when I arrived and would be capable of overcoming all the obstacles that would be put in my way. My dad said to me "We never thought you'd get through it all, Son!" It raises the question of what would have happened if I had failed but I did fulfill my side of the deal. I did get through it and I am still owed, I have received nothing for my efforts so I am left to consider that it was not of any great significance in the scheme of things. The most precious thing I have ever wanted was Catherine, who is not mine and there's nothing that I can be given to compare so maybe that is the reason I have been given nothing. There is of course, another reason that I have received nothing and that is because I have made the whole thing up and that it all arises from a hallucination I had while I was in cloud cuckoo land. Where does all the time go? I am nearly 32 years old and I still haven't grown up much along the way. I'm the forever teenager who once believed that after the age of 16 all the years were the same. There was a life before Catherine and there is a life after, so I will just have to get on with it. Why was my life so mapped out before I was born? There was something different about me that separates me from you. My mum and dad knew I was different. My dad had been saving the dressing gown with the Wolf's head on for years in anticipation. But nothing seems to explain what it was that made me different. Had I chosen a different route in my life, would I have been hated for doing so? Someone out there must know some of the answers to these questions. I do not believe that I am the only one who was born for a mission and it makes me wonder what happened to the others. Another thought is that in the main I've hurt people when I haven't intended to do so because I am such a deep person; other people tend to think that everything I say or do is what I meant, when in fact, I am just being silly. If I was a more lighter minded person who does not take much notice of the world around me with all its problems and all the pain and misery that ensues, I am sure I would be a more happier person in myself. Why was it that I was fated to wait and wait, to forget, to deny, to die inside myself and become nearly brain-dead in my life in order to get to the day when I met my other half. When I get there I get a girl who doesn't give a toss whether I live or die. She cannot comprehend the fact that if I didn't exist she wouldn't either. What did I do so wrong in my past life that I had to pay such a heavy price in my life today? The events that took place in 1987 have changed my life forever, but even though I am free of the burden that weighed me down so, I cannot deny the unhappiness that I went through in order to achieve my aim. My past cannot be denied. But I do not want to live there, and hope one day I can forget so much of it. All of these thoughts and the images they bring to me cannot overlook the fact that I did not get Catherine. She is the only human being on this planet with different coloured blood other than myself. But the blood will now be only red because the time for colours other than red have now passed by. What a pity and what a waste of time and effort, I must be born under the stupid bastard star sign and maybe that's what made me different to the rest in the first place.

I am still on the sick and taking the tablets which keep my head stable, but I have been having some dizzy spells and seeing stars, plus when I stand up I go faint and have to hold on to a wall. The Zeebrugge incident that happened on the same day as I went into hospital was commemorated and it was hard to believe that it is now six years since I went into hospital. I never thought that in 1993 I would still be suffering from the breakdown and still feeling drained from my mission after all this time. The time when I was in hospital and my dad told me if I ever did it again I would end up in Middlewood appears like a joke to me now. If I even considered the thought I would deserve to be put away because there is no way I could get through for a second time. Once was more than enough for me, and if you feel left out and would like redemption, remember not to get in touch with me because my time thankfully, has passed by and I can try to live life just like everyone else from now on.

7 Sex

I started to have strong sexual feelings when I was eight years old. I can remember exposing myself to some of the girls where I lived while we were out playing. It seemed like it was the right thing to do at the time and it made my heart beat faster when I did expose myself to females and some of the girls would do it to. I suppose it was a very natural thing to do as we all did it at sometime. I can recall dropping a needle on the floor so I could look up a teachers dress when I was at junior school but I was not the only one being a child pervert.

When I started Myers Grove school I was eleven years old. It's not to surprising to say I felt sexual urges towards my female teachers. I fancied all of my female teachers except for one who took us for French, her name was Oldfield and she did not like males and from what I saw of her I doubt very much if males liked her to much either. The Biology teacher I had at the time was the one I was attracted to the most. It was she who went through the facts of life with my class and I wanted her body. There were very few of the girls in my classes who I fancied, maybe I wanted the guiding hand of experience. The urges increased and by now I was playing with myself all the time. I would play with myself for ages and see how many times I could come. One night I was still in my school uniform and I was talking to one of the girls who lived nearby and I put it to her that we could go into the woods and take our clothes off. When she had agreed and we were going to go her mother called out for to go into the house and I never did get another chance which was probably for the best, but what might have been? So much for the plans of mice and men, I think its how the cookie crumbles. Even at this early age I knew deep down I could not be like other children even though I felt the same urges as those around me, it was a case of being patient.

With the age of puberty came acne which always upset me, maybe because I am so vain. It always seemed to be the end of the World when I got big boils on my nose and sometimes I wondered whether I was starting to grow another nose. I used needles to pick at the boils and the pock marks on my nose to this day are a reminder of those horrible boils. I did go to the Doctor about them but none of the creams or tablets worked. This in my mind made for a kind of barrier between me and the female sex or more importantly I hid behind it to shield myself from any advances that might arise. I hope that does not sound like I was expecting girls to fall at my feet and begin worshipping me even though on the other hand it does sound like a good idea.

Of cause when I started to reach my teens the urges began to increase and intensify. Luckily for me my left hand had started on a beautiful friendship. I was having doubts about my sexuality, that is I wanted to have sex with a female but I felt deep down that this was not possible and that I had to hold my emotions in check. This for me meant emotional turmoil and with my teens I began to go into a deep depression. My moods from this time would alter very quickly from a high to a low and would effect my schooling and my life in general. A large weight would seem to be resting on my shoulders and to alleviate this condition I would spend a lot of my time dreaming about women and making love to them if only in my head. I so much wanted it to be real life but all I got was my imagination, which I was lucky with because I have a great imagination.

The school years were hard because the other lads would tell stories of their experiences. Of cause a lot of it was made up nonsense, with some of them saying they had sex over twenty times a night or some such rubbish. Some of my friends at school would go to the Top Rank club on the Saturday and asked me to go with them but I never went. It was a club for young teenagers, held in the mornings till lunch time. The reason I didn't go was not just down to acne I was starting a withdrawal from life because I could not join in with the usual activities of a puberty teenaged randy male. Don't get me wrong there was a part of me that wanted to join in but deep down inside of me I knew there was no point in me starting something which I couldn't finish and that something was sex.

When I was about fourteen there was a film on at the Classic Cinema, which was known as the flea pit, to us all. The film that we went to see was I think called Naked Over The Fence and turned out to be a poorly dubbed foreign film. The Cinema was packed on the Friday night we went to see the film and there were six of us. We ended up sat behind some girls from our school. The Cinema looked like it was going to fall to pieces because of thee strain of having a full house, which was filled with sex starved half wits, namely us all. The place couldn't have been so full for years and no one was paying much attention to the films, even though I can tell you the films shown us were total crap but it was a great laugh that night which everyone seemed to share in. It was very much a be there experience and I enjoyed it immensely.

There was one girl in my year who I really liked and I had known her for a long time, she was called Julie. I can recall her taking Assembly one morning and it must have taken a lot of guts to face hundreds of fellow pupils. The speech she made was about saving the Whale, whose sperm was being used in women's make up, which is quite a thought. It is one of only a very few number of Assemblies that I can remember having. Julie was too much in the main stream of events at the school, while I was part of the background scenery.

I can remember having a nude magazine with the image I can still remember being of a nude woman eating a water melon. The dance groups such as Legs and Co or later Hot Gossip were my fantasy women and I love seeing women's legs when they're wearing stockings in particular. When we were in our last year at school there was a film on at the Ritz Cinema at the Intake and it was called Black Emmanuel 2. Even though some of my friends had already seen the film the week before they went with me to see it again. Altogether there were five of us and one or two had seen Black Emmanuel 1 the previous film. The Ritz Cinema on the Friday night had only us and a couple of Dirty Dan the Dirty Old Mans in. It was only a soft porn movie but I still came in my pants. The woman in the title role was beautiful and she was certainly worth one; what do you mean I am only a wanker? So much about sex was discussed by my friends and I usually went a bright red colour when the subject was brought up. Well school was tough to get through but work was waiting just around the corner with even more ridicule to come my way.

I joined the Sheffield Works Department and was an apprentice painter and decorator. In the site cabins there was usually plenty of girlie magazines in stock, plus some you couldn't buy in your newsagents, such as Orgasm or Climax, which left little to the imagination. Sometimes they would be passed around at dinnertime and a woman's vagina was nicknamed spam fritter. When I was still new to the job, a lad no older than fourteen gave me a load of hard core porn for the cabin. By the end of the week they had all but gone, with the men trying to blame me but they were just trying to cover there tracks. It made you think what their wives thought about it or if they took them just for themselves, you never know. When the discussion was sexual I would usually get called a virgin and for that matter - so did the other apprentices. They would ask who your girlfriend was or how many times you've had sex and then start telling some tripe about what they got up to when they were my age. After a while it no longer bothered me, I am very fortunate I was born with a very broad back. On some of the jobs where the men knew who I was they would be helpful rather than hurtful. One of the men on one job I was working on would start off a load of jokes for my benefit such as "I gave my wife nine inches, I fucked her three times!" I used to say "It makes you sweat just thinking about it!" When we had a laughter session it made me feel a lot better about things and certain days would pass a little quicker.

When I was eighteen going on nineteen I went on holiday with the family after going on holiday with a friend the previous year and thankfully I would be going abroad with friends in future. The relationship I had with my parents was not so hot and I was going through the process of wanting to decide things for myself. We went on Holiday to the Isle of Man and booked into a cheap boarding house for half board. There was a little bar in the boarding house and one night when my parents and my Brother had gone to bed I got talking to a girl who worked in the kitchen. She was called Susan and she had come from Liverpool to gain some employment. We arranged to meet the next day and went around the sea front and into a bar. I fell in love with this girl or so I thought at the time. It made my holiday to not have to be with my parents all the time and it felt like freedom. I spent the evenings with Susan from now on and the two weeks flew by. The girls who served the food were a little jealous of the attention I gave Susan but that was there hard luck story for the day. When it was my last night I can recall being very upset and I even cried on the way to my bed and thinking that the World was against me and that I would never see Susan again.

I wrote to her and she wrote to me during the week after my holiday. She should have stayed on the Isle of Man for another month but she left the job so she could return to Liverpool. I decided to go and see her at the weekend and we talked over the phone to confirm the time I would be arriving by train. My dad gave me a lift to the Midland Station and we had an awful beer in the bar before I went for my train. The train was on time and when we were coming into Lime Street Station my heart beat faster. Susan was there and we kissed and made our way to a bus stop. I was carrying a small black bag which had my shaving gear and some fresh underwear inside it. Susan was not living at home but at a friend's who didn't mind me staying there. The place in Liverpool was called Speke and I think it was the place where George Harrison came from and looking at the place, with the state it was in I bet he as never been back.

When we got off the bus we only had a short walk to the house. The Lady whose house it was had seven children one of whom was in borstal. When we went in the house there were no carpets and no paint or paper on the walls, even Stone Age man had some form of paint on the cave walls. The Lady whose name I have forgotten had a child to a man who was living with her at the time whilst the other children's father had remarried.

Me and Susan went to the Catholic club for a drink that night, which was on the same road as the house. The Ladies mother was visiting that night so me and Susan didn't sleep together that night, things would be different the following night or so I thought. I got on really well with the children and they were the nicest kids I have ever met, who deserved a lot better. We talked during the day me and Susan and went for a walk to the local newsagents. The newsagents had wire cageing on the windows, which at that time was not in use in Sheffield. The shop was half bare which reflected the area sadly. When it was night fall we got ready to go to the club again, this time with the Lady whose house I was staying at and her man friend. The children could watch the television in the house, which was on the second floor and also had a carpet where it touched. The television was a slot machine operated one. The bedroom windows had bars across them for some reason and to all purposes it resembled an out post in Outer Mongolia than a place in Britain. The whole place when I walked around it looked like the Second World War had just ended.

I bought some drinks in the club where there was a really awful turn on. I can remember one of the fab duo throwing his hat on to the floor saying "That's Chuck Berry!" sadly this was the funniest and most memorable part of their sorry act. The night passed away and when the club was ready for closing we left. Tonight me and Susan would sleep together in the television room, which also had an electric fire; wonders never cease.

We both got undressed in the dark and we started to kiss and when it came to the moment when we were supposed to have intercourse I could no longer get an erection. This was most strange to me because I had always managed to get one before. But my night of supposed passion was not to be. I couldn't let people down having got this far, not that this made me feel any better at the time. If I had made love to Susan it would not be possible to give redemption when the time came.

On the Sunday we said our goodbyes at the train station and I got onto the train to Sheffield with a confused mind about the weekend. It was back to work on the Monday and all the jollies that brought me. I couldn't think about anything else as you can imagine, of what had taken place at the weekend or more precisely what had not taken place.

Me and Susan talked on the phone and I arranged to go again to Liverpool at the weekend. My mind was trying to make some sense of all that was going on but I was a fool in that I had fallen in love with someone who I couldn't have. In some ways it was just that fact why I didn't date girls too much in my teens because I would not be able to fulfil my promise; if I made love to only one girl before the time was right it would all be over. Looking back on it I was doing a social study but that hides away the fact that I was in love with Susan even though it was just a teenage crush.

The weekend arrived and I caught the train on the Friday night and when we got to the Lady's house both me and Susan were in a bedroom with two single beds. The children were in bed when I arrived because I had caught a later train than the previous week. In the morning the children were happy to see me and I was glad to see them.

On this particular Saturday there was a little fete being held with a local radio station taking part also. There was a little parade for the children and it seemed odd that this was happening in such a desolate place. I bought some of the children an ice cream and I can still recall those who missed out complaining. The event helped the day pass on but I was glad when it finished. One of the younger children had been with me during the day and I took him back to the house where his mum was waiting for him. It was strange but on the second visit I was more concerned for the children than my hopeless love life.

When we were ready to go out we went to the Catholic club yet again and downed some beers. Me and Susan didn't talk much in the club with the act being worse than last week, which if you had been the previous week you would have said was impossible, so much for Liverpool being the home of humour. When we went back to the house I knew I had been stupid with my crush for Susan and I put it down to my lack of experience in such matters. My head was full of emotional turmoil which would not go away no matter how hard I tried to break through the other side. If only I could be like your average teenager but then again no one ever said life was easy. When Sunday came I was not feeling too good and I had made up my mind that this whole charade had to come to an end. The Lady and her man friend were going to Town and I caught the bus with them, I said goodbye and felt terrible about the whole thing. The journey back to Sheffield seemed to take for ages. There was a family on the train who were having a row and I got a packet of biscuits on my lap when one of them threw the biscuits at one of their tribe.

I was happy with being back in Sheffield and it really did feel like home after my visit to the reservation in Liverpool. The Lady called a couple of weeks later to tell me of a change of address and how much the children wanted to see me. I did think of going to see the children but I thought it would be for the best if I just let it drop. I hope the kids got a better deal than it looked like they were going to get when I saw them last. I had finished totally with Susan and it all reminded me of the fact that I still had to wait if I was to make any difference to the scheme of things when my time would come, unlike me, well me and my left hand were still good buddies. What if I was wrong and I was punishing myself just for the sake of it, I was racked with doubt which would not go away.

My teenage years were quickly coming to a close and I felt unfulfilled with me withdrawing in to myself, which made me more insular with every passing day. I was still the most talked about member of the painting division and my ears were always ringing. The taunting and abuse in general which came my way, I would let fly over my head because I was immune to it all and anyway it was like water off a duck's arse. On my holidays that followed with me going away with friends, I never met anyone who I fell in love with again and maybe the time with Susan was just down to my age. The fact is I had the urges but the great weight I felt on my shoulders kept me away from carrying them out. In my life it was a case of waiting for things to happen and I had to believe in that he who waits gets everything when it comes around eventually. The trouble with my life being that I never did believe there would be a happy ending to my story and for that matter I never thought my other half existed. For me it was a case of my faithful left hand and a great imagination.

When I started to go to the O level classes I had paid to do I met a woman who took my English class who I was attracted to, not because of a physical thing but very much because of a mental attraction. She helped me a great deal by marking my work down through the course, which after reading this you no doubt can see why, and pointed out some authors to read, which could help with the development of my writing. Don't get me wrong I am not saying she was unattractive but I had grown up, even though if I had been her pupil when I was at school I would probably had a crush on her. She was there for me when I needed someone to talk through what was whirling around my head when it was time for action in 1987. I will always be grateful to Ms Emsworth even if she did speak Received Pronunciation.

Having mentioned other people's vices of looking at pornographic magazines I will come clean and say that I enjoy watching porn videos and find it entertaining to see so many ways of doing the same thing. The porn video scene is something I have done since being turned down by Catherine. Whether I have become a woman hater through my experiences, I don't know but that is what some people would say I am, even though I think it is a flawed argument. Just because you watch someone shoot somebody on the television doesn't mean that you will go out and do the same thing. Maybe that's a bad comparison to make but I also have a few homosexual videos where men are the ones making fools of themselves. Those who say porn is degrading must be watching different films to me as it is only natural bodily functions on view whether some people like it or not that is shown.

By having had to repress my own sexuality in my life may well make me see things in a different light. I don't really know how much of a pervert I have become if one at all. In other countries in Europe they show porn films every night on the television but I have noticed that abroad people seem to take a more adult view of life yet in Britain we seem to be treated like children by the people who run the country and make the decisions.

When I was in Hospital sex was something I thought about quite a lot and that there was now no reason to not take part. The person I wanted to have sex with the most was of cause Catherine. Looking back on it I wish I had wrote letters about my feelings towards her but I was in a right state. Why she never contacted me to talk things out I will never know. I know one thing I am worth one conversation of everyone's time.

Sex is certainly something that is not going to go away that's for sure. There were times when I had to walk away from offers of sex in my time on the council, because I met many lonely women. I can recall one woman who was single with a child who was more than friendly and I had to leave her house before things go out of hand. I hope you don't think I saw myself as some sort of stud because I only ever got a few offers which if you had seen me at the time you would not have believed it was possible but that just confirms that the women were desperate and lonely.

The thing with sex is that sometimes you can't think of anything else. When I see a woman with black tights on with good legs it's a real turn on, unlike my leering depraved expression. But on looking back on my none sex life as it is, the best feeling was as a kid to early teenager. The feeling of sex that I had was such a great one, the way it could just lift up your day with an excitement from exposing yourself to a girl. I hope no one reading this is going to start exposing themselves in public for I will no doubt get the blame should it happen.

Sex to me is about a feeling not just a product you can buy at the supermarket, even though some people would probably like to buy it there if they could. In the press a week doesn't pass by without another guide to sex or the Zodiac of sex pullout. Sometimes it's the confession of a page three model who will claim that they are not involved in pornography, which seems strange to me as some of the most well known models in the country have appeared on the covers of girlie magazines. Because they print pictures of nude or semi nude women in newspapers some people try to get these photographs banned. I don't understand how people being in their birthday suit is such a threat to the minds who see it. People who put forward for censorship don't seem to believe that the rest of us can take or leave it and possibly make up our own minds. These people are the sort of people who really at the end of the day don't want other people to think for themselves.

I am willing to admit to my vice but are these people who act so concerned on our behalf willing to admit theirs. What harm can watching nude men and women of consenting age do to anyone who is an adult. I can not see the sense of this argument at all. We are all sexist by choice whether some like the fact or not as they see it. By sexual preference we choose our partners whether they be heterosexual or homosexual. To me this is the right of every individual and they should be left to make up there own preferences by themselves.

No one should be allowed to stop someone else finding out there own sexuality and hide behind politics to do so. It is the right of all to make fools of themselves as some would have it but it is also an essential part of growing up and gaining experience about life in the process. Maybe in many ways I am not the one to judge having had such a limited weight of experience behind me because of the burden on my shoulders, however real or imagined, to reach my destiny.

That's about all I have to say on the subject of sex (or the lack of it) for now at any rate. What would I have done without my left hand is anyone's guess. One thing for sure is if I had given in and had sexual intercourse with just one female before the right time my life story would be a very different one. I very much doubt that I would be trying to write a book about my life if I had chosen a different route and let down the people who were counting on me.

I got offers when I was going round the pub circuit after Hospital from a few women but at the time I was still very much for having Catherine and so was not interested. Going back to my time at Myers Grove and being in my English lesson taken by Mr Daniels, he used to ask "How's your sex life?" It goes to prove that some people are all heart and never hit a nerve of frustration but others... well that's another matter.

8 Symbolism

If you're wondering how come I got the job and you didn't, I don't really have an answer for you but I do feel that there was a power, which exerted a force, which was linked to symbolism. To begin I will go back to the time when my parents met for the first time. They were both on holiday in Blackpool where they first got together. My mother claims she was born in the sound range of Bow Bells, which makes her a cockney. My Father was born in Sheffield so is a born Yorkshire man. When they were married my mother moved to Sheffield and they both lived with my grandparents, as was the custom on those days. My granddad's house was near the Wadsley Bride Club and it was situated on Wolfe Road. The Wolfe will appear again in this story. My granddad was a little Mester Knife maker, with the knife being very symbolic. I think I can recall that my grandmother who dies while I was still young said "Don't hit this one, he's the one we've been waiting for!" Maybe this is just wishful thinking on my behalf to back up my claims to what really happened during my illness. Whether I was taken around the houses for people to know who I was could also be an over active imagination. Yet if my story is true, there must have been something that was different about me when I was born, for people to take notice.

My mother's parents divorced when she was still a child and her mother remarried a man whose surname was Angel. On one occasion there was a great storm that hit Sheffield and Tommy Angel came to Sheffield to see how my mother was. If I claimed I had something to do with it you might rightly think me paranoid, yet there was the time when I had my appendix removed and that week Sheffield had some of the worst weather it has ever endured.

By giving me the knife to cut into people's minds I was capable of looking into the workings of people's heads and able to attack certain areas, which would bring about a change in a person's mind. When I visited my dad just a week or so before my ordeal In Hospital to smoke the pipe of peace, I wasn't sure which house his was, but I made a guess that the one with all the rubble outside was his. He came in his car just at the right moment and I waited for him to open the door of his house and noticed that the doorknocker was a wolf's head. That didn't make me think much about it at the time so I just acknowledged it but said nothing about it.

When I was throwing the paint all around in Myers Grove School I thought I could see people from another time with paint daubed on their faces dancing around a big fire. The rituals of the ancients were before me and you can't get much more symbolic than that. The release I experienced was quite fantastic at that moment in time and I'm sure some of the reasons behind me having the power stretch right back in time.

After the orgy of enjoyment of course you already know I ended up in hospital and my dad brought me a dressing gown that he had been saving for the occasion. On the dressing gown pocket there was a wolf's head, symbolizing the leader of the pack. My fellow patients took note of my dressing gown whilst I had it and I can remember one patient saying "You're good you are!" when I was wearing the gown. The way certain events came together hint at a long awaited plan that even precedes my being born. The way after such a long wait I met my other half who just happened to be in my history class, who happened to be a former workmate's sister, who happened to like U2 and was now living in Stannington. That my tutor in English should be a man who was washed out and in a terrible state, just at the right time asking for redemption. This is too many coincidences and a magician would pay a million quid for such a trick except this was real magic. In days gone by, all this might have been put down to being the work of witchcraft or some unholy alliance with the devil. But such times have passed by and I don't have three sixes on the back of my head, believe it or not. Some life force made all these things come together just as Catherine wouldn't exist if it was not for me but that is too much for her to comprehend and for that matter I'm sure it is difficult for a lot of people to comprehend either. Getting back to the subject of how come I got the power and not my brother or sister. It's a question we can all ask yet I don't believe I will ever have a satisfactory answer. I was born with the gift or curse, depending on your point of view and given a great burden that weighed down on my shoulders for a quarter of a century; maybe all I did was draw the short straw. I do think though that there is something to do with this in my history and that this could be viewed by using symbolism. That symbolism holds the key to my power in completing my task is an interesting thought.

I can recall that one evening class that was being taken by John Edwards was him talking to me about a man he had known while he was a child, during the lesson. The thing is I am sure he was talking about my granddad, of course you might say it was all a flight of fancy on my behalf and I'm trying to make something out of nothing, but the way John Edwards was talking this particular evening, which had nothing to do with the subject he was supposed to be talking about, I'm sure he was addressing me. If he had known my granddad it would reaffirm the circuit, which was there before I was born and made even large during my lifetime. I do not know if there was any symbol for the circuit by those who knew who I was and what I was trying to achieve. The circuit itself though was a symbol in my mind and it was the five years on the council doing something I hated so much, yet I knew it had to be done whether I liked it or not. In many ways this was how something symbolic was turned into something that people could see and when the mist I had created come down to change some people it was all definitely real and not just a case of my imagination working overtime.

My time on the council when it seemed most of the time that I was taking on everyone was essential to the whole that I was attempting. You could say my ladder and stepladder were my crosses to bear as I worked off them and then moved them to another position to paint an area. It was very much a job of putting weight on my shoulders when I was moving the big ladder around an outside of a house that I was working on. This was also very much to do with the process of joining up areas so they would be effected when the time would come for me to do my redemption act. Not everyone on the council was behind what I was doing and some feared the power I had and were bewildered by the whole thing. It could be put down to them, fearing change, which is a very common fear to have or that they could not understand what was going on around them so went for the simplest answer they could think of trying to upset me. I got a bad reputation in my time on the council and I can say that I couldn't care less what anyone thought of me during that unhappiest part of my life. I got moved to an estate, which meant painting the outsides of houses and the charge hand said one dinner time "You don't talk much for a trouble causer Wayne!" I replied "Who Me?" then men in the cabin all laughed. In the main I was quiet which is the way I am normally with most people that I know and I think I caught on early in my life to be more of a person in the background rather than someone in the spotlight. The way I painted always taking my time over he job brought many a comment over the years. Some thought I was the slowest painter they had ever seen; others thought I should be the one who the time in motion people should study if they could find me making a motion. The thing is I knew I could only ever do it the once and that meant doing the job in a careful way as in the old saying if a jobs worth doing its worth doing well. It might well have made me unpopular but I had the wall around me and I could take the flak that came my way with ease. The wall is something I believe I was given to make sure I got through my task and it was built up so I feared no one. The wall would stay with me as long as my blood would stay pure because in order to go through everything I needed the blood to not be tainted by an act of intercourse that is something I've already written about. My body had to be pure not for just the people it would help, but so I could have my bride because I was given the incentive that once I had done for everyone else I could have what I wanted, and that was Catherine.

While I had the dressing gown with the wolf's head on the pocket, everyone in the hospital seemed to know who I was instantly. In fact some of the patient's feared me but I don't know why. The day I went off to find Catherine while I was still at hospital, I threw the gown away and also my shaving gear. This meant I started to grow some stubble on my chin and other areas of my face and this was very much noticed by the Matron on my ward, who always seemed to be giggling when near me. The Matron asked me "Are you going to grow a beard?" "I haven't got a razor!" I replied. The symbolism of the beard to do with someone of legend in the past was brought to the fore of stereo typing me, to much amusement of the laughing Matron. The very fact that I can't even grow a beard had no relevance to this very poor taste joke in saying that most of my life had been a poor taste joke, if I say so myself.

While I was in hospital, I thought that I had used a symbolic knife to attack other people's minds so they would think in a slightly more different way, to what they had before. I can recall Geoff Hammond who in particular seemed to have been under a great emotional stress. He was bordering on the paranoid and for that matter maybe he was paranoid. Just before my time to go to hospital, he actually said "I've never had a student who wanted me dead before!" This statement was directed at me and I still don't know why he thought I was out to kill him. I don't ever remember saying anything remotely vindictive to him or being malevolent towards him at any time. It certainly upset me at the time because I thought I was doing something that would be good for people and I wasn't planning on scaring one of my tutors to death. There's no doubt that I did affect people's minds and part of the process was losing out on a nights sleep for a couple of nights. The day when I had ran around Hillsborough and went to college where only two other students bothered to turn up was down to me but if I said I had done it, no one would have believed me. The symbolism that invades our minds every day can be used to alter people's usual thoughts and bring about a change that might only be temporary but a change none the less. One day in an early part of my stay in the Northern General I came across an article in a Reader's Digest book that was about mind travel and trying to get into other people's minds so you could find out what they were thinking. In part of it there was a young lad in an emergency ward who this person, who I thought of as myself, got into the lads mind but it only lasted for a few minutes because the lad didn't survive but he was the first attempt and wouldn't be forgotten even though he turned out unsuitable. When I had read this I thought back to an incident that happened while I was a child and we were still living at Holme Lane. I was doing the William Tell bit with my brother as my assistant and instead of a bolt from a crossbow I was using a dart. I threw the dart and it landed a couple of inches above his eyes and I rushed towards him as he started to cry. There's no doubt in my mind that it was one of the most stupid things I have ever done in my life and only somebody shit for brains would even attempt what could turn out to be a horror story for some poor bugger dumb enough to be the target. While I was in hospital and had just been reading about mind travel it occurred to me that maybe I had been trying to get into my brother's mind and find out all his fears that were present inside his head. He was one of my first guinea pigs. Of course on the other hand I was trying to push off some of the guilt for a very stupid and potentially blinding experience for my brother. The funny thing about it all is that a couple of inches away from my eyes in the middle of my head there was a mark. I know my brother to this day doesn't like me much because of the way I treated him when we were young so he'd definitely take the guilty part of the story. But the thought I had been given a power to go into other people's minds wouldn't go away easily, it would answer so much of why in times I had suddenly felt like the lad who was going to get caned at school and I didn't like the feeling beforehand or go through an event first hand such as the day I got the sack from the Council. I feel I had to go into other people's minds so I could perform what I was being paid for a lot better. I had to know why some people hold onto nothing yet won't let go, just as people who have everything feel there is nothing to believe in anymore. Maybe I wasn't just dreaming in my school days because I had a purpose to perform in learning about other people's dreams and aspirations. The symbol at our school was the acorn but come to think about it, they don't have too many oak trees together in a wood so maybe there's only ever enough room for one oak tree, which would certainly explain why very few of my school chums are doing that well in the big old world out there and probably point to the fact that I thought it was just a ramp from the start and I've peen proved right after all this time.

The biggest part of the process was in tackling the paranoia's that gets inside people's heads as they go through their journey through life. The affect that society has on people's prospective is great and they have a problem admitting to their weaknesses. I could tackle these problems in my 'A' level courses because the accent was on making a challenge to the accepted order of things and unlike at school debate was encouraged in the class to try and work certain questions out. The status quo could be put to the sword even though nothing major would change so you can all sleep well in your beds, don't worry because believe me, there's nothing major in the world of thought on the horizon.

This was the arena that I could use to express some of my deepest held beliefs and I had changed from being a beetroot face at school, when I was ever asked a question, to being someone who could put forward a well thought out opinion. On the other side of the coin, maybe I was deluding myself into thinking I could possibly make a difference and that I could not face the major disappointments in my life so I was just playing out a charade. I wanted to believe my observations on certain topics were worthwhile and had a greater significance, than the fact that it was just a load of garbled tripe.

I've put forward guilty conscience or knowledge able mystic it is up to you to decide which has the ring of truth to it or maybe you will end up disregarding both viewpoints for one of your own.

Before I ended up in hospital, I was going through the dictionary a lot and playing a game where I started off with a word and looked up its meaning and then looked up the words given as its meaning, and so on. I got an idea that maybe if I am whom I think I am, my name will be in the Bible of words, the dictionary. When I looked I found a word, which was taken from the Maori language, and it was spelt WAHINE, its definition is that it means woman. It made me think back to my time as a painter when I was working with John on a school and he was telling some of our workmates that I farted like a woman, well perhaps not the most complimentary thing to say about someone, but one that has stayed in my head ever since. My mother, being a southerner who has lived in Sheffield for years, still pronounces my name in what, to me, is a high-pitched way of talking and when she calls my name it sounds a lot like WAHINE when she says it. I don't really know if this is all just a figment of my own making or really has something deeper behind it.

When I threw my glasses away on my adventure to go and see Catherine while still at hospital, I needed to replace them, so I could watch television. I went for an eye test and my dad paid for the new pair but they were not as good as the pair I threw away. A strange thing happened when I wore the new glasses, I could see a yellow glow and all the dark parts of a room were very refined and very dark black. At first I was nearly sick on seeing this optical illusion, in some ways it made rooms seem like they had coloured glass windows. The effect made the rooms appear like chapels do when the sun hits the coloured glass. It must have been some sort of side effect from the drugs I was taking but it was definitely not an imagined one. I couldn't really handle it at first so I took off my new glasses and went for a walk outside and hoped that I was not going mad because of all the pressure that my mind and body had been through in recent times. It took me a few days to get used to seeing a yellow light hitting the room I was in, with all the very distinct black outlines. The world around me certainly appeared different to what it had been before and I was told when I mentioned what was going on, that the drugs could sometimes bring on a yellow optical effect and that there was nothing to worry about. That was very easy for them to say but it was me who was going through hell and it all at the time, appeared to point to permanent damage to the workings of my mind. The symbolism I thought of that the rooms were turned into instant chapels was an interesting one or so I thought, maybe at that moment I was more open to a religious angle than I would have liked to admit. But in the end it was just another side effect to my medication and I got used to it after a while.

When I looked down at my hands I felt there was imaginary handcuffs, which restrained my every move and also had an effect over all thoughts that I might have. I think it was because of all the responsibility that rested on my shoulders and my very limited way of life to reach my aims. When I started work and was doing my time at college with the other apprentices, it was like being thrown into the lion's den because of the bitterness that some of the lads had inside of them. I became in a way a vent for some of their deep held hatred and also posed a question because of the mystery that surrounded me. In other words I was not someone you could work out easily and this in part put doubts into minds and created a little bit of fear of the unknown. To get through would not be easy because my hands were tied so all I had were words rather than actions to combat my enemies, which was also of course the way I got through school in the main. My minor problem of having my hands bound was nothing compared to the problems that those around me were going through and I would be selfish to not acknowledge this. The day one of the group started to cut my strap on my rucksack I thought of it now having more significance than had appeared at the time. When I said " don't cut me off!" to stop the strap from being cut right through with a Stanley knife, it was a plea that I made because it was only the start and I hadn't got going yet, in breaking people down yet in the group, which was my task. I sewed the strap with strong cord to show that I could make a difference to these people who hated so much and now the game was on. All I had was kindness to get me through while so many of the group only could offer violence to get them through the day.

The first couple of weeks were typical of my life, when I was in hospital because it was me with my hands symbolically tied, faced with twenty four hours a day to get through. My parents taking it in turns to see me were by my side for just an hour but I had the other twenty-three hours to negotiate for myself. This task before me had always been in front of my life waiting for the day it came together.

When the police came for me after I had painted the rainbow I had my arms put behind my back and a pair of handcuffs were placed on me for real. So here the symbolism was pushed aside and I could fee the real thing, maybe it had not been just the thought of symbolism but a vision of the future. It's funny that from the time the handcuffs were put on me I was on the path to be free from my bonds. The trip to the police station made me think of all the films I had seen about prison. To give the prisoner the ultimate hell they were placed in solitary confinement but if I were ever in prison that is the place I would rather be in. I wouldn't go to pieces just because there was no one to talk to and it must say a lot about my character that being alone is something I have had a lot of and yet rarely in my life have I felt alone. Some of this is bared out when I think back over my late teens and early twenties, when I went out with friends I didn't go out every night; they did and I was accused of being a bit of a hermit.

Now that the imaginary handcuffs are no longer needed I no longer feel they are there. But the memories are very much alive and kicking. I still think that the parts of the story that encompassed the wolf simply backs up my claim of symbolism playing a major part in the whole story. I do believe that my family tree can point to some sort of reason for the power that I carried from birth to a good twenty-five years old, when I was a fair bit more worldly than I was in getting there. Of course you might think it is a very weak argument that symbolism played a very important part but a lot of other people who knew who I was, who nearly had a heart attack when they realized how much power I possessed, will believe any old rubbish that I write because they also know that some people would not come out of things for the better when all the dust settled. The wolf in sheep's clothing is very symbolic and of course precedes my life in the annals of time and if you happen to see a wolf's head on a doorknocker, please get in touch as soon as you can. Symbolism is out there and it affects all of our lives and I bet it still has a part to play in my life and also in yours.

9 Pieces at the end

There to start this final chapter I ask myself, well I've certainly come a long way since the start of the book and its opening chapter. I've gone through most of the ups and downs that have confronted me in my life up to now. The amazing details of my life that I claim are true but you may still have doubts, if you actually got this far and have read the book I hope you have enjoyed it up to now at any rate. I very much doubt if you have not enjoyed the book you will get your money back, but look on the bright side, with all the charity shops there are now you will have no problem in putting your copy of the book to good use. Maybe charity is not something you believe in so maybe you could hang the book on a rusty nail on the back of your toilet door and put the paper to better use! Of course if you are a lot more imaginative I'm sure there are a thousand and one uses that you could put your copy to, when you have read it. You may even want to look after your copy of the book but be sure to take medical advice if this is the case; I don't want to be blamed for any backlash that may arise from people reading this story and I will state clearly that you have read this book because you wanted to and no one forced your arm to do so. There's nothing like passing the buck, is there? When I started to write about my life, I never thought that I could write such a long book. There was certainly no precedent of writing long stories or long essays as the written word followed the spoken one in my case and that means devout silence. To think that I have put together so many words is something some of the people from my past would not have thought possible and in particular, my last English teacher at Myers Grove School, Mr Daniels, who could only get about half a page out of me because of my complete lack of interest, even though he was my favourite teacher. If he ever gets to read this he will no doubt deny any knowledge of ever having taught me and I can't say that I would blame him for doing so. My later confidant, Ms Emsworth, my 'O' level tutor from Stannington College, would no doubt notice an improvement in my ability to speak my mind through the written word but if she was marking the story, I dare say I would not get more than fifty out of one hundred for my efforts. For her I did try harder because I wanted to succeed but I would doubt if I would take any notice if she criticized my work

221

this time, for it would take longer than a couple of hours to rewrite this story. If Ms Emsworth or Mr Daniels ever does read this story, I would like them to get in touch and give me their honest opinion on what I have written. In the main though, I hope both of you have enjoyed reading a bare arse painter's recollections on what has been a very unusual story and used a sprinkle of salt in doing so. Putting them aside, I'll get back to the last chapter.

There is something I have not yet told you and that is that I walk down Stannington Hill virtually every day. I bought a pair of boots and had only been wearing them for six weeks when the sole broke and they started to let water in. I know that I do a fair bit of walking but this was ridiculous and the boots were a total waste of money. It meant buying another pair of footwear and I got some Doc Martens shoes, which I know to be a good brand and guaranteed. The people who live along Stannington Road must see me and think there goes that silly bastard walking down the hill again because he's too tight to pay to go by bus. I've done it when it's been pouring down with rain but now I will catch the bus if it's a rainy day. In the main, I catch the bus to go up the hill but sometimes I do walk up the hill as well. It gives me time in the morning to come round and it gets me out of my flat that I have now been living in for over four years. The flat is great and I'd hate to loose it because I am happy where I am. I sometimes see a man who was on the same landing as myself but he stayed in the flat that he was moved to, and we usually say hello to each other. When I'm early in the morning, I see some of the children going to school but there is nothing like as many pupils as there was when I attended Myers Grove. I think the part of the school that was for first and second year students is now part of the college, which has changed its name from Stannington College to Loxley College.

The thing that appeals to me about this final chapter is that I can go over my past one more time in a reflective way, but I would hope not in a repetitive way. The large part of my life is very much in the past because I have been taking it rather easy in the present, so that I can hope to build myself a life after the event. The whole job lot bag of mashings was no easy trek to walk away from because the asking price was very high. Only myself as far as I knew, was the carrier of the power that could with real magic, change people's lives for the better. So it is only I who know what took place but I was under heavy sedation at that time. The thought in my mind at the time and for that matter very much previously, was that I would become one with myself when the whole part that I had been born to play was over. This idea didn't seem too clever after my time in hospital, for a very long time, because all my energies felt that they were drained. But slowly I no longer asked the question of why I am here and I have nothing to prove to myself or anyone else. There are no barriers for the first time in my life. I can do what I like without feeling that I am doing wrong and breaking my promise. In many ways I have become more mature in my outlook to my life and so I should when I'm coming up to my thirty-second birthday. Of course, you might say finding yourself is alright but that it is very selfish to do so yet I have no responsibilities to a wife or children like most who are reaching the same age as myself and this is where the sacrifice of what I have done with my life comes into the open. I wanted the same things when I was a teenager just like any other teenager, but it was not possible to have both what I wanted and also the way it had to be. It meant self sacrifice on any account even though, don't get me wrong, I'm not looking for any sympathy, I went along with the deal with open arms. The thing that I am trying to say is that the whole thing is a two sided sword, which cuts both ways and if you look at it in this way, selfish or sacrifice are very close companions in my tale at any rate. They became connected and it becomes very much the angle from where you are looking from that decides which is which.

Taking on the whole world was too good an opportunity to let pass by. I had a chance to beat the world, or if not beat it, at least get a draw. How could anyone let such a chance pass by and not take up the challenge that was set before me? I knew I couldn't even when I so wanted to get out of my part of the deal in order to be like everyone else. To some it would come as a shock that it was me who did the deed, while those who knew made sure they stayed out of my way when I was working towards my goal. The power I had was hard to gauge but it had to be immense in order to affect as many people as possible. I was left in a state of being an empty vessel; the strain took its toll on me for many years to come. I had a great deal of problems with my sleep patterns because all I wanted to do was go back to bed and lay down again after my breakfast and I cannot over stress that this was like one big trip to hell every day. This also meant I wasn't tired enough to go to sleep when the night came, when all I wanted to do was go into deep sleep so I could forget about all the events and suffering I had been through recently. I think sadly but very honestly that no one else really understood the problems I was facing and perhaps didn't want to either. The whole event had nearly pulled my body apart, firstly my head felt like a burning pot of pain with it also seeming like someone was inside squeezing my brain, then the rest of my body felt like I had been beaten up with all my body aching in reaction to the physical strain I had put myself under in order to complete my mission. All this for what I may ask, for me it was worth absolutely nothing except a lot of pain and payment of a debt to a lot of people I no longer knew. The whole episode is something I can look back on as some sort of nightmare and who could say that it was not so. If you believe my story then some would call you gullible, stupid or just crazy; and to those who do not believe, well I honestly couldn't care less what you think. In my life I have grown used to being alone, which some have seen as being unsociable but this is the way I lived my life and I am used to it. Don't get me wrong, I like going out for a few beers with friends but I don't have to do it every night. The way I have kept to myself a lot in my life also affected my relationships inside the family. I could never talk to my dad and we were never very pally with one another in my childhood years. Even the relationship I had with my mother was not that good and I always felt she got on better with my brother and sister. My sister, who is three years older than me, and I never seemed to be on friendly terms and we were not close. My brother grew up hating me because I beat him up a fair bit while we were growing up. So my family and I were not exactly bosom buddies.

When I was in the Scouts and went camping at the weekends I never wanted to go back home for I wanted to stay camping and going home on the Sunday evening would mean a bath, sleep and Monday morning and worse of all, school. By all accounts there has been plenty written about the middle child in a family because for some reason it is a noted fact that they usually have problems that don't affect the other two members of the family. So being the middle child of three, I have a written excuse for being stupid, so now you know. I don't know if I am a typical case or not, but in some ways I never felt that I was part of the family in the same way that my brother and sister were. It's sad to say that for some reason I looked on myself as some sort of outsider and I didn't feel that I belonged with my family. The person in the family who I felt more at one with was my granddad and I think this is also something that has been much written about, when a son is more able to be with his granddad than his own father. I can't say I know the reason for this, maybe I could feel more for my granddad because in some ways he was like me in that he was also an outsider. The way he dressed was old fashioned and the furniture in his house had seen better days. There was something else about my childhood and for that matter in my adulthood also and that was a sense that I was out of my time. What I mean by this is that I felt out of place, this was not the right time for me to be living in. Sometimes I felt that I belonged in the past and that the world I would have liked to live in was now long gone. Other times it was the very opposite that I definitely belonged in the future and before my time. Getting back, when I say I got on more with my granddad, that is not much of a statement because my dad and me were rarely close. In the main, when I saw my granddad I would listen to him telling his tales and look into the fire, which was still solid fuel. These were very much my childhood years as far as getting along with my family was concerned because I am a lot closer to my family in the present. I usually visit my dad once a week where before I went a good three years without seeing him before my time in hospital. My relationship with my mother is now a lot better than it was and I see her the most in a week than any other member of the family. I'm also a lot closer to both my sister and brother than I ever was when we were growing up.

Continuing with a family theme I am now a three times uncle, with my sister having Richard and Leanne and my brother's daughter, Madison. With both my younger brother and elder sister I am now the odd one out in the family with not being married or being a parent. The subject of me being a parent is something which I have given a great deal of thought to in my life and I feel that I could not live with myself if I had a child which was in anyway like myself, the very thought of bringing another child into this world doesn't much appeal to me anyway. But to think that a child of mine had the same ability as I was born with, who would have to go through all I have done is something that I could not do because the child would have a right to hate me for putting them through the same ordeal that I have had to go through. To actually think that such a gene could be passed on from me is not a happy thought. You might think that it would be a good idea but you do not know what it is like to carry such a heavy burden of responsibility, which you cannot share with anyone, it is down to you. The very idea that my path could be followed with a similar climax, that when you reach the end of the journey and find out the cupboard is bare is not something that I could wish on anyone. Only I know what it is like to be affected in this way and the disappointment is still with me to this day. My whole life that I lived before the psychiatric ward was a form of a test of my ability to survive and somehow I was able to overcome the obstacles that were in my way. The reason I survived is that I am good at it and deep down I am a mean competitor who doesn't like giving up. My life was mapped out for me and if a baby did come along who had the same abilities as myself they too would be restrained in a certain code that they would have to abide by. I would feel inside like a failure because I would not be able to justify such a selfish desire to have a child and weigh up the way of life that child would have to live by in order to have the burden around their shoulders to be lifted off them. It would be hard to watch someone else hide away their feelings in order to get through the ordeal facing them. Of course, they could leave the course set them and live like the rest and that would make me happy because they could have a choice to change their destiny. Maybe though, it is not just the thought that I would feel guilt, which is going through my mind over being a father, but could well be the bitterness that I have tried to hold back with regards to Catherine. With her not wanting me and my receiving nothing, has clouded my judgment over the whole affair and in the main, I have concentrated on the dark side of things because of my disappointment.

At the end of the day though, I know what it takes and I can say there is no way that I could put someone else though what I have been through. The job certainly is not for anyone with plans such as buying a house, getting married, falling in love or making a commitment to someone that you just cannot keep, before you finish the task that is marked out before you. Probably the biggest part of being able to pull the job off is a liking for pain or being able to live with pain because there is plenty to deal with, believe me. When in hospital it was very much a physical pain as well as a mental one and the proceeding years had brought much pain with them because of the life I had to lead in order to carry out my task. Having gone through it all I know that deep down it was a mammoth task that I had to take on and I made it into a game to get over the very serious nature of what I was attempting to do.

The problem of dealing with my emotions is something in the past that I somehow locked them deep inside and lived without them. Only now after six years that have passed by since my time in hospital, am I starting to come to terms with my life. The way the illness affected my health after the event has made it very difficult to walk away and say that's behind me because every time I've felt like I was getting better and feeling good inside another obstacle has crossed my path of recovery. Many times over the last six years have I thought it has passed by and many times have I been proved wrong. This has taken a long time to sink in, that for the rest of my life I will, in some way, be affected by what took place in 1987 and no medicine will ever be able to change this fact. I have thought of a tablet that could take you back in time but I don't think I would choose the week before my time in the psychiatric unit in 1987 but I would return to the third of June 1961, the day I was born, and live my life differently this time and sod the rest. This is all just wishful thinking of course, and very much an after event thought. I suppose not getting Catherine has made my thoughts rather anti what I achieved and you have to take into account that I always was a bad loser when I was a child and some of this has reappeared in my adulthood. To myself, I feel that I failed because I did not get what I wanted but I do feel that I did do some good and perhaps I did change some people's lives for the better. For me there are the memories of my dreams even though they did not come true so my views are blurred to the good that I performed.

Looking back at what I did to get admitted to the Northern General Hospital I think the part where I got out ten books from the Hillsborough Library is something even you might like to think about. What ten books would you choose to spread out on a desk if you had the choice? I think it is a very good question, which you alone can answer.

If you were capable of waiting for twenty five years before you came to face the partner you had made and been waiting to meet for such a long time, what would you like your partner to be like? In my case I was waiting for a female but you can choose the sex of your partner to suit yourself, if not one of your friends. In my case she was blonde, nothing unusual about that you might say. She had, and still has no doubt, very creamy looking skin. A feature of her face was that she had no pock marks from acne and in fact, looked like she had never even had nappy rash, never mind a spot. She was about five foot six inches in height with shoes on so she could just be below that. Her body was, even when she was just wearing jeans and a shirt, very languid looking and she was so feminine that she could look good in dungarees, or even for that matter, wearing nothing. The day I visited her after leaving hospital on the Monday, she came out of her house without any shoes or socks on and her toes didn't look too bad either, which is not the case with my feet. I have bent toes because I wore shoes that were too small for me when I was a child. Her voice was nice enough; her teeth pearly white and she looked like a goddess if there is such a thing. Her eyes were so bright, yet she was still very innocent and I bet now she knows how to manipulate men to her advantage. With her looks it would not take much for men to offer their favours to her. Of course, I was a lot luckier than most, in that I actually got the chance to choose how my other half looked and then even got to meet my creation. The problem with looks is very much what is behind them, yet Catherine was a very nice person who liked dirty jokes, yet that word I have already used keeps coming to mind, that of innocence. There was no doubt she had been kept in a cotton wool existence and that her father was very protective when it came to his daughter. I have wondered if I did create her, did I make her faithful to her husband who I the plan of mice and men was going to be, played by me but there is someone else in my role who has taken something that is far more than he understands and far more than he deserves. Maybe that sounds terrible that I talk of Catherine as if she was a mere thing, but Catherine is not someone who is a mere anything. It is my jealousy which is coming through and even though I might write that time is a great healer, there is still a little bit inside me that will always remember Catherine whether I like it or not. Of course you might say this is the biggest whopper of a story that I have come up with so far. How can anyone create someone else without being part of their making, such as being involved in the sexual intercourse that needs to take place or by artificial insemination? For those who don't believe I don't think there's anything that could back up my story but myself, because I am living proof that some things cannot be explained away. The workshop gaffer at the hospital did say to me when he had shown a group of us a nude woman on a rock that "It's not as good as you son!" In reply to my saying the nude ornaments were great! You're there saying this is flimsy evidence to back up my story and that I'll have to think something up a lot better if I am top be believed. When my dad visited me one day he just asked me "What's her name son?" without asking anything else. He didn't say is there a girl mixed up in all this that I should know about, but he had already worked out that I had met my other half before I ended up in hospital. I told my dad her name was Catherine and I gave him her address so he could arrange what had to be done. Am I making any headway into those who do not believe it is possible that another human being can be made for the sole purpose of a deal that the said person has absolutely no prior knowledge of being struck. This is why I made the effort to go and see Catherine to try and explain what was going on and what was going to happen and that reality does contain dreams that cannot be explained away very easily. I was allowed a choice of a woman and as you know, I chose Catherine, but I did not get what I had been promised from the deal and maybe some of you think that the disappointment I have been given is fair because such a deal over a person should not have been agreed to in the first place. But would I have gotten through the ordeal without the thought of gaining Catherine afterwards? The fact is she gave me something to look forward to when all I could feel was pain. I do not know if I could have gotten through all that was necessary if there had been no Catherine in the story but even though she turned me down, she did play a major part in the whole affair, because I believed for the first time in my life that I had a bright future before me and some great times to come. Catherine today could well be married with children by now, yet I will always remember how she looked when she was a teenager and had seen little of life and was so fresh, yes when Catherine crosses my mind this is how I will think of her.

The thing with having a dream and in this case a dream girl, is that dreams don't come true but in some ways a dream is just that and can not become reality and dreams are really something to hope with when you're feeling down and nearly counted out. So Catherine's rejection of me was because to her there was no dream in her mind and she had no feelings for me at all. The fact that she wouldn't exist if it weren't for me is too much of a thought for her to understand, I suppose.

Moving on I got the job of painting the wall at the front of my mother's house. When you become a painter to earn a crust you become a painter for the rest of your life, whether you like it or you don't. So my mother paid for the masonry paint and I was given the job of slapping it on. In the past I had done the decorating reluctantly but thankfully I no longer went into a sea of depression over it and could now take it all in my stride. I got the ladder ready and my brush and paint. Now I faced my biggest problem which was climbing up the really wobbly ladder, which when I got near to the top, I started to shit myself. All I could manage was to move up the ladder very slowly and move up one rung at a time. My heart was in a big beat mode and I feared falling off the ladder. It had been such a long time since I had been up a ladder that I had lost my bottle for the job. The usual passing of neighbours ensued with me being just able to smile through my grimace to acknowledge them. Two lads were kicking a football and I just hoped that they did not hit the ladder because I would be close to having a heart attack! Because I was so scared I could not do more than a couple of feet either side of the ladder. To me I was on the top of Mount Everest and it was far too high to be. It seemed to be taking forever to do and it was a case of biting the bullet and just plodding on. I was thinking such jolly thoughts to myself such as if I fell off from this height I would end up dead, which was a great thing to be thinking about whilst performing a chore. My whole life passed before my eyes, well about twelve seconds of it, which were the best bits. It seemed to be taking an eternity to get the paint from the bucket onto the stone, but I couldn't do much about it as I had one overriding thought and that was to survive. I don't believe my mother knows anything what you have to go through if it isn't related to sewing. I was, to say the least, really glad when I had finished for the day but there was a dark cloud on the horizon; the whole wall would need another coat. Why do I always get the shit jobs; I wonder if someone could turn that line into a song and I would have it as my theme tune. I gave my mother my leather jacket so she could put a zip into it because the present one had broken, that was the best part of a year ago but have I got my jacket back with a new zip? No, of course I haven't because it would take too much effort on my mother's part to get the job done. Yet its Wayne do this, and Wayne do that when it comes to jobs that I can do around the house. Anyway, I got back into painting the stone wall the next day but it was still a matter of holding on for grim death. I overheard two lads say that I was taking ages over the job but I would gladly have changed places if they were feeling brave and their insurance was up to date. It seems that even children are born critics these days, all I can say is: wait until it's their turn and then we will see who is who. While I was up the ladder I thought I hadn't felt so bad for a long time and it was a job that didn't help my nervous system any, I can tell you. It was a day that could not finish fast enough and I was glad when I was putting the finishing touches to the stone wall. If I ever went back to painting I would have to get my head examined to find out if there was a brain present inside my head. This is not the only painting I have done for my mother recently because I've also done most of the rooms in the house again.

There is one question which you may or may not have though of, and that is did I ask to be born. It's such a mind blowing thought because we somehow end up here but we don't choose to do so, for it is others, namely our parents, who decide to bring us into this world that we live in. The reason I've brought the question up is because my life was waiting for me to come along and play join the dots and see what I find when I get to the end. I must admit that I don't think that I did make myself happen and that I waited throughout the ages to make a prophecy come true in this life. It is really a very posing question because after all I do claim that it was I who made my other half appear when the time was right. This does not add up yet I knew from a very early age that a deal had been made and if I kept to my side of the bargain I would be rewarded when the time came. I somehow always knew that I did not fit in and that I was different to other children but that I was definitely not superior to them. As I have already written I had plenty of problems to deal with as a child which must have had a great effect over me, with my lack of self confidence being very evident from my school days. If I did bring myself into this world I chose a very poor body in which to do so. Of course if I was born because I wanted to be then I have no one else to blame than myself for the way my life has worked out. I've mentioned my liking of history and I think at the back of my interest I was always looking for people like myself who had the same ability and the same problems that they had to deal with. They would have had to stand against the tide that was against them just as I have had to. I have always felt that I have gone against the grain in my life in order to be myself, for I think that society is very against the individual other than those who follow an economic form, which is not individualism as I refer to it. Certain people pretend to be individuals, so they can appear in the media's eye as much as possible and to me these people are totally obnoxious and how they can be held up as an example to follow is beyond me. Getting back to the question of whether I asked to be born I do know that there must have been something different about my birth. The only problem is that I do not know what it was that made certain people know I was someone who was different to the usual born baby. If I did appear by my own request I must have been stupid even then, for to agree to such a demanding path that I had to take was not exactly a bright move. Maybe in order to be granted life in the first place I had to agree to the deal that I owed and would have to pay back the debt before I could get on with living my own life in a way that I wanted to. I don't think that there is anyway to prove that I had wished myself to be born and the question will still stand. But one thing's for sure, it will always take some explaining to how I was born with this destiny before me that I have now accomplished.

What have I gained from going though such an ordeal is another question you may ask, I think the answer is that I am now at one with myself. I no longer feel the world is on my back and that everything is against me and that everything I say or do is going to be held against me by those around me. At long last I am free you might say, yet it is a phoney freedom because I could well be affected for the rest of my life from what I have been through in order to fulfil my promise. Of course some of you out there are saying that I am just a lazy bastard who does not want to work but this is not the case, and I am not just hiding behind my illness. If I could find a job I like doing and there was very little stress attached to the job, I would be well away. I no longer get obsessed by anything because it can lead to a lot of emotional turmoil that I do not need. My life is fine by me at the moment and is a million miles away from my worst times on the council or even my time at school. I've already stated I hated both school and my job as a painter on the works, yet there were times, especially while I was working, that I could never see a happy time in my life in the future. There's no doubt in my mind that the worst years of my life were when the council employed me. It was brain numbing and an awful price to have to pay in order to achieve the overall effect. Those five years will never be totally erased from my thoughts because I was on the edge of my sanity for most of those years. No one should have to go through such a bad experience but the fact is I had to, even though I was not cut out for such an environment. I was a fish out of water when I think back to those times, which everyone seemed to want to have a go at, mainly because they could not understand me. It's a good job I was made of sterner stuff because if I had not, there is no doubt that I would not have got through it. I somehow did manage to hide away the real reason for being on the council, that of building the circuit even from myself most of the time.

The world before me and the people who were around me were pretty simple, that of school, work, marriage and eventually death with very little in between or so I could see, when trying to view the world from their prospective. My life in this period was pathetic when looking back on it but so were most of the men who were around me but I have managed to move on, whereas they are still living pathetic little lives. Don't I sound like the superior one, which was something I have denied in this tale up to now. With me still having some work to do when I got the sack, via the 'O' levels that I had paid to do, it would not have been a more changed environment if you had been trying for one. Doing 'O' levels was a planet away form being a painter on the works and I think I handled the transition very well. This period of time was the beginning of education as far as I was concerned for I now had plenty of time and much more importantly, I had the motivation, which was something I never had in my time at school. It was time to open my mind to new thoughts and perhaps change some of my own perceptions along the way, education had begun and I was the swot on the job. The year was 1983 and I read hundreds of books during the year because I wanted to and it opened up a whole new world for me. I've already written about the help I got from my English tutor and for once all the good things seemed to be going my way for a change. From being a television junkie I was now a bookworm and I felt great about the whole thing. Looking back to whether I did gain anything from the programme my life was based on I would say that the education beef was the most telling of what I gained in this time. To me in the main, it was something new to read books but not just read them, to actually enjoy reading them was something I would never had thought possible after my time at school where I was unhappy and thought book reading was for arse licking wimps. The thing with reading is that it is a personal thing with you and the writer and I'm sure we all get different images in our heads from reading the same pages. The trip through education was also a means to an end of carrying me to the day when I could offer my redemption gift, but the good thing was that I could enjoy myself without a clash of interests.

On another theme, I manage to go out with my mate Tony a couple of nights a week at the present time. There is no doubt it helps me to unwind and I feel a lot better for having been out and not be totally isolated as I have been in the past. I sometimes go into a pub on my own if there is a football match on and I have seen a fair few games in pubs this year. I try not to drink much because I am not supposed to drink alcohol with the tablets I am taking. The main thing is that I have got a bit of a social life going, which can only help chase the blues away. Of course I haven't got too many brain cells left but you might say I didn't have too many of them to start with by agreeing to the deal.

The main problem I have now faced for six years is coming to terms with my illness in a way that I can move on to better times but unless I face up to the past I will not find a more greener park than the dark one that I have occupied for many years. The pain of depression and anguish that I went through was not imagined they were real and very hurtful just like they are for everybody. The pain of living a life where I could see no outlet to better times was soul destroying and something that I could not wish on anybody. The years of depression that I endured were wasted yet all I could do was scrape myself off the floor and try as best I could to get on with my life. When you're facing depression every day though, it is easier said than done to snap out of it. Depression over such a long period of time like I endured without medical help is a hard trip to get through, but my obligation meant I had to stand my ground, even if I knew that if I got away from my life I could perhaps start to live a more normal existence.

The mental anguish that I felt is hard to describe and in a way it had to be and my personal feelings were of little consequence in the bigger game that was being played around me. These words can become like labels yet they're a lot harder to cast off than labels on clothes, for they stick to your inner skin, where it's hard to erase the stain. Just because I felt like casting them away there was no easy way of doing so for there was no one that I could turn to because the whole thing revolved around me and I was the only one who had the answers that I could only use when the right time came along. The thing was really about facing up to the fact that this was a real life I was leading and not just something that I was making up along the way, and whether I was enjoying my life or not, it was me who had lived it and I had to accept the consequences of my part of the deal. Because it was a job for a lone person who could handle being alone, over many occasions there was no one I could look up to and say that I was going through this here problem, I had to sort it out for myself and hope that I was right in my final decisions. These were some of the things that I really had not faced before my time in the psychiatric unit at the Northern General Hospital. The years of depression from my childhood right through to the present day was a massive build up that I had finally come face to face with and I certainly could not run away from it because there was nowhere left to run to. The whole thing was after a time, going to start poring out of me for the first time and I was going to bore the staff silly telling them my life story that had brought me to this moment in time. Of course I might had had an even better reason for being at the hospital, but there was plenty to treat in the way my life had made me bottle up my emotions so much so that I rarely cried or ever said sorry in a way that had meaning to it. I cannot stress how difficult this was for me to admit to myself, just because I had induced my ticket to ward 54 I thought that I was fine with there being nothing at all wrong with me but this was just not the case. The task itself had brought these problems, with there being part of the course. I keep returning to the word depression but somehow it does not seem to transmit all those days and years where I had the face on and felt that I was an alien from another planet. No one else seemed to be going through the turmoil that was going on inside my head and at times I wished to be somewhere else in the world instead of living in the city of Sheffield. It's not that it was Sheffield's fault, but if I were somewhere else the whole game would have to come to an end and I would be, at last, free.

When you go into a depressive stupor, it is one of the most brain numbing experiences that you could imagine. Of course everyone goes through some depression in their teens in particular, because they are such important years, but the difference with myself to the others was that I was going through an all time whopper, which would not budge. I got pronounced as a manic-depressive, which was of no surprise to me and I still have days where I feel out of it and wonder why I was so earmarked for such a sob story and why things have always weighed very heavily upon me?

We have gained a new addition to the family, with a cat called Beauty, which was one of the litter by a domestic cat that had been abandoned on the back of my Mum's old shop, the Sewing Box, which was now closed. At first she ran away from me and went behind the cooker or the washing machine when she felt like it. In a little while she got used to me and not before long, she was jumping on me to give her a love and for that matter she is a very affectionate cat. Because Beauty is a female, we made sure she didn't go out of my mother's house until she had been spade at the Vet's. One of the best features of Beauty was that she always went to the litter tray to do her business. Well perhaps that isn't really her best feature, which is that she has a black half nostril, which always makes her look cute! She is black, white and ginger over her fur with a mainly white body. Of course cats are a law to themselves but she does seem to know her name. Where she first was at my mother's house she would hide in one of the units in the dining room. I would look all over for her and she would be there, staring at me and thinking he's a right banana, this one! At first, my mother thought she as going to get a ginger cat because she had been feeding a wild ginger cat, who used to visit her back garden, for quite a while but I was glad that she got Beauty because she looks different to any of the other cats in the area. The thing about Beauty is that she loves to play and sometimes she likes to bite, but in a friendly way because she just puts on very little pressure in her jaw as she has sharp teeth. The only problem with having Beauty indoors all the time of course is the smell, in particular, when she dropped one. She also has a habit of scratching the wallpaper, which she had done a lot of damage especially in my mother's dining room. She was ripping the paper around the fireplace so we pinned some plastic bags to stop her from doing so. In the early months she was not let out of the one room because she was still only a kitten and she was still getting to know us. When my sister and the gruesome twosome turned up during this time, she hid behind the washing machine and I can't say that I blame her. But in time she no longer ran away from them, which was her big mistake. She loved jumping on your lap and also she loved jumping into bags, so much so we also nicknamed her the bag lady! I would pop down when my mother was out working so Beauty wasn't lonely because she had been surrounded by people all the time in her life so far. When my mother opened the washer door Beauty would jump in to see what it was like and when it was in operation she would watch the washing going around for ages, it really fascinated her.

I got the task of going to the RSPCA to make an appointment to have Beauty spayed, but it was going to be many months for us to wait so it came down to whether we wanted to pay for the operation ourselves, and we decided that we would have to pay. I asked how much it cost at the vet's surgery on Holme Lane and I told my mum that I would pay. So I booked an appointment for Beauty and took her around to the vet's and left her there and I would go back for her the following day. I used a box to carry her there and back and she was very hungry when I got her back to my mother's. She ate a lot and slept most of the time and didn't go running about as she had normally done.

There were some stitches where they had cut her open and they were to be removed in a week's time. I took her back to the vet's and she had her stitches taken out and that was that. She moved around a fair bit though when the stitches were removed. It didn't take her long to get back to her usual mischief and we now let her go up the stairs and into the bathroom, where she was soon trying to rip the paper off - the little bitch! We still didn't want her to get out because she was still just a baby compared to the other cats who roamed about outside. The smell in the litter tray could be smelt as soon as you entered the house and we used some air freshener to try to tone it down a bit. The big day arrived soon enough when we let her outside and after about 30 seconds she ran into someone's house and hid behind the cooker before I took her home with her clawing me. The next time she got let out she didn't come back and we thought we had seen the last of her but after a day and a half, my mother spotted her and Beauty couldn't wait to run into the house. She had grease on her head and was mucky, which made it look like she had been in someone's garage and couldn't get out. My mother was really upset when Beauty didn't come back but was really glad when she did come back and for that matter I was glad to see old stinker myself. At first all she did was sleep but she got back to her usual self and she gets let out fairly often now.

I think its time for a recap to try and help make up your mind whether all I have written is just a figment of my imagination. Who out there is going to believe that by running around a park you can release a powerful force that you just had been carrying for a quarter of a century. Then when you get greatly out of your head and end up in a psychiatric hospital the nurses and staff look upon you as something special and not an everyday looney tune that they usually get in their unit, in saying that I am the biggest looney tune of them all and there is no doubt about that. The proof is in the fact that I received nothing for my efforts and for that matter why should I; that your Dad had just been saving a dressing gown for you with a wolf's head on the pocket just in case you happened to get put in hospital; that the very same dad, on one of his visits, wore a checked jacket, a dark brown shirt and a cream tie which made him look like a forties gangster and it was a night that was one of great pain to me and my Dad kept saying "You're the governor, Son, you're the governor, You're the best there's ever been!" Now that does take some swallowing, doesn't it just? That when it is nearly time to leave the hospital you get blue and yellow blood extracted from your right arm, which most would put down to an hallucination except I wasn't going through any hallucinations at the time. Then there's the small matter of people looking like they are wobbly jelly or some sort of ape and not forgetting the red eyes that made people cry. Such things really do take some explaining and I doubt very

235

much that I would be able to put forward a very convincing case to back up what I thought took place. There was also the little matter of everyone knowing my name no matter where I went in Sheffield when I was going for long walks around the city. I wonder if there are any takers of my very condensed story that I have loosely just gone through in order to hold the story up to the light and it is far too easy to see right through it and see that it is all make believe or is it so out of the ordinary that it can only be viewed as true. Well it's very much up to you to decide. I wonder if I could have gotten away with much more in terms of playing the fool. Would such stupidity as I could have got up to made any difference to the final outcome? I cannot move forward without facing up to my past and I need to find someone which will not be easy because I set a very high standard as in the case of Catherine.

What to do with the rest of my life is a question I have given very little thought to and I honestly can say I have no direction in mind at the moment. I can look back on what I have written as a truly great achievement in managing to write my life story from a position of not really believing that I could do so. For me now there is no quest or burden for me to carry and I hope because of this that I can become a lighter minded person in regards to the world I see around me. Will I ever find true happiness in my life is something I hope the answer will eventually be yes to. I certainly don't know all the answers to life but I'll keep on searching because I am made that way but I no longer ask what am I here for, thankfully for me I have overcome such a depressing thought. I have received great support from my mum and dad and this is one of the best things that have come out of the whole episode. To leave you on a happy thought: the sight of the neighbour who lived opposite us when we lived on Woodend Drive, with two red circles is something that makes me smile to this day. His eyes disappeared under the weight of red and I had done it to him, such satisfaction over a job well done. Well it's a lot better than finishing on a sentimental note, don't you think?

ORDER
'STRONGER THAN EVER'

The Report of the First Survivor Worker Conference UK
by Rose Snow

PUBLISHED BY ASYLUM

Price for individuals and small groups **£6**

Large organisations **£24.97**

MAKE CHEQUES PAYABLE TO: Asylum

SEND TO:
Asylum Associates, Limbrick Centre, Limbrick Rd, Sheffield S6 2PE

Name _____

Organisation _____

Address _____

_____

_____

_____

Postcode _____ email **(Optional)** _____

4 issues
Individuals UK £12
Organisations UK £24

International Rates
Individuals:
£18 by non UK currency
Organisations: £30

Make cheques payable to:
Asylum

Send to:
Asylum Associates
Limbrick Centre, Limbrick Rd, Sheffield
S6 2PE
subs@asylumonline.net

Please copy these forms or just send these details to the above addresses

Name

Organisation

Address

Postcode   email **(Optional)**